I0810421

IMAGES
of America

The Kiwanis Club of Birmingham

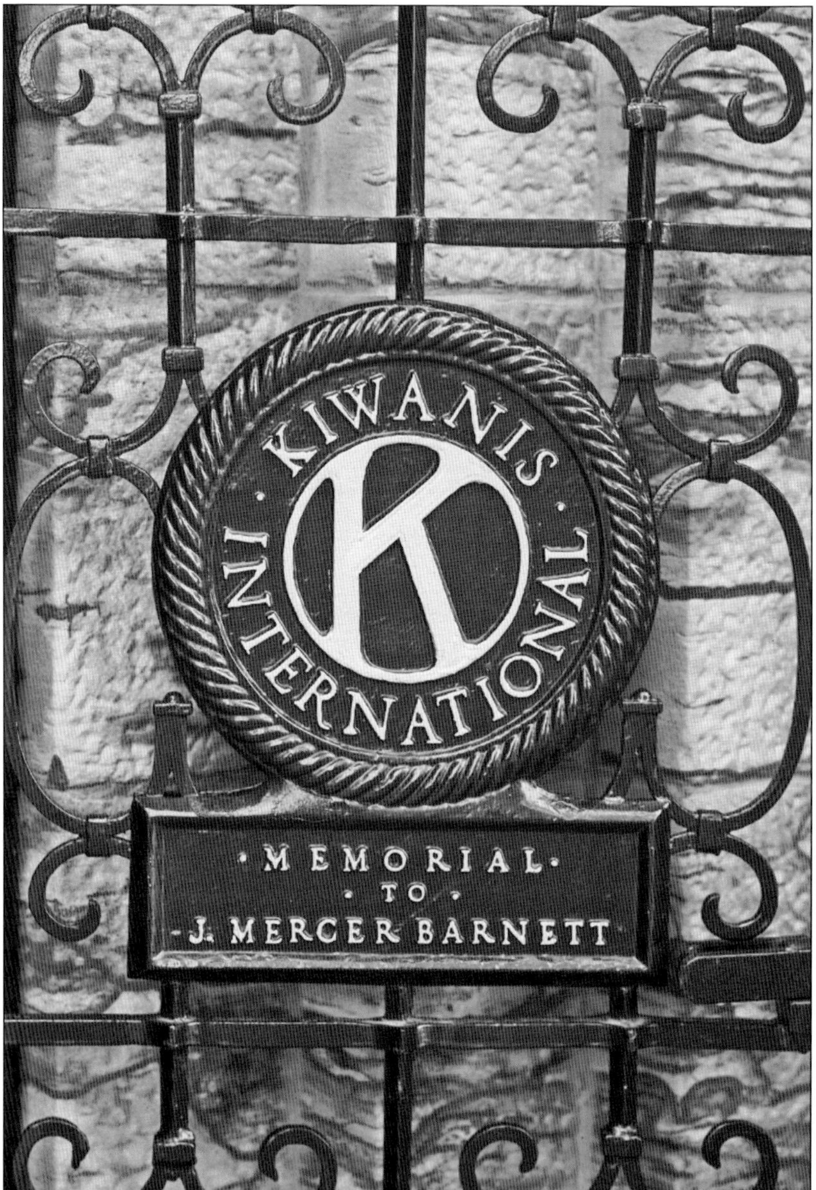

This image offers a detail of the so-called Kiwanis Gate, donated to the city in 1950 to commemorate Birmingham's hosting of the historic 1919 Kiwanis International Convention and to mark the Kiwanis Club's role in erecting *Vulcan* atop Birmingham's Red Mountain. During a renovation of *Vulcan*, the gate was removed and kept at the Kiwanis Club in downtown Birmingham; it has since been returned to its original location. (Kiwanis Club of Birmingham.)

On the Cover: Famed singing cowboy and Saturday matinee idol Gene Autry had set aside his guitar and spurs during World War II to join the Army Air Forces; during that period, he found time to visit Birmingham's Crippled Children's Clinic, where the Kiwanis Club's financial support was memorialized with a sponsored bed. (Kiwanis Club of Birmingham.)

IMAGES
of America

THE KIWANIS CLUB OF BIRMINGHAM

James L. Noles Jr.

ARCADIA
PUBLISHING

ISBN 978-1-4671-2624-3

Published by Arcadia Publishing
Charleston, South Carolina

Printed in the United States of America

Library of Congress Control Number: 2017942087

For all general information, please contact Arcadia Publishing:
Telephone 843-853-2070
Fax 843-853-0044
E-mail sales@arcadiapublishing.com
For customer service and orders:
Toll-Free 1-888-313-2665

Visit us on the Internet at www.arcadiapublishing.com

To Elizabeth, my wife and friend of boundless patience and steadfast love, and to the late Mike Klyce, who introduced me to the Kiwanis Club of Birmingham

Contents

ACKNOWLEDGMENTS

Thank you, Pres. Tom Thagard, the board of directors, and the Kiwanis Club Foundation for supporting this book. Thank you, Gail Vaughan, Janet Byrd, and Darcie Plowden for your unflappable good natures throughout this project. Thank you, Linda Self and colleagues and staff here at the firm. Thank you, official and unofficial club photographers over the years, such as Ivey Jackson, Harold Williams, and Ben Jackson. Many of the photographs credited to Kiwanis Club of Birmingham likely were taken by Ivey and Ben in particular. Thank you, helpful archivists too many to fully mention for finding (or trying to find) various and random photographs—at the risk of slighting anyone, I will tip my proverbial hat to Don Veasey, Meredith McDonough, J.D. Weeks, and Angela White in particular. And thank you, everyone, in advance, for tolerating whatever mistakes you might find this volume. Mistakes and errors are unintentional but mine alone.

KEY TO PHOTOGRAPH SOURCE ABBREVIATIONS:

Alabama Department of Archives and History	ADAH
Birmingham Public Library Archives	BPLA
Indiana University–Purdue University Indianapolis	IUPUI
Kiwanis Club of Birmingham	KCOB
Library of Congress	LOC
National Archives and Records Administration	NARA
University of the South, Sewanee	Sewanee

Introduction

There are certain years in America's—and the world's—history when the forces of the past gather and converge with unexpected impact. Sometimes, a historian must wait for the dust to settle and for history's lenses to clear before looking back through the intervening years and appreciating the catalytic turmoil of a particular time. But in other instances, even the people of that time can appreciate the change afoot.

The spring of 1917 was such a time.

In Washington, DC, Pres. Woodrow Wilson had begun his second term in the White House and, despite his best intentions to the contrary, found himself leading a nation embroiled in the First World War. That spring, Congress not only declared war but also began military conscription. For the Allied Powers, America's entry came not a moment too soon. Russia, with the abdication of the tsar, teetered on collapse. Meanwhile, in the trenches of France, entire French regiments mutinied as the weary British and their Commonwealth allies soldiered on.

Even aside from its entry into World War I, the United States was a nation on the verge of seismic change itself. In New Orleans, the Original Dixieland Jass [*sic*] Band released "Livery Stable Blues," the first commercial recording of jazz music. A train journey north, the Chicago White Sox, led by such legendary players as Shoeless Joe Jackson, Eddie Collins, and Eddie Cicotte, embarked on a campaign to a record-breaking 100-win season that would culminate in a World Series championship. In New York, the first Pulitzer Prize for Biography was awarded for Laura Richards and Maud Elliott's biography of suffragist Julia Ward Howe, while in Washington, DC, Montana's Jeannette Rankin took her seat as America's first female member of Congress.

Perhaps more than most cities of the age, Birmingham, Alabama, quivered with the resonance of the new era. In 1917, Birmingham was only 46 years old. It was a city born of the deliberate juncture of two railroads amid rich deposits of iron ore, coal, and limestone—the key ingredients of modern iron and steel. Its rapid growth not only earned it the moniker "The Magic City" but also attracted businessmen and entrepreneurs, as well as immigrants, miners, and mill and factory workers, to what would become the prototypical New South city. Over a 20-year span, Birmingham's population exploded from 38,415 in 1900 to 178,806 by 1920.

In such a city at such a time, perhaps it was no surprise that the prospective organizers of civic and business clubs found fertile ground. One such man was Dr. Alfred Durham, of Oakmont, Pennsylvania, tasked with organizing a Kiwanis Club in Birmingham. At the time, the parent Kiwanis Club organization, founded two years earlier in Detroit, Michigan, was growing across the nation and into Canada. Kiwanis—with a name derived from a Native American phrase meaning "We Trade"—was a civic association of businessmen with shared aspirations of commercial success and civic improvement.

Birmingham was the logical seat for Alabama's first Kiwanis Club, as men like Charles Miller, the advertising manager for the *Birmingham News*, agreed with Durham's vision. By the spring of

1917, the infant Kiwanis Club of Birmingham had organized and held its first meetings, and on May 19, 1917, it received its charter from Kiwanis' Detroit headquarters.

William C. Bonham, employed by grocery wholesaler Collins & Company, became the Birmingham club's first president; other early members included C.E. Mason of Empire Laundry; Joseph E. Loveman of the Loveman, Joseph & Loeb department store; Wallace V. Trammell of Wells Mercantile Agency; Herbert E. Steiner of Steiner Brothers Bankers; Walter S. Brower, attorney with London, Yancey & Brower; Frank W. Bromberg, jeweler; Thomas H. Joy, architect; and E.F. Stovall, general agent for the Central of Georgia & Illinois Central Railroad.

Club records from that era reveal the membership requirements for the Kiwanis Club of Birmingham at the time: "Any white adult male of good moral character, and who is an American citizen, who is engaged as a proprietor, partner, corporate officer, agent, or manager in full charge in any legitimate professional or business undertaking in the City of Birmingham shall be eligible for membership unless engaged in an occupation already represented by a member." Understandably, many of the club's early board meetings were devoted to discussions as to how to vocationally classify would-be members. Happily, these strict restrictions would ultimately fall to the wayside, as would the club's limitation of membership to "white adult males."

In the meantime, however, the Kiwanis Club of Birmingham achieved national prominence within two short years of first receiving its charter when the international Kiwanis organization held its annual convention in Birmingham. At the Birmingham convention, the various local clubs mounted a successful coup against Allen Browne, the founder of Kiwanis, who still wielded financial control over the organization. With Browne ousted, the member clubs charted a new and independent course for Kiwanis in closer alignment with the civic ideals of their members. In short order, Kiwanis' motto changed from "We Trade" to "We Build."

The following year, the Birmingham club's president, Mercer Barnett, a local lumber company owner, became the international organization's president. This would be the first and last time a Birmingham Kiwanian served as Kiwanis International's president, but in the decades that followed, the club, led by a veritable who's who of Birmingham's business leaders, would have a remarkable impact on its hometown.

In the 1920s, the club catalyzed the creation of the Parks & Recreation Board for Birmingham and the commissioning of a master parks study by Boston's acclaimed Olmsted Brothers landscape architecture firm. The following decade, the club spearheaded the effort to place Birmingham's iconic *Vulcan* statue atop Red Mountain. Club members made the ultimate sacrifice in World War II, and in the 1960s, the club sponsored a series of professional football exhibition games at legendary Legion Field that established the corpus of a foundation destined to provide hundreds of thousands of dollars to children-focused charities. Most recently, in 2016, Kiwanis embarked upon a $4.5 million project intended to enhance *Vulcan*, build the Kiwanis Centennial Park, and establish a key link in Birmingham's growing urban trails system. And these are just a few of the club's civic and charitable contributions.

As the Kiwanis Club wove itself into the fabric of Birmingham's civic life, it naturally reflected, for better or for worse, the tumultuous (and sometimes tortured) history of the city it called home. As reflected in the club's minutes and programs, the club witnessed, firsthand, Birmingham's experiences with the Progressive Era's labor unrest, a pair of world wars, the Great Depression, the boom years of Eisenhower's America, the civil upheaval and uncertainty of the 1960s, the urban malaise of the 1970s, the Sunbelt optimism of the 1980s and 1990s, the Great Recession, and, today, what many are calling a new Birmingham renaissance. In short, the story of the Kiwanis Club is the story of Birmingham. Therefore, whether the reader is simply interested in the history of this storied civic club or, more broadly, seeks a unique perspective into the last 100 years of Birmingham's history, we hope that *The Kiwanis Club of Birmingham* will be worth the time spent among the pages that follow.

One

The Beginnings

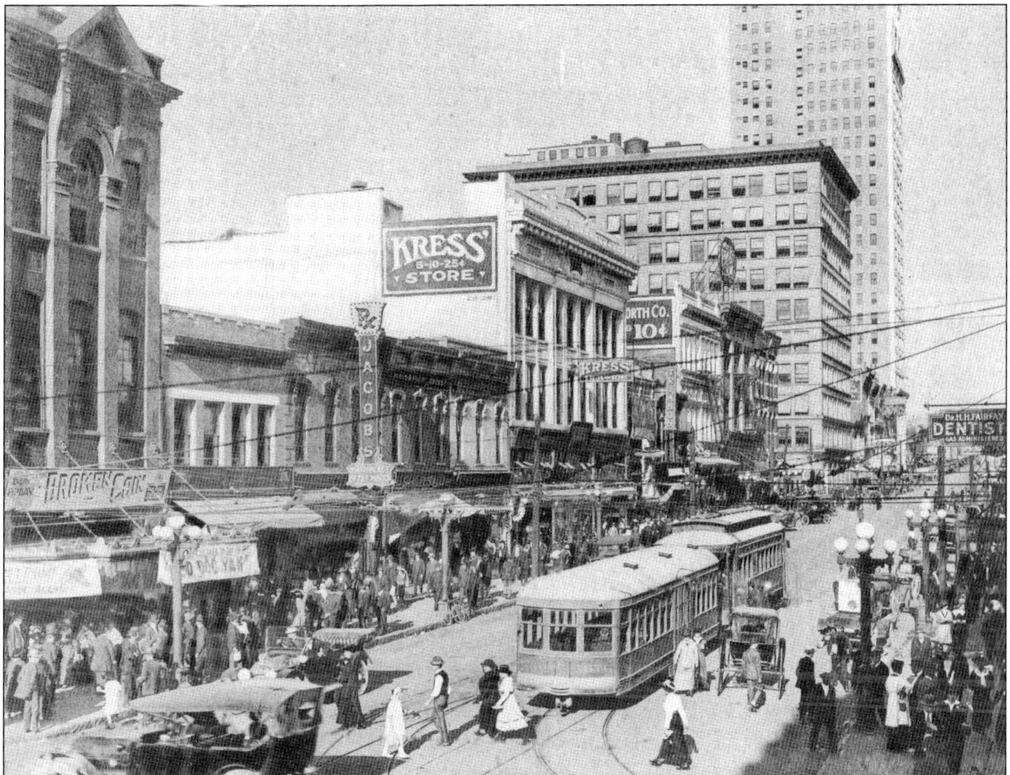

This photograph, published in 1915 by the *Birmingham Age-Herald*, was originally captioned "A Busy Scene on a Busy Street in Busy Birmingham." Although it was taken two years before the Kiwanis Club of Birmingham formed, the photograph accurately captures the bustling downtown environment that gave birth to the club in 1917. (ADAH.)

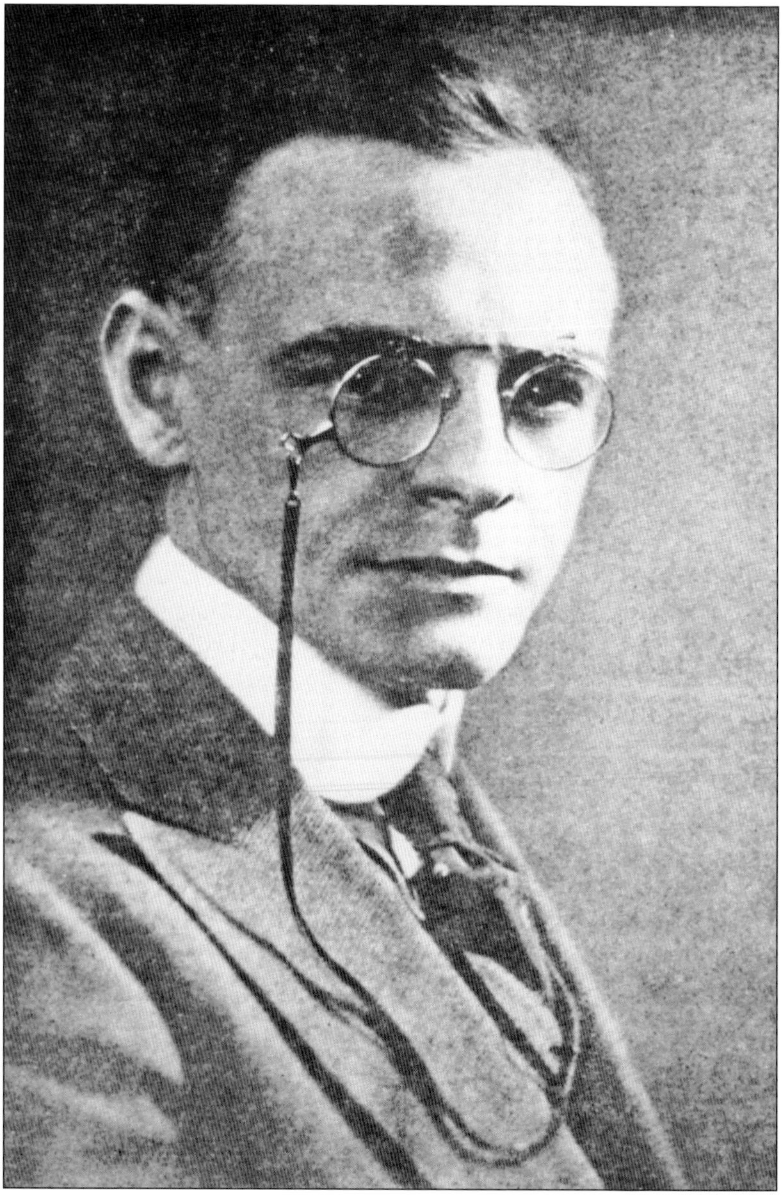

Allen S. Browne was, according to *The Men Who Wear the K*, a "personable, persuasive supersalesman" who, in 1914, earned his living in the Midwest by organizing and recruiting for such associations as the Loyal Order of Moose. But whereas the typical business model for such clubs relied on offering mutual sickness and accident benefits to its members, Browne envisioned a club with membership limited solely to businessmen and professionals and without the traditional insurance component. Joining forces with Detroit, Michigan, tailor Joseph G. Prance, Browne organized a new club aligned with his new vision. The organization's first name, Supreme Lodge Benevolent Order Brothers, did not last long—"Who wants to be a BOB?" one early member groused—and was soon replaced with the name "Kiwanis." *Nunc Kee-wanis*, according to Detroit's city historian, was an Otchipew phrase meaning "We Have a Good Time," "We Make a Noise," or "We Trade." Regardless of the precise translation, the BOBs liked it better than their current moniker and so, in January 1915, they became Kiwanis. (IUPUI.)

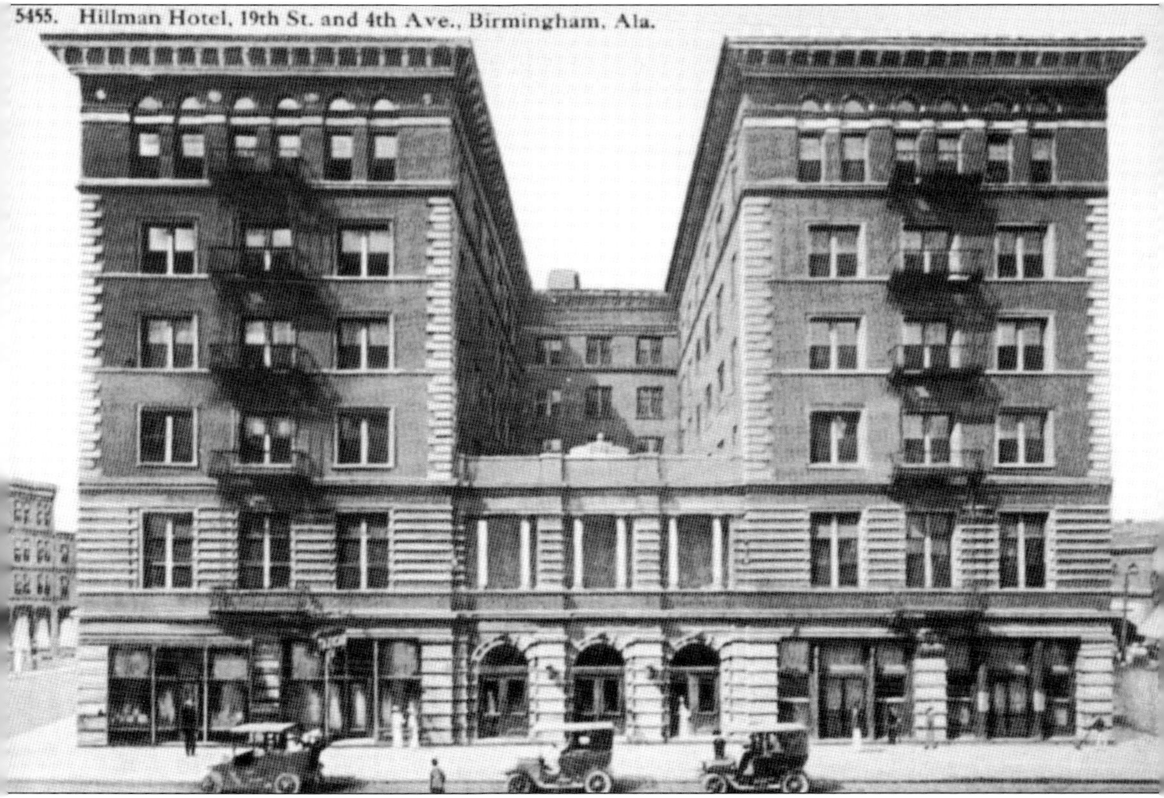

Within two years, Allen Browne's Detroit-based Kiwanis Club had chartered some 40 new clubs across American's Northeast and Midwest (and even in Hamilton, Canada). No one welcomed the rapid growth of the club more than Browne, who was receiving $5 for every new recruit to each club. By early 1917, southern cities such as Dallas, Nashville, and Birmingham were organizing clubs as well. On January 24, 1917, the nascent Birmingham club held its first organizational meeting in a private dining room at the Hotel Hillman (pictured here) and applied for a charter with the Kiwanis Club shortly thereafter. Charles Miller, advertising manager for the *Birmingham News*, called the first meeting to order in the Hotel Hillman as its acting chairman. Located on the southwestern corner of Fourth Avenue North and Nineteenth Street North, the luxurious Hillman Hotel no longer stands. In 1967, it was demolished for a parking lot. (J.D. Weeks.)

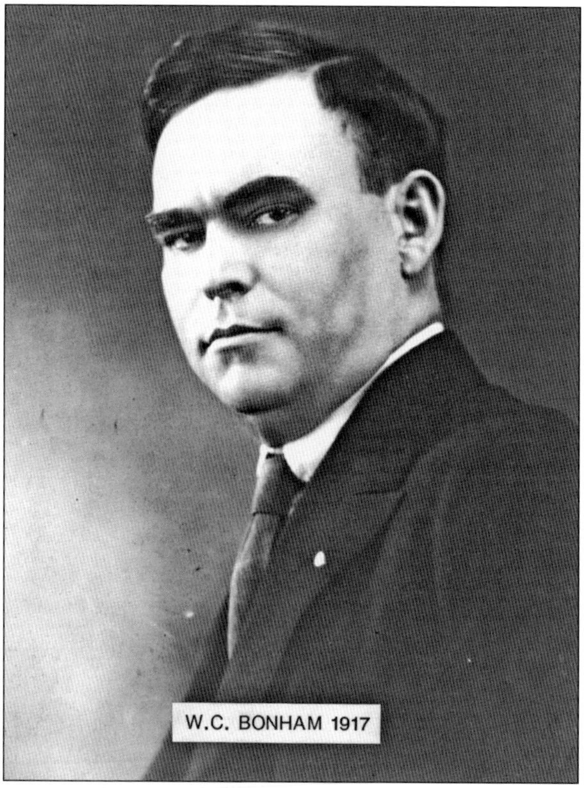

The Kiwanis Club of Birmingham received its charter on May 19, 1917, with William C. Bonham as the club's first president. The 34-year-old Bonham was a native of Wilcox County, Alabama. In 1917, Bonham was working for Collins & Company, a grocery wholesaler, but he soon moved to the C.C. Snyder Wholesale Cigar and Tobacco Company, one of the largest cigar wholesalers in the American South. (KCOB.)

The Kiwanis Club held its first meetings at the Southern Club, a private gentlemen's club. Among the club's earliest resolutions was that "an alarm clock be purchased and put upon the table at the luncheon each week to facilitate prompt adjournment." Although the club's insistence on "prompt adjournment" survives, the Southern Club does not. It was demolished in 1967, its site is now home to Regions Tower. (KCOB.)

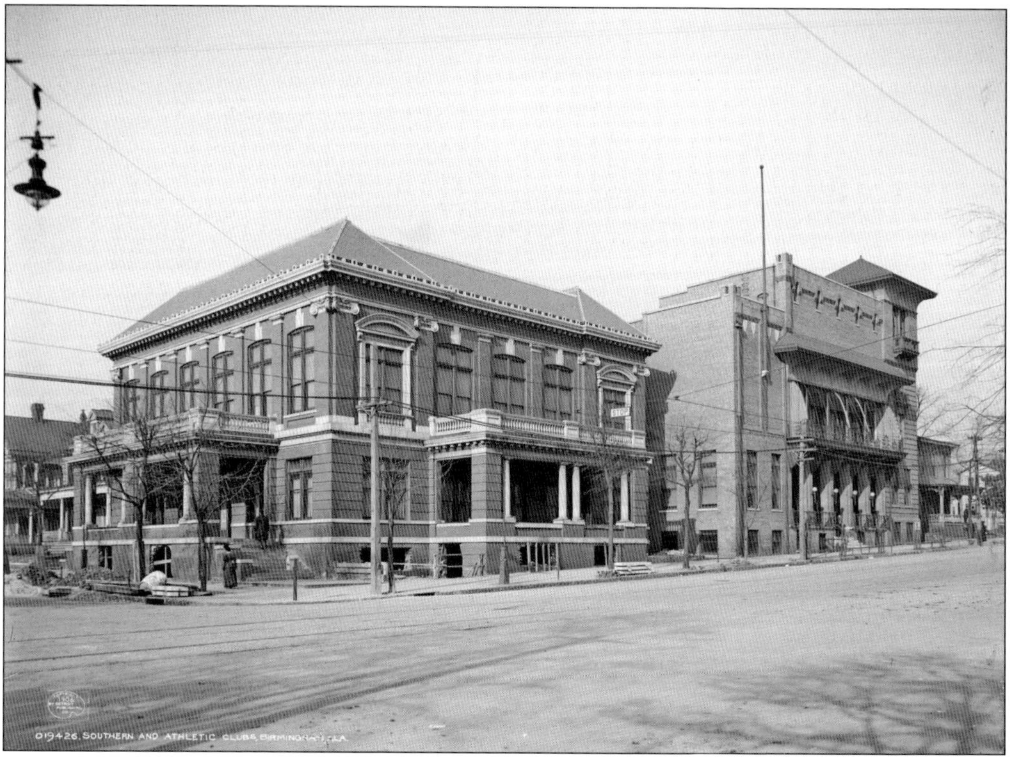

On April 6, 1917, the United States declared war on Germany and entered the First World War. To finance the war, Congress passed the First Liberty Loan Act to issue Liberty Bonds and raise $5 billion. When George Ward, president of the Birmingham City Commission, boldly committed Birmingham for $100,000 in Liberty bonds, the Kiwanis Club commended his patriotism and pledged its individual members would purchase the bonds. (LOC.)

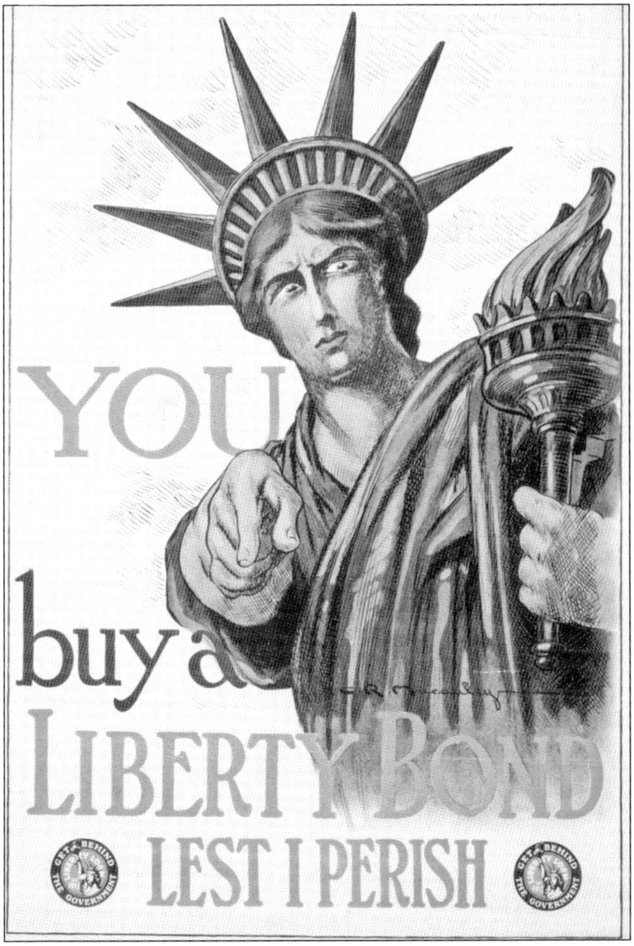

Club records indicate that the first guest speakers spoke to the club on April 18, 1917. On that day, the speakers were delegates of the US Good Roads Association's convention, meeting in Birmingham that week. This contemporary photograph, of a traveler braving a road through the swamps of south Alabama, illustrates the motivation of such associations in the early days of the 20th century. (ADAH.)

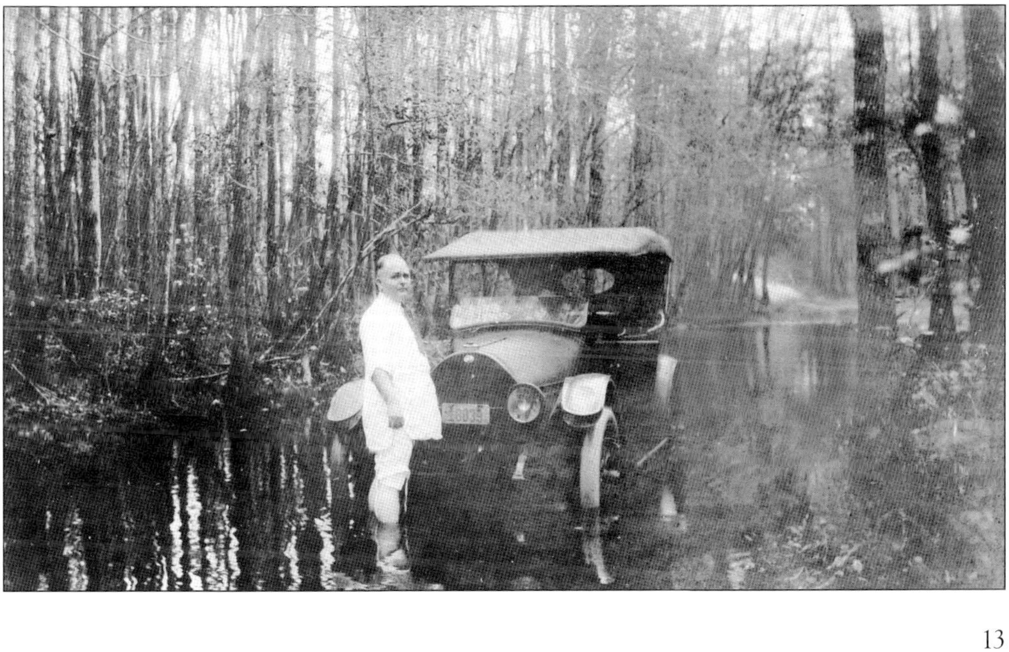

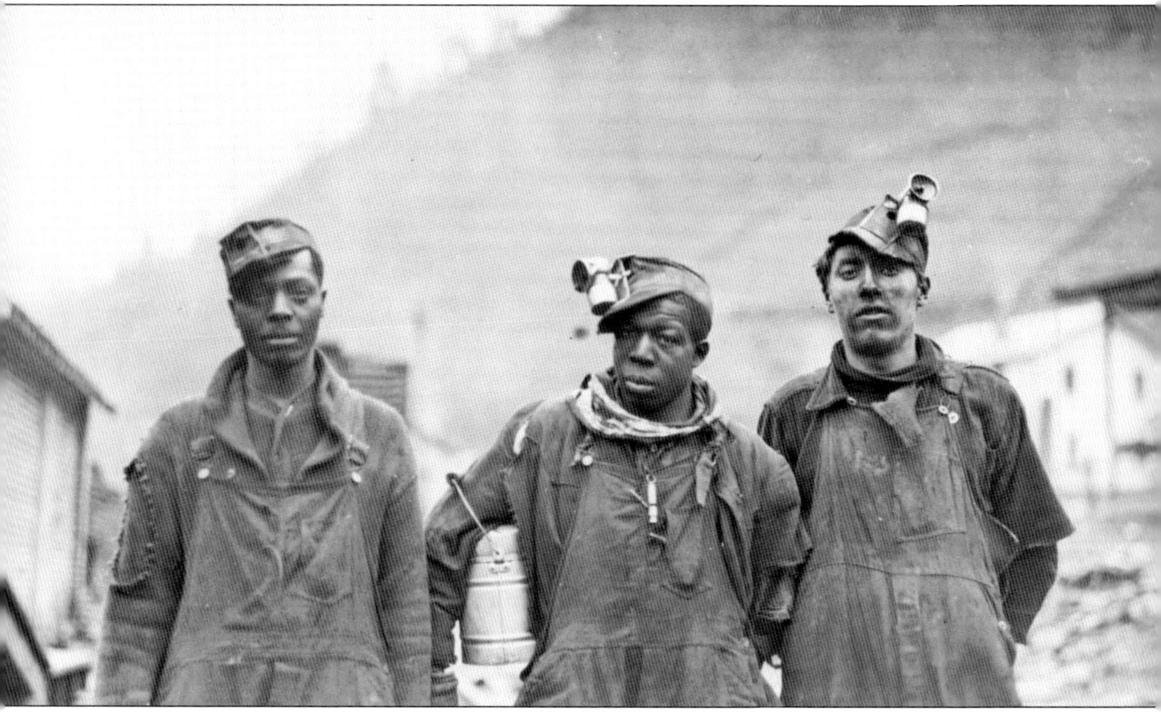

In 1917, Birmingham was home to a number of civic clubs, notably the Civitan Club (founded in Birmingham in the spring of 1917 as the genesis of what would become today's Civitan International) and the Rotary Club, founded four years earlier. Marking the beginning of a long tradition of cooperation with such clubs, the Kiwanis Club voted on May 17, 1917, to "cooperate with the Rotary and other organizations in devising some means to stop the exodus of [African American] labor from the Birmingham District." At the time, Birmingham's economy depended on the region's mining of coal and limestone and its production of pig iron and steel. A wave of migration from Birmingham to the coalfields of Kentucky and West Virginia (perhaps personified by the three West Virginia miners shown here) was of such concern that it even warranted an investigation by the US attorney in Atlanta. (LOC.)

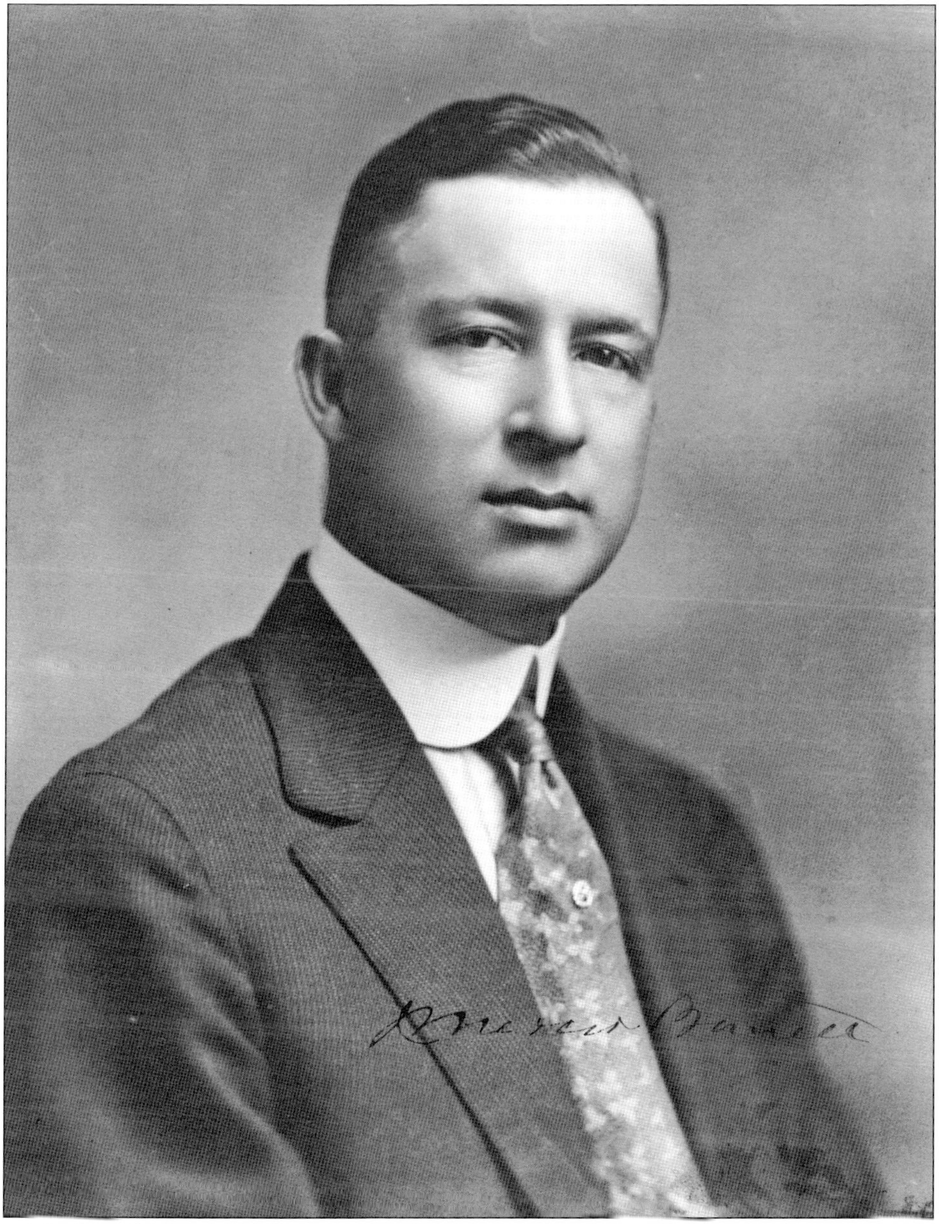

The club elected 34-year-old James Mercer Barnett its president on May 31, 1917. Barnett owned the Barnett Lumber Company and later acquired Jefferson Motors Company. A native of Eufaula, Alabama, he had graduated from the Virginia Military Institute in 1902. Barnett would ultimately serve two consecutive terms as the club's president (1917–1919). While attending the Kiwanis International Convention in Providence, Rhode Island, in 1918, he secured Birmingham as the host site for the 1919 convention. His success set the stage for Birmingham to occupy a key page in the annals of Kiwanis history, for it would be in Birmingham that leadership representing various cities' club would successfully negotiate to purchase the right to the name "Kiwanis" from founder Allen Browne. "Kiwanis, organized on a basis of trade, has found for itself a basis of service," Barnett later famously declared. In 1920, he would be elected the president of Kiwanis International. (KCOB.)

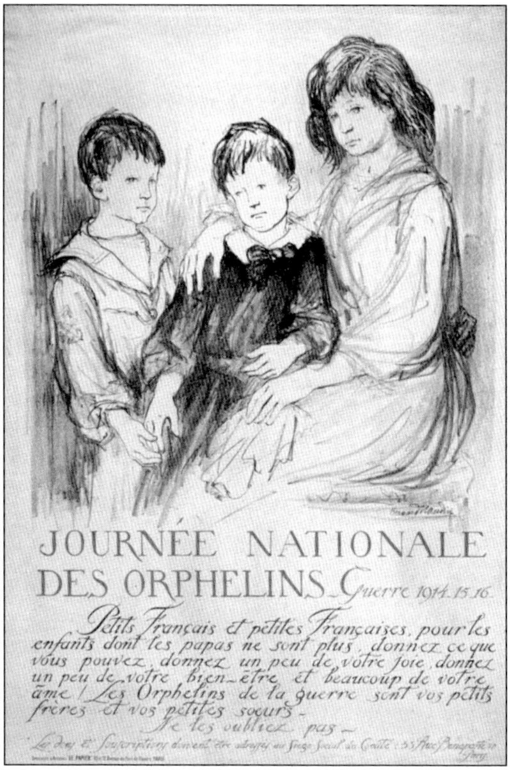

Elinor Fell, an Englishwoman with France's Orphelinat des Armees, spoke to the club on May 24, 1917. Fell's organization was dedicated to raising money for some of the 1.1 million French children left fatherless by World War I. By Fell's estimations, a donation of $73 a year would keep a child with his or her widowed mother rather than committed to a public orphanage. (LOC.)

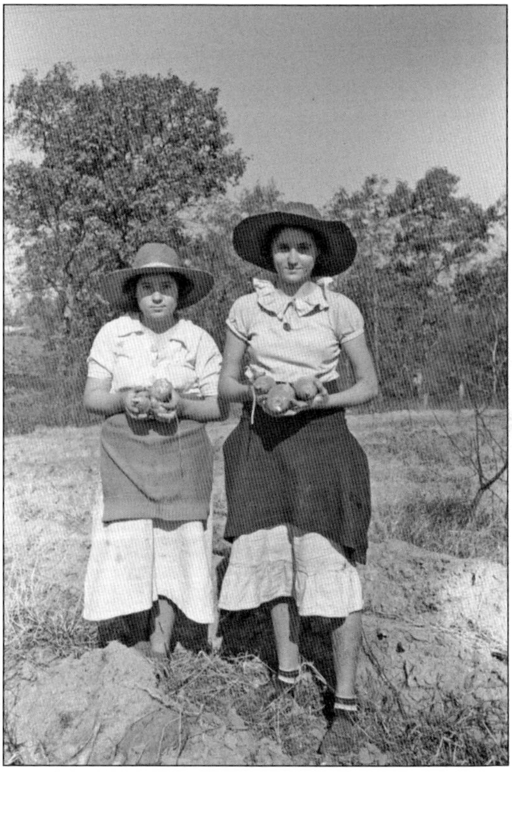

According to the club minutes from October 2, 1917, the Kiwanis Club voted "to have sweet potatoes on [its] menu," perhaps the very ones pictured here. The reason for this particular motion, as well as the identity of the Kiwanian who made the motion, are lost in the dusty annals of history. Maybe he felt that the club's annual dues of $12, plus the cost of meals, warranted sweet potatoes on the menu. (LOC.)

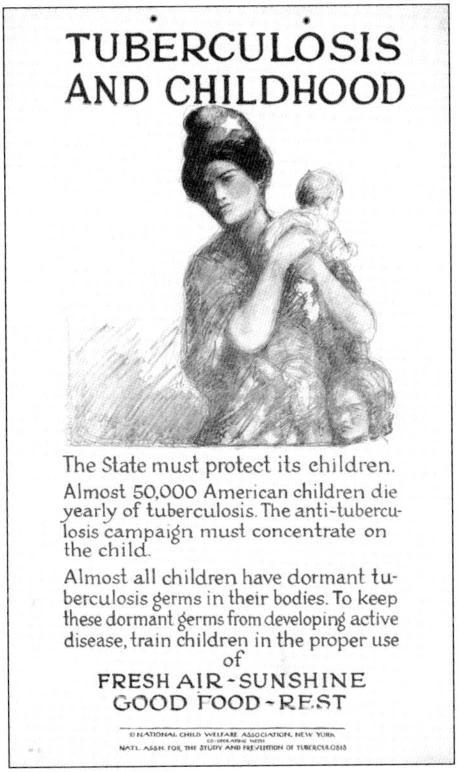

According to the National Child Labor Committee's study *Child Welfare in Alabama*, Alabama suffered 3,207 cases of pulmonary tuberculosis in 1917, with 2,689 deaths reported. At the time, tuberculosis was known as the Great White Plague, called that because of the extremely anemic pallor of its victims. Perhaps it was not surprising, then, that the Kiwanis' first recorded charitable endeavor was a raffle on October 30, 1917, that donated proceeds to the city's Anti-Tuberculosis Camp, likely similar to the one pictured here. The camp, later known as the Red Mountain Sanitorium, was located in the vicinity of what is today's Mountain Brook's English Village. The camp operated under the auspices of a missionary Englishman, George Eaves, DD, with Kathryn I. Malone as the camp's superintendent. (Both, LOC.)

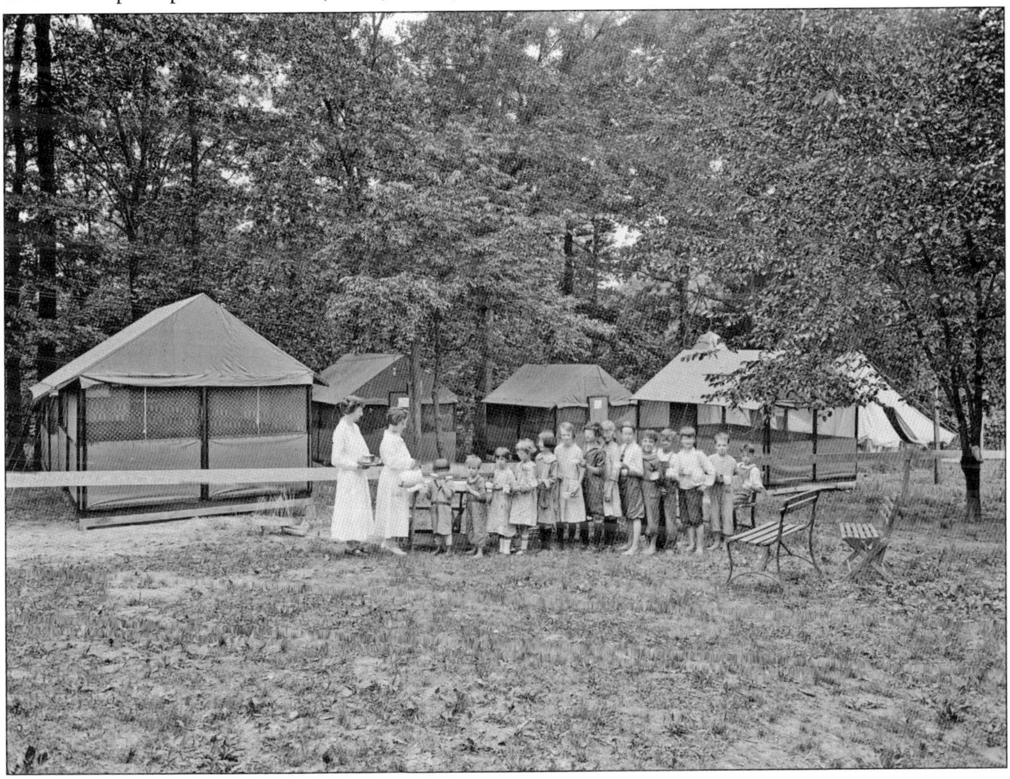

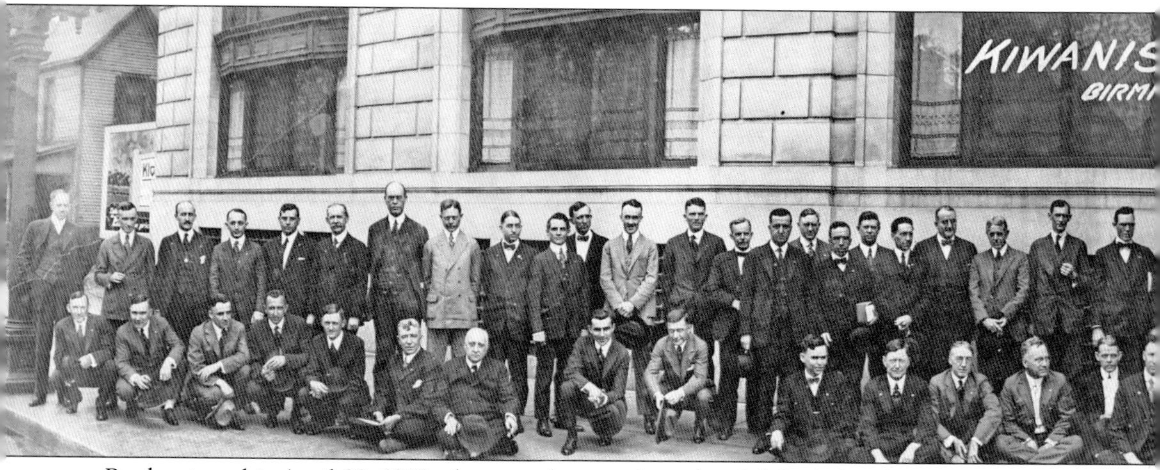

By the time this April 30, 1918, photograph was taken, the club had already had a busy year. In the first four months of 1918, the club had held a smoker at the Southern Club, donated $100 to buy wool for the Council of National Defense, entertained the Rotary Club, celebrated its one-year anniversary and, according to its club minutes, formed committees to "cooperate with city officials to establish safety zone markers" and to "investigate the matter of providing ways

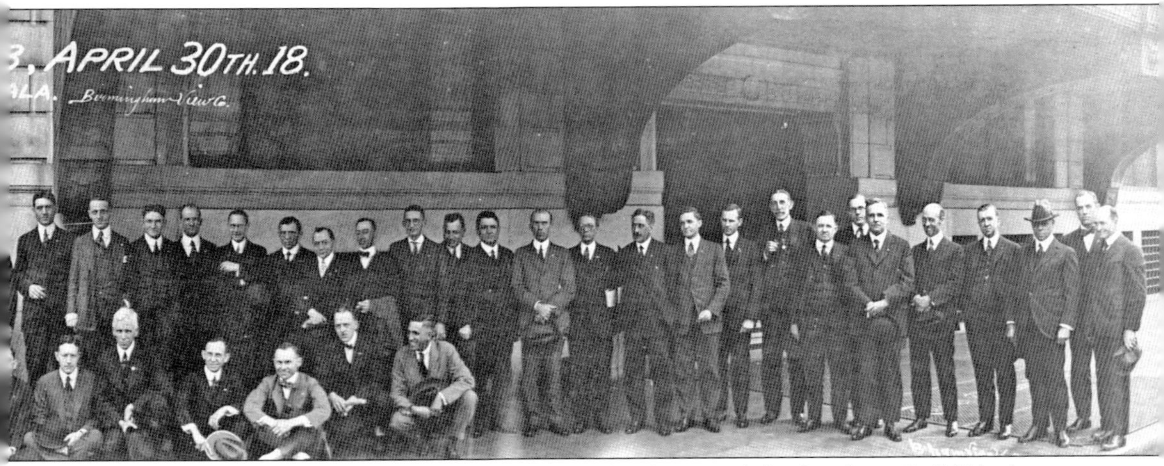

and means of securing new quarters for the Girls School," visited the Southern Bell Telephone & Telegraph Company and Tennessee Coal & Iron Company, welcomed guests ranging from a British army general to "a lady from Romania describing the conditions there on account of the war," and heard a talk on "what the Government is doing at Muscle Shoals." (BPLA.)

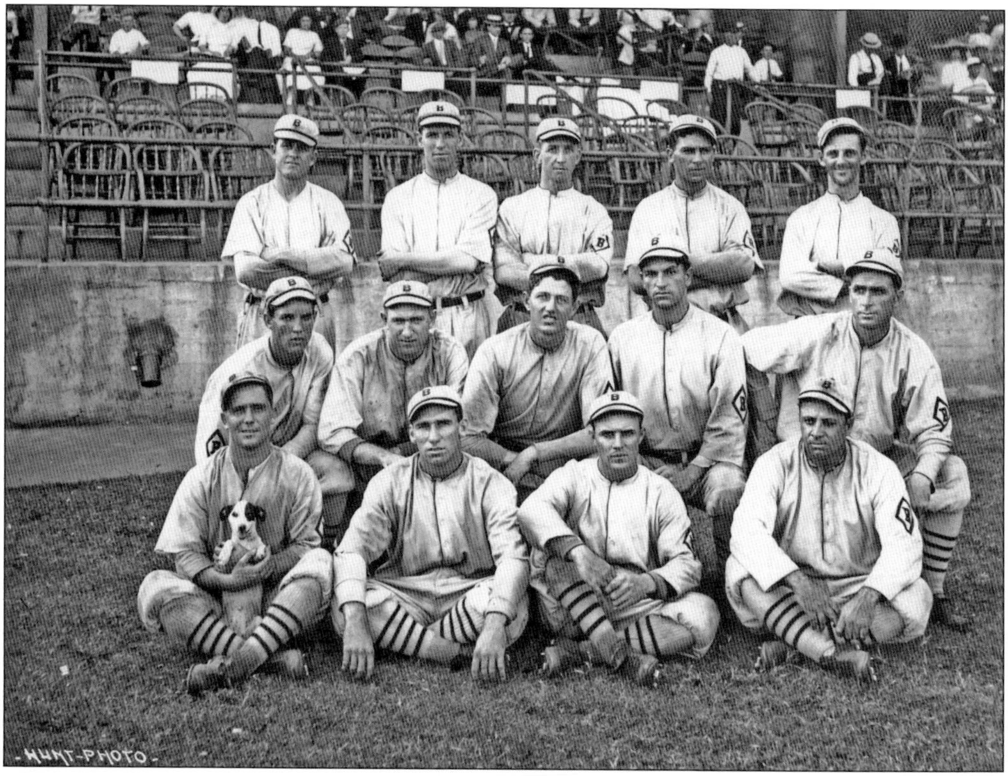

Birmingham had been home to professional baseball as early as 1895, when the Coal Barons barnstormed across the South. By 1918, the team was simply the Barons, with still-new Rickwood Field as their home ballpark. Club records reflect that on May 14, 1918, the Kiwanians adjourned their lunch meeting early and headed for Rickwood Field en masse to watch the Barons battle the Little Rock Travelers. (BPLA.)

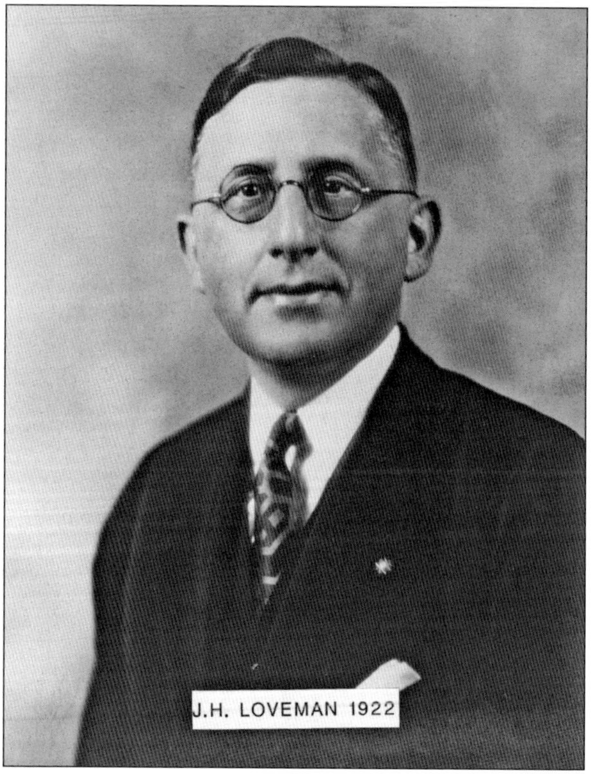

Joseph H. Loveman, shown here, was one of the club's charter members. Loveman would ultimately become the president of family retail operation Loveman, Joseph & Loeb, but first, in 1918, he offered a baby buggy to the first Kiwanian to have a son. D.C. Picard, of Picard Laboratory, claimed the honor on May 28, 1918. Four years later, in 1922, Loveman would become the club's fifth president. (KCOB.)

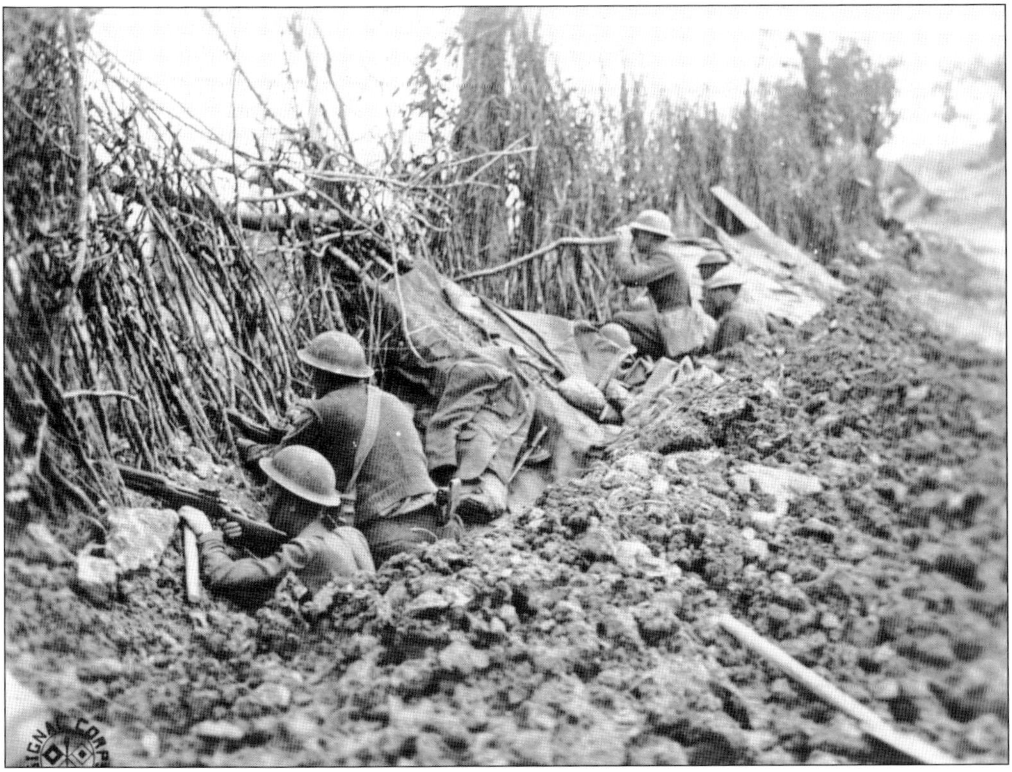

Overseas, the spring of 1918 marked the first offensives of the American Expeditionary Forces (AEF) in France, as American doughboys like the ones pictured here took the fight to their German foes. Kiwanians such as Priestly Toulmin had sons serving in the AEF. In the near future, the Kiwanis Club would count many veterans of the First World War in its ranks. (LOC.)

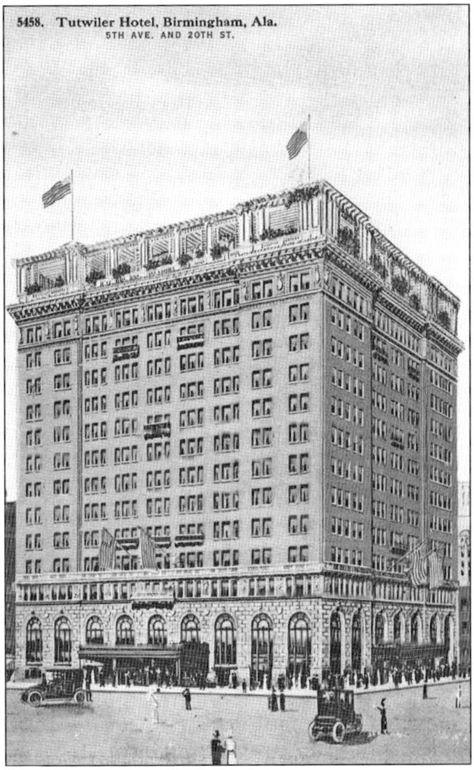

On May 19, 1919, Kiwanians descended upon Birmingham for their annual international convention. At the time, there were nearly 100 Kiwanis clubs, spread from Winnipeg, Canada, to El Paso, Texas, and from Los Angeles to Philadelphia. As local newspapers heralded their arrival, Kiwanians convened at the Tutwiler Hotel, Birmingham's premier hotel, pictured at right and located on the southeastern corner of Fifth Avenue and Twentieth Street North. (J.D. Weeks.)

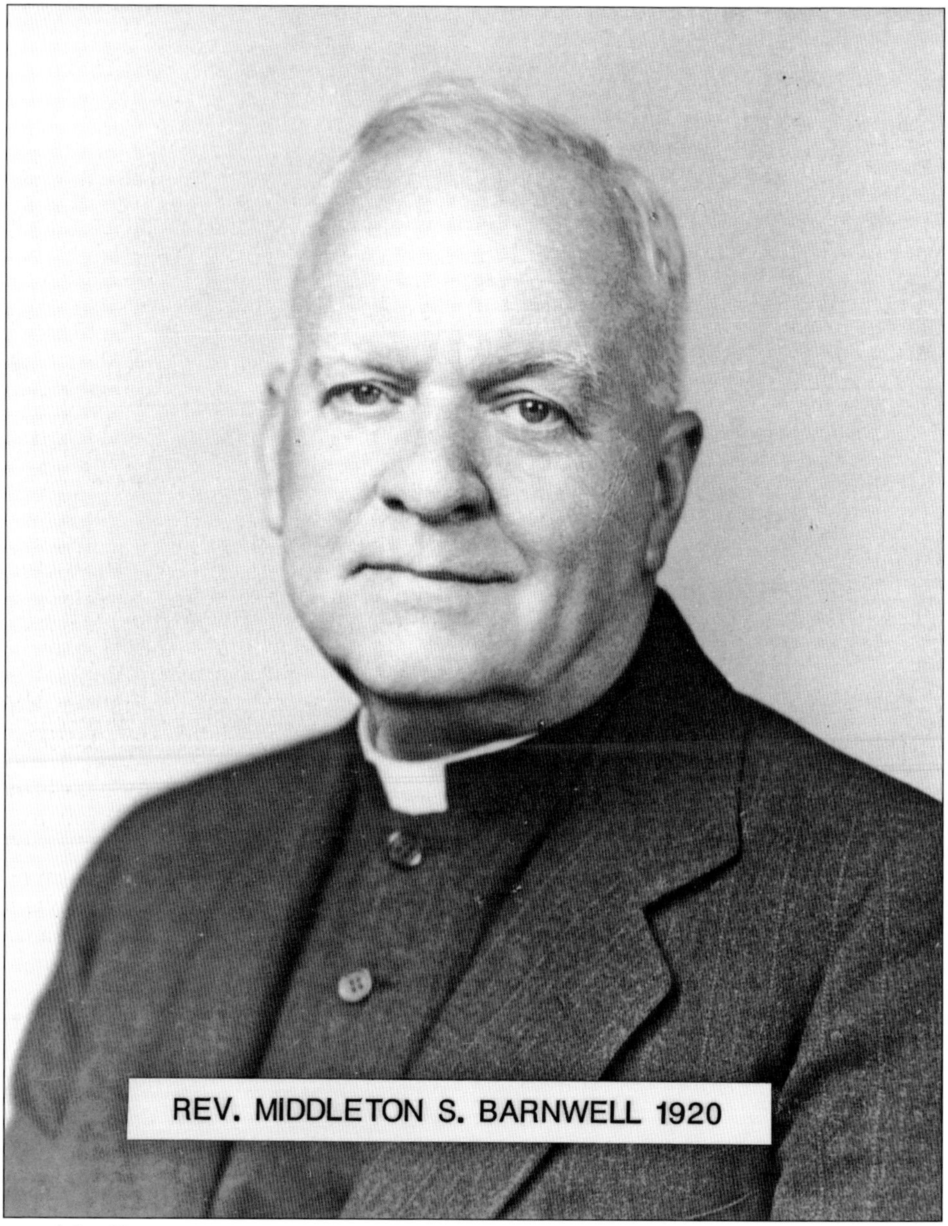

Many of the Kiwanians convening in Birmingham in the spring of 1919 were dissatisfied with founder Allen Browne's mercantile focus on creating platforms for an "exchange-of-business" between members, as well as his lucrative commission (in 1919, up to $15 a head) for each new member. Some Kiwanians also felt that he seemed to be better at recruiting—and collecting commissions—than managing the paperwork associated with a growing international organization. Accordingly, inside the Tutwiler Hotel, a cadre of negotiators from the far-flung clubs, including Birmingham's Mercer Barnett and Rev. Middleton "Barney" Barnwell (pictured), worked to distance Browne from Kiwanis International. Barnwell, Episcopal rector at Birmingham's Cathedral Church of the Advent, lent a measured and spiritual voice to the negotiations. A year later, Barnwell would become the club's third president. In 1925, Barnwell became the bishop of Idaho; in 1936, he became the long-serving bishop of Georgia. (KCOB.)

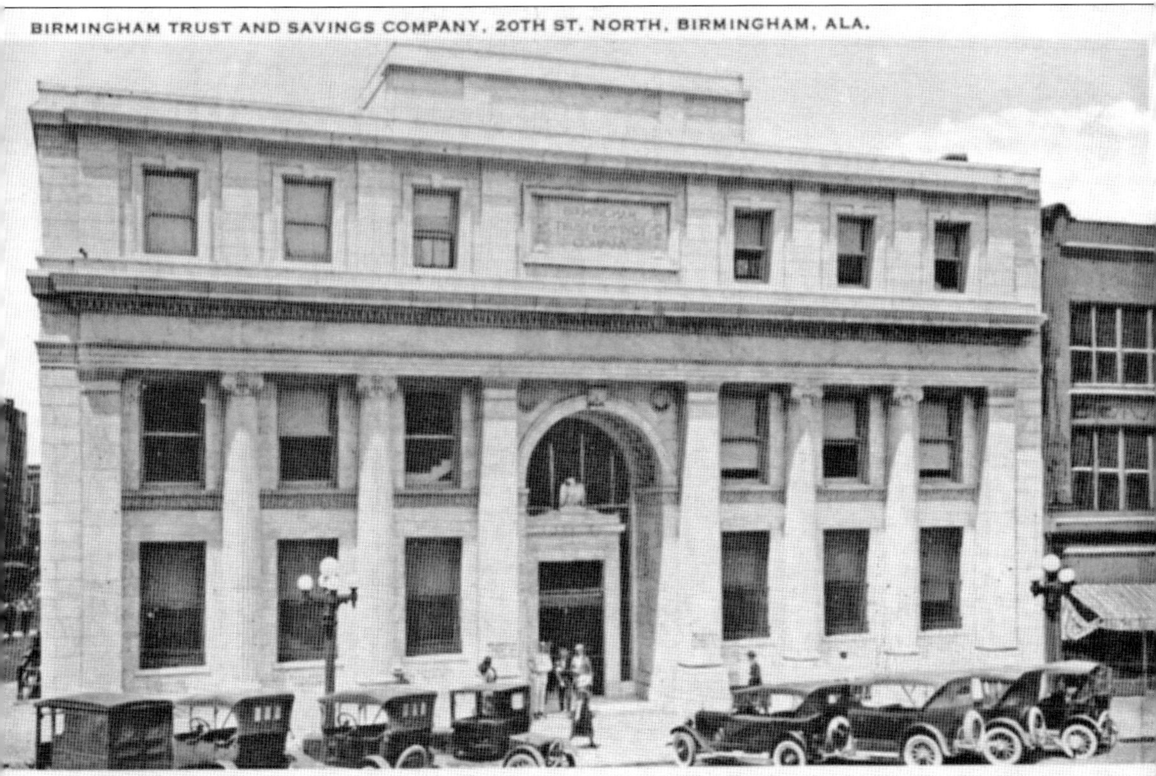

Negotiations to separate Allen Browne and the Kiwanis name continued until the early hours of the morning of May 21, 1919, when Browne finally agreed to be bought out for $17,500 in cash. Glad to be rid of Browne, the delegates literally wrote hatfuls of personal checks to buy their peace. However, the checks needed to be converted to cash, and Mercer Barnett personally guaranteed each of them to Col. Thomas O. Smith. Smith, a veteran of the Spanish-American War who ran the Birmingham Trust & Savings Company, was a fellow Kiwanian and one of Alabama's foremost bankers. In short order, Barnett's young assistant, Joseph H. Brady, trotted the four blocks to Smith's bank (pictured at 112 Twentieth Street North), cashed his satchel full of checks, and returned to the Tutwiler. The transaction completed, Browne, with cash in hand, wasted no time catching a Louisville & Nashville train for unknown points north. (ADAH.)

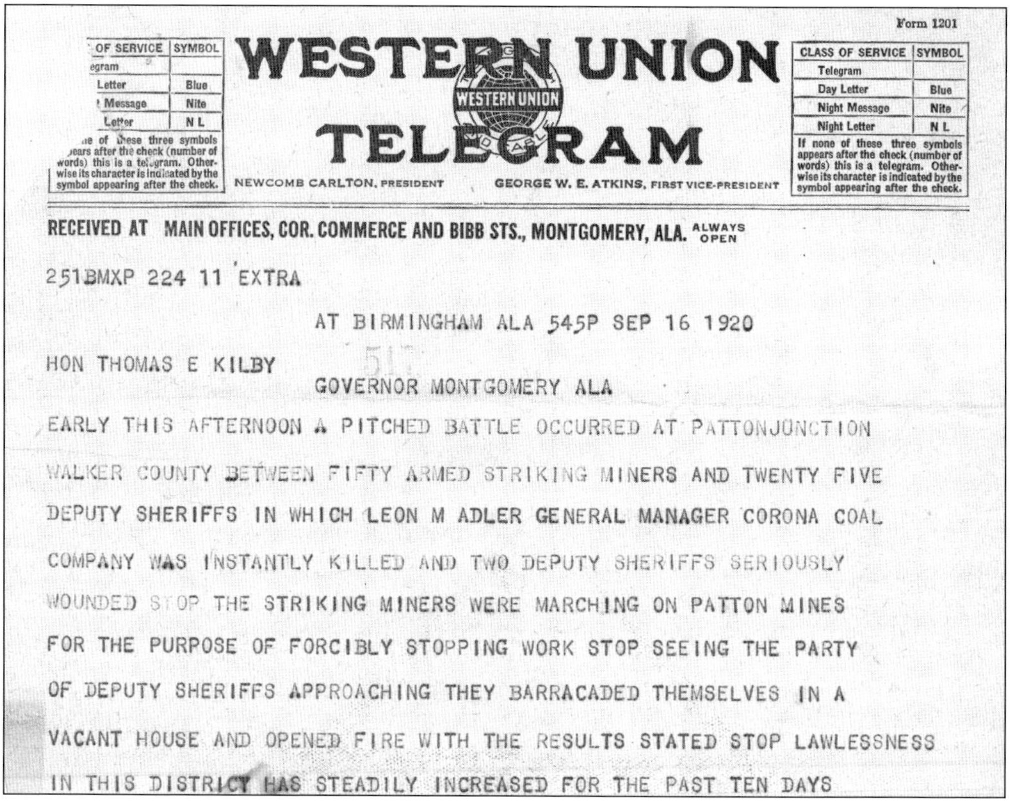

Form 1201

CLASS OF SERVICE	SYMBOL
Telegram	
Day Letter	Blue
Night Message	Nite
Night Letter	N L

If none of these three symbols appears after the check (number of words) this is a telegram. Otherwise its character is indicated by the symbol appearing after the check.

WESTERN UNION TELEGRAM

NEWCOMB CARLTON, PRESIDENT GEORGE W. E. ATKINS, FIRST VICE-PRESIDENT

RECEIVED AT MAIN OFFICES, COR. COMMERCE AND BIBB STS., MONTGOMERY, ALA. ALWAYS OPEN

251BMXP 224 11 EXTRA

AT BIRMINGHAM ALA 545P SEP 16 1920

HON THOMAS E KILBY

GOVERNOR MONTGOMERY ALA

EARLY THIS AFTERNOON A PITCHED BATTLE OCCURRED AT PATTONJUNCTION WALKER COUNTY BETWEEN FIFTY ARMED STRIKING MINERS AND TWENTY FIVE DEPUTY SHERIFFS IN WHICH LEON M ADLER GENERAL MANAGER CORONA COAL COMPANY WAS INSTANTLY KILLED AND TWO DEPUTY SHERIFFS SERIOUSLY WOUNDED STOP THE STRIKING MINERS WERE MARCHING ON PATTON MINES FOR THE PURPOSE OF FORCIBLY STOPPING WORK STOP SEEING THE PARTY OF DEPUTY SHERIFFS APPROACHING THEY BARRACADED THEMSELVES IN A VACANT HOUSE AND OPENED FIRE WITH THE RESULTS STATED STOP LAWLESSNESS IN THIS DISTRICT HAS STEADILY INCREASED FOR THE PAST TEN DAYS

On September 16, 1920, former club member Leon M. Adler, manager of the Corona Coal Company's mines in Jefferson County, was murdered in strike-related violence. Birmingham business leaders appealed to Gov. Thomas Kilby for assistance in keeping law and order in the nearby mining towns in this telegram. Meanwhile, an angry Kiwanis Club quickly passed a resolution that "deplore[d] his untimely death as a loss to ourselves and our country." (ADAH.)

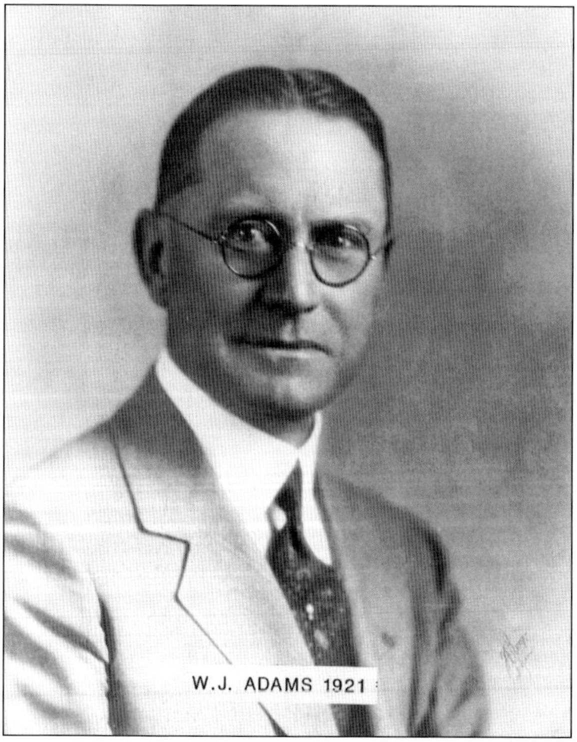

W.J. ADAMS 1921

The club elected W. Jack Adams its president in 1921. A native of Opelika, Alabama, Adams came to Birmingham as a child. He owned and operated Adams Drug Store. Adams was one of the founders of the city's Boys Club and was also a founder of Independent Presbyterian Church, where he served as chairman of its board of deacons. (KCOB.)

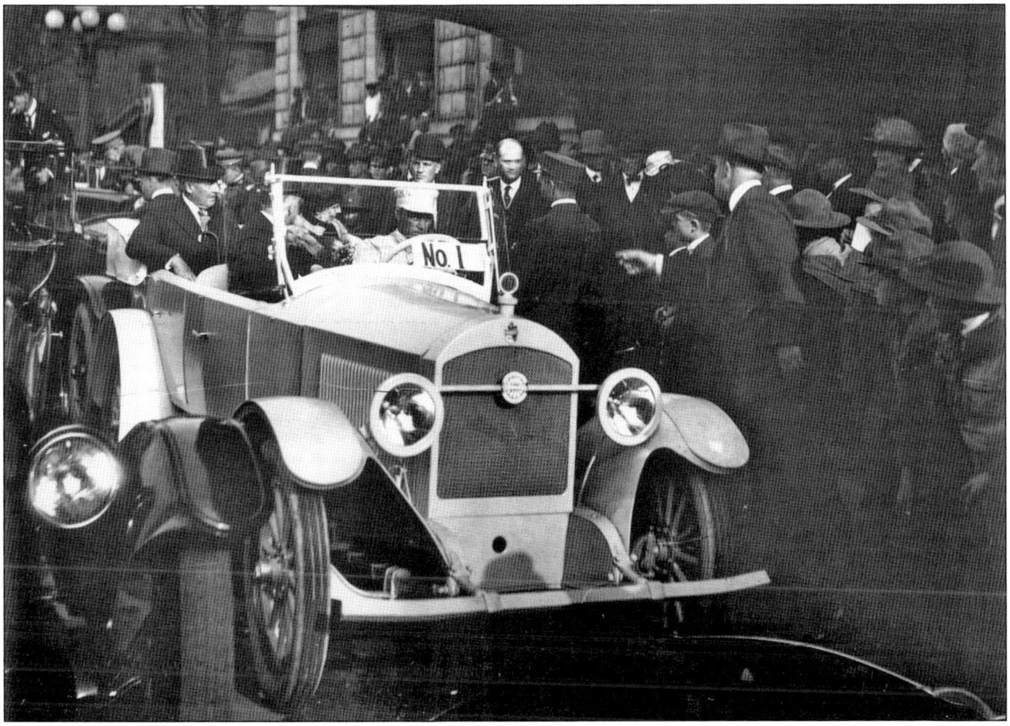

On October 26, 1921, Pres. Warren Harding visited Birmingham as the city marked its 50th anniversary. He arrived from the city's train station in a gleaming white Premocar, built in Birmingham by Preston Motors, and attended a luncheon hosted by the Kiwanis Club at the Tutwiler Hotel. In a speech made in Birmingham during his visit, Harding made national news when he declared, "Let the black man vote when he is fit to vote; prohibit the white man voting when he is unfit to vote . . . whether you like it or not, unless our democracy is a lie, you must stand for that equality." (Both, BPLA.)

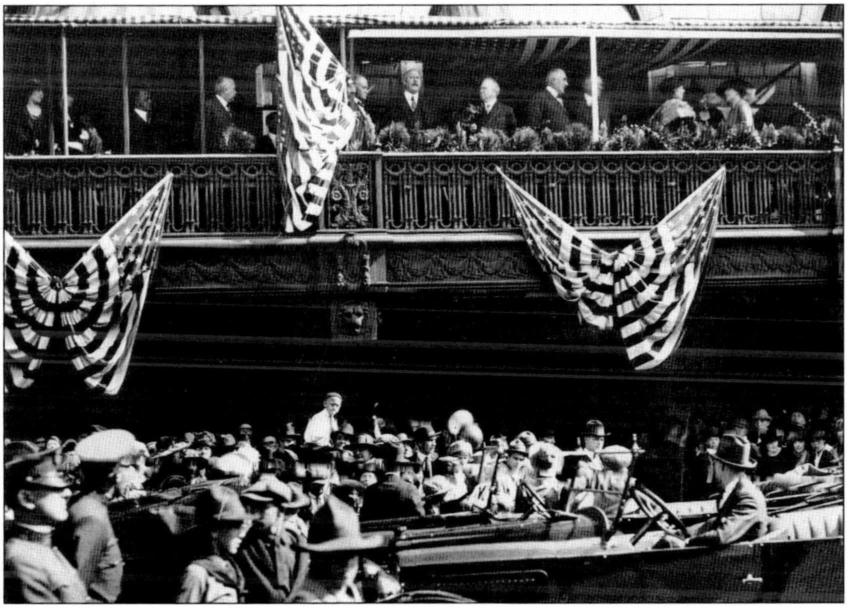

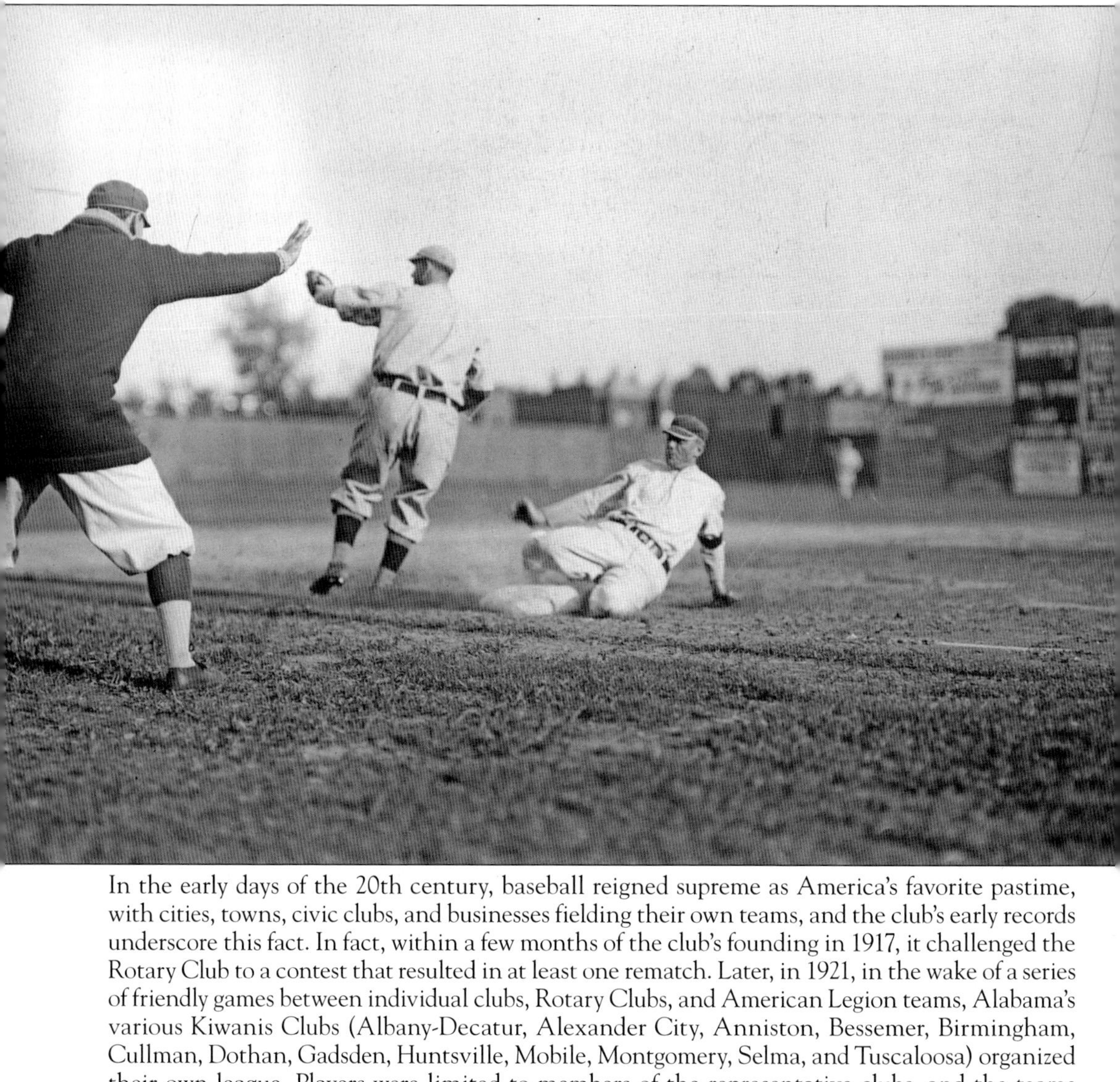

In the early days of the 20th century, baseball reigned supreme as America's favorite pastime, with cities, towns, civic clubs, and businesses fielding their own teams, and the club's early records underscore this fact. In fact, within a few months of the club's founding in 1917, it challenged the Rotary Club to a contest that resulted in at least one rematch. Later, in 1921, in the wake of a series of friendly games between individual clubs, Rotary Clubs, and American Legion teams, Alabama's various Kiwanis Clubs (Albany-Decatur, Alexander City, Anniston, Bessemer, Birmingham, Cullman, Dothan, Gadsden, Huntsville, Mobile, Montgomery, Selma, and Tuscaloosa) organized their own league. Players were limited to members of the representative clubs, and the teams battled for the Bailey Pennant (presumably in honor of Waldo E. Bailey, Kiwanis International field organizer) and the Arrant Loving Cup. Unfortunately, records do not indicate what club claimed the pennant or the cup. (LOC.)

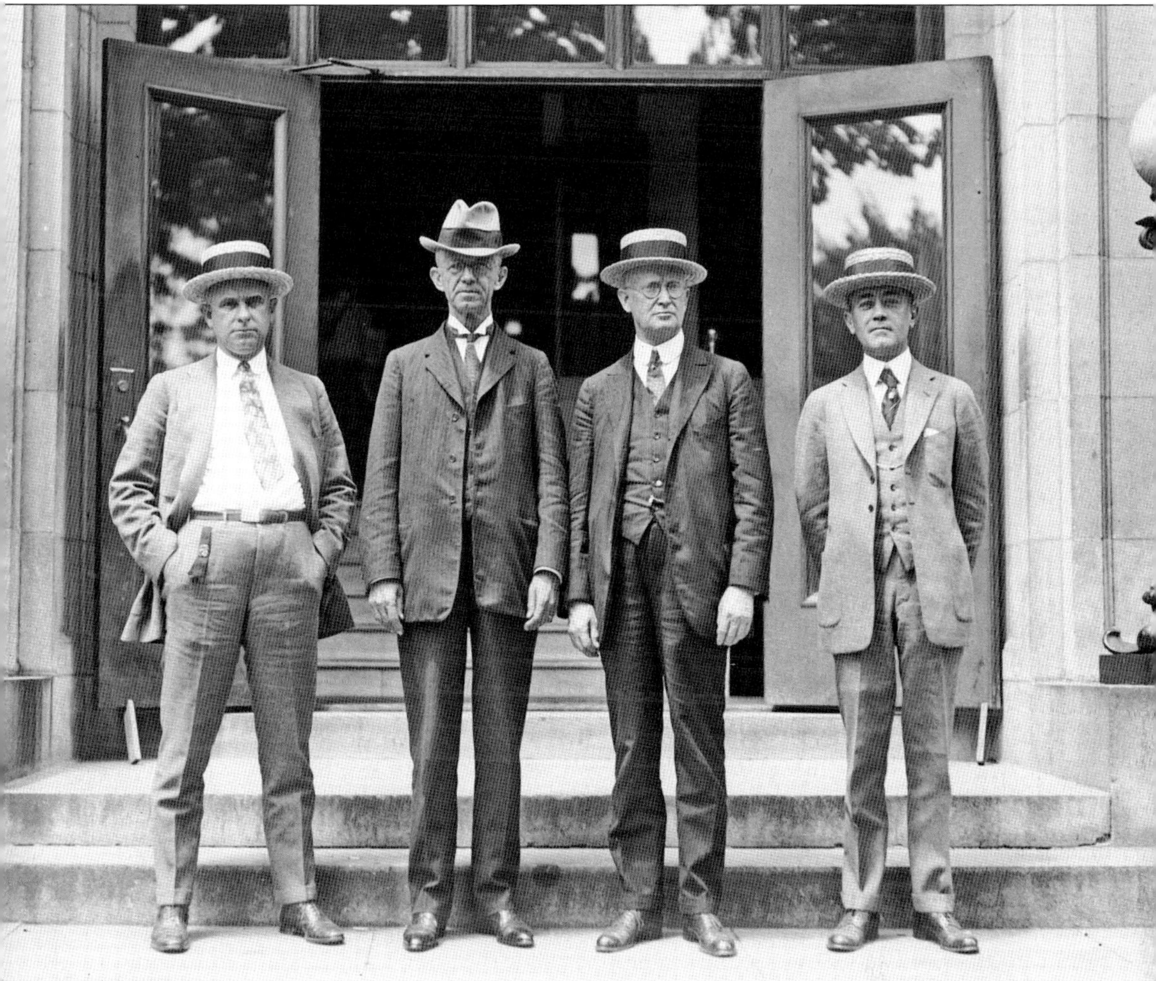

The remarkable Erskine Ramsay (second from right), who became the club's president in 1923, was a legend in his own time. He came from Pennsylvania to Birmingham in 1887 at the age of 23 to work for the Tennessee Coal, Iron & Railroad Company; struck out on his own in 1901 into Birmingham's coal, coke, and real estate markets; and, by 1904, had reportedly "ceased counting his money except in thousands," according to *The Presidents of the Kiwanis Club of Birmingham*. For 20 years, Ramsay was the president of the Birmingham Board of Education and a member of multiple other civic and corporate boards as well, including Protective Life Insurance Company, Avondale Mills, and Buffalo Rock. The namesake of Birmingham's Ramsay High School and various buildings on college campuses across Alabama, Ramsay was renowned for a seemingly boundless spirit of generosity. This photograph shows him and three other Birmingham coal operators in 1922 after a meeting with Commerce Secretary Herbert Hoover, a testament to Ramsay's national stature at the time. (LOC.)

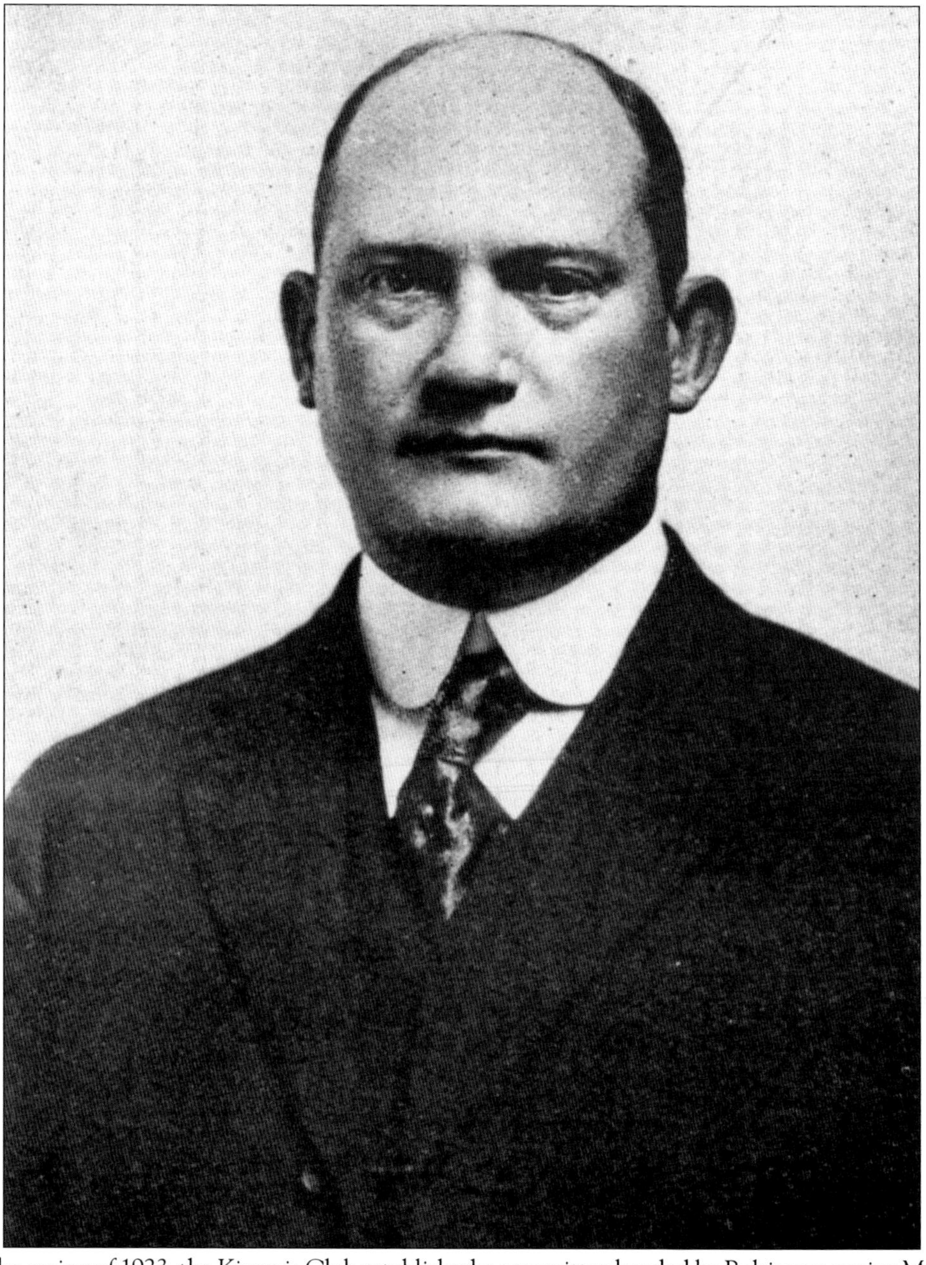

In the spring of 1923, the Kiwanis Club established a committee headed by Baltimore native Major Paul "M.P." Phillips to pursue the enactment of a parks bill in the Alabama Legislature that would enable Birmingham to create the Parks & Recreation Board autonomous of the Birmingham City Commission. Consulting with the famed Olmsted Brothers landscape architecture firm and in cooperation with state representative Lewis Bowen, Phillips succeeded in securing passage of the necessary legislation on September 29, 1923. Selected as one of the new board's first commissioners, he designated Olmsted Brothers to craft a master parks plan for Birmingham. When Phillips died scarcely two years later of a heart attack at the age of 52, the *Birmingham Age-Herald* lauded the president of the Steel City Lumber Company as "a man of strong conviction . . . and who had an intense passion to be of the public service." (BPLA.)

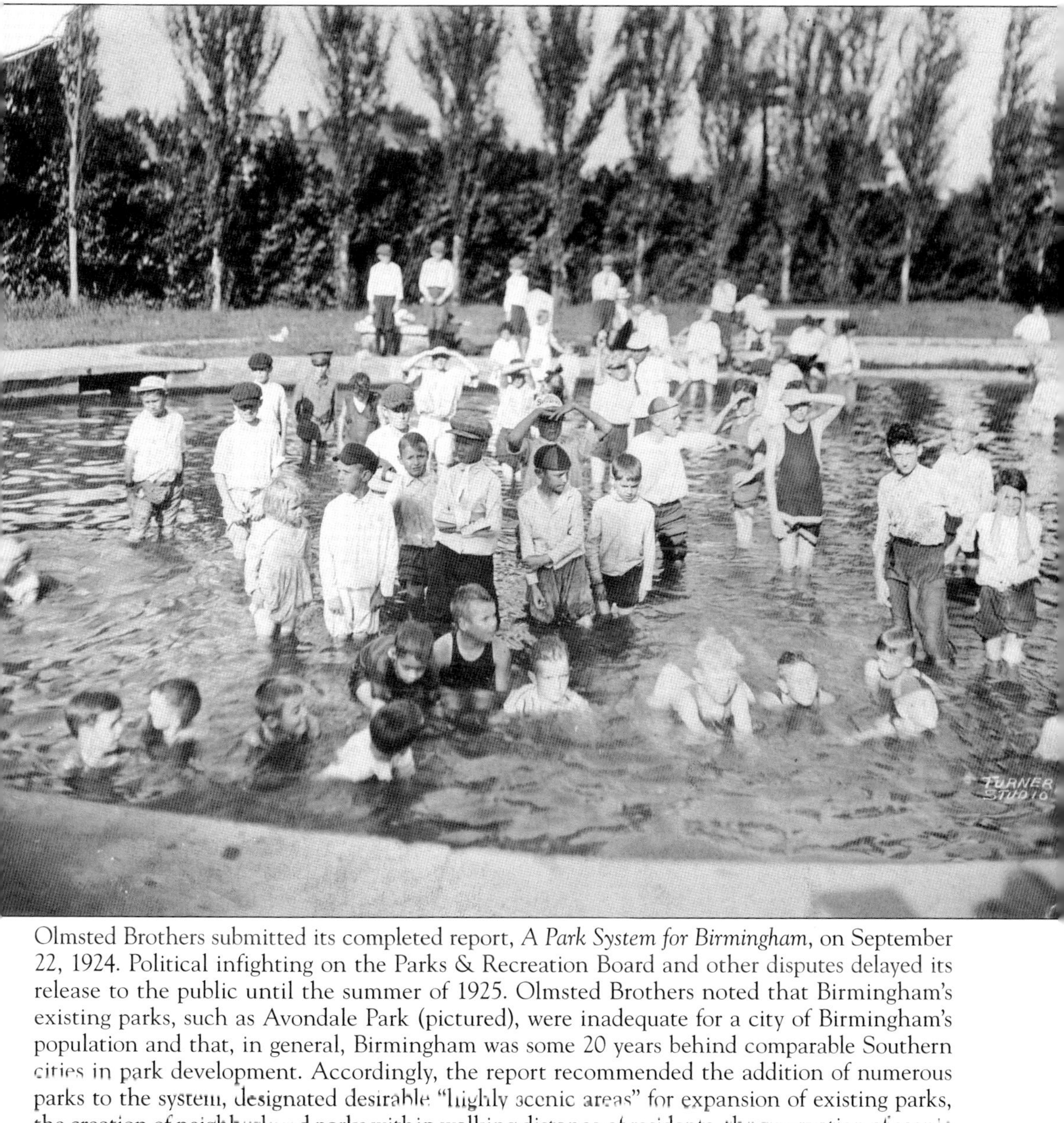

Olmsted Brothers submitted its completed report, *A Park System for Birmingham*, on September 22, 1924. Political infighting on the Parks & Recreation Board and other disputes delayed its release to the public until the summer of 1925. Olmsted Brothers noted that Birmingham's existing parks, such as Avondale Park (pictured), were inadequate for a city of Birmingham's population and that, in general, Birmingham was some 20 years behind comparable Southern cities in park development. Accordingly, the report recommended the addition of numerous parks to the system, designated desirable "highly scenic areas" for expansion of existing parks, the creation of neighborhood parks within walking distance of residents, the reservation of scenic parkways along the city's ridgelines, and large creekside parks in the city's floodplains. Although swiftly changing urban priorities would stymie many of the plan's more ambitious visions, the urban park and trail initiatives funded by the Kiwanis Club's $4 million centennial celebration project in 2017 will help bring the earlier club members' and the Olmsted Brothers' vision closer to fruition. (ADAH.)

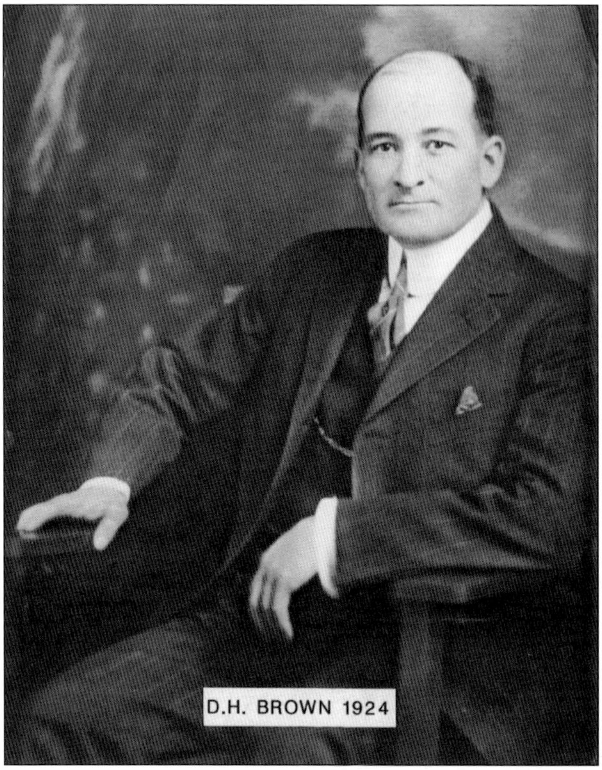

Darby H. Brown was the club's president in 1924. A native of Sumterville, Alabama, he left a teaching position in Mobile to pursue business success in Birmingham at the turn of the century. Brown was the president of D.H. Brown and Company, a sales agent in Birmingham's lucrative coal and coke industry in the early 20th century. (KCOB.)

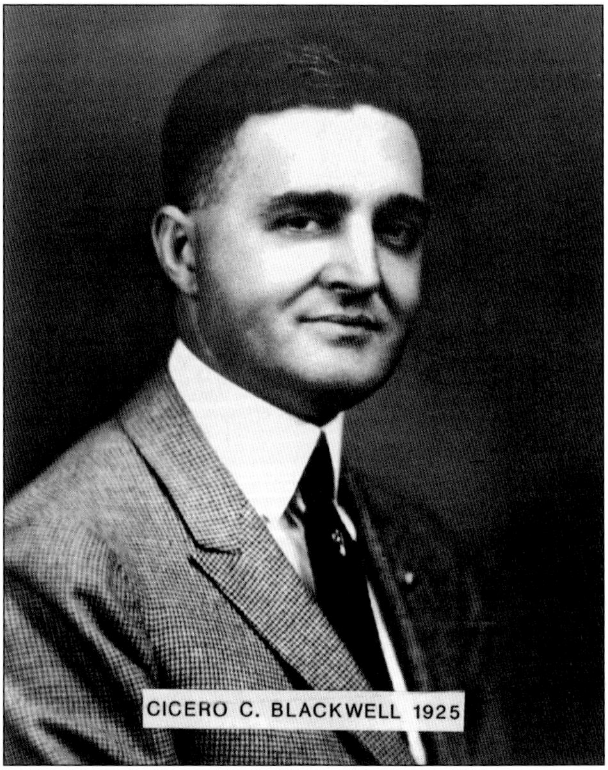

In 1925, Cicero Claude "C.C." Blackwell became the club's president. Working at Moore-Handley Hardware Company, Blackwell rose through the ranks from office boy to become the company's vice president. He was one of many Kiwanians who championed the cause of the Birmingham Boys Club. "He worked hard at every job and he interested in everything right up to the time of his death," *The Presidents of the Kiwanis Club of Birmingham* would one day recall. (KCOB.)

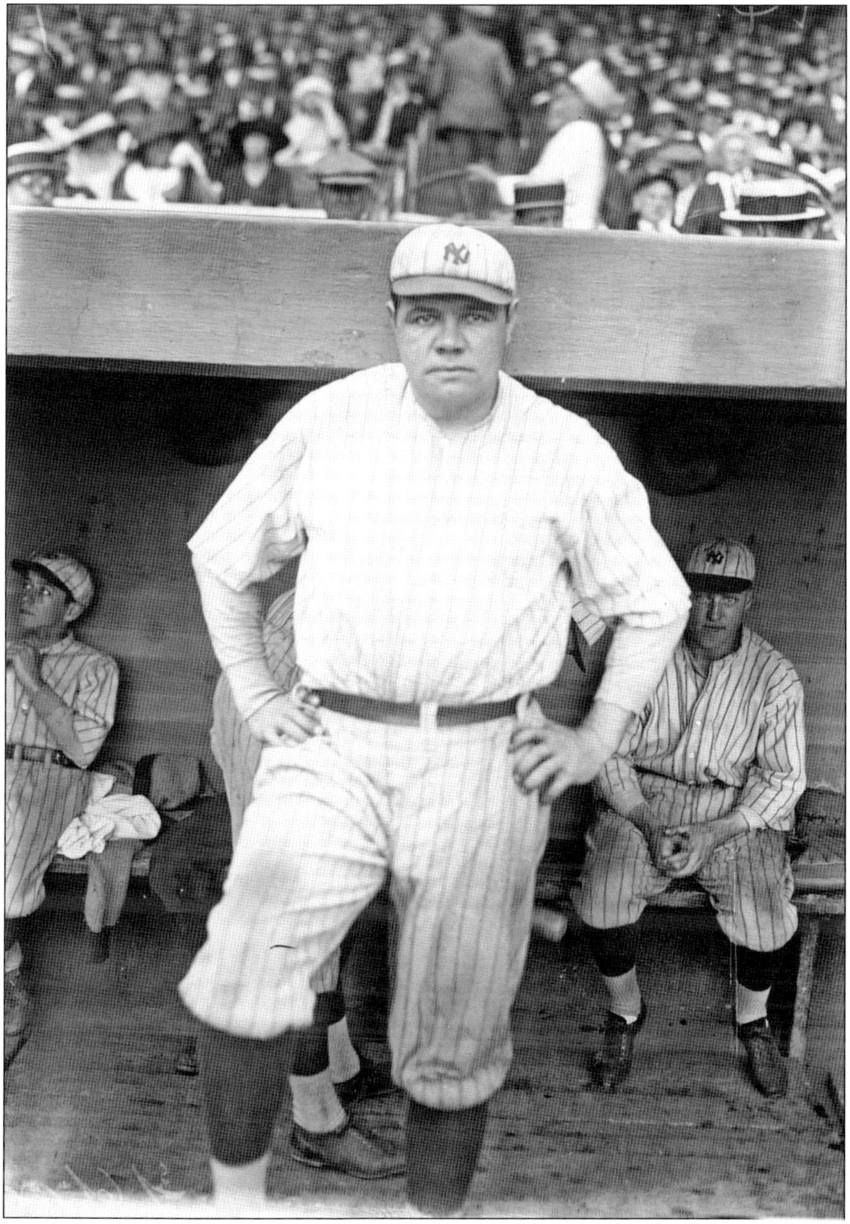

On March 30, 1925, the great Babe Ruth visited Birmingham as Ruth's New York Yankees played the Brooklyn Dodgers in an exhibition game at Rickwood Field. On that spring day, the "Sultan of Swat" hammered a grand slam in the second inning to lift the Yankees to an 11-8 victory. The next day, before the two teams boarded a train for Nashville to continue their traveling southern series, Ruth was the honored guest at the Kiwanis Club's weekly luncheon at the Hillman Hotel. Reflecting on the event, a writer for the Birmingham Chamber of Commerce declared that "the youngsters who were lucky enough to get a peep at the big giant at the Kiwanis Club are prouder of the fact than if they had been invited to spend a week at the White House." That same series of games, however, took a toll on Ruth's health that, by the time the Yankees reached Asheville, North Carolina, culminated in the infamous "bellyache heard 'round the world" and a six-week stay at St. Vincent's Hospital in New York. (LOC.)

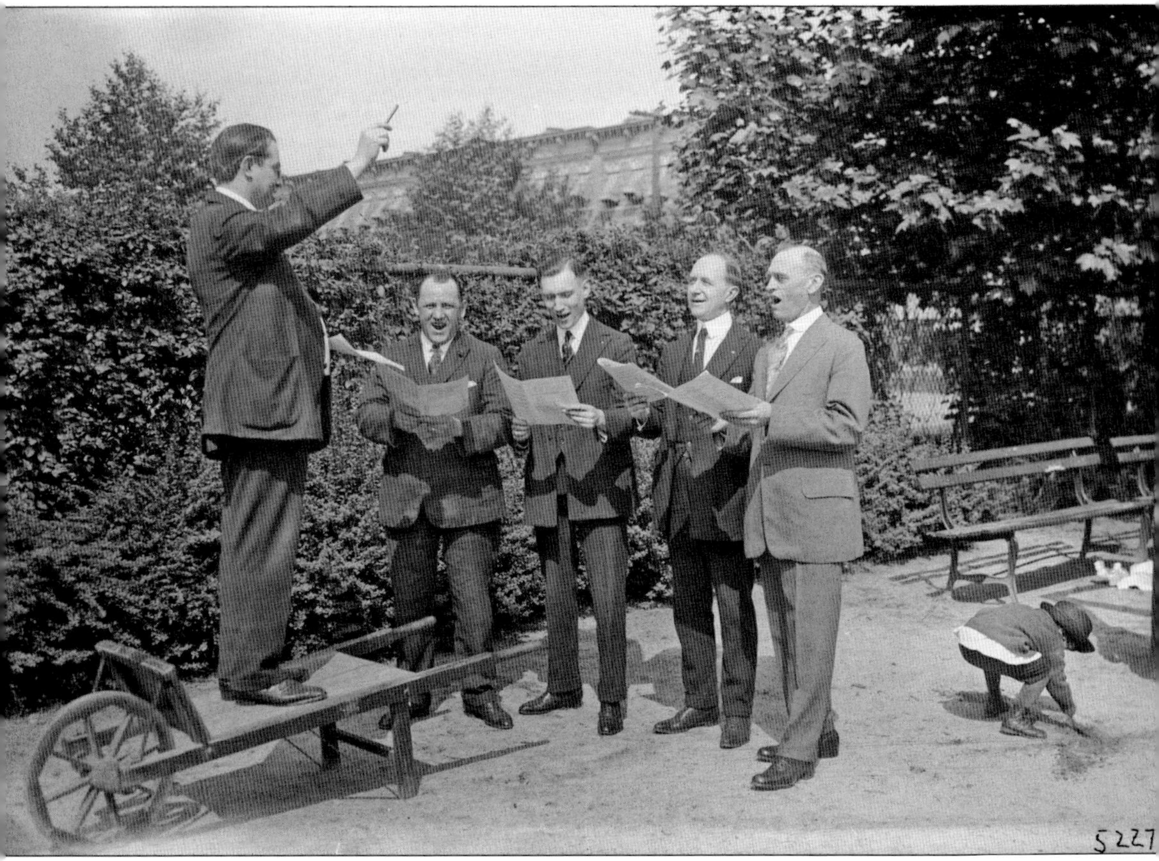

Singing was an integral part of the fellowship of the weekly club luncheons at the Hillman and later the Tutwiler Hotels, and the club's budget even accounted for the services of a professional singer to lead the weekly serenades. Official songbooks available to the members included such standards as "God Bless America" and "For He's a Jolly Good Fellow" and lesser-known ditties like "I'm Crazy 'Bout Kiwanis" and "The Kiwanis Booster Song." "It is now universally recognized in Kiwanis that music is one of the most important features of the program," the foreword to one such book reads. "The saying that 'A singing club is a good club' has a most practical significance, as proved by experience. No matter how vital the other activities may be, the fact remains that the spirit of congeniality and good fellowship, which is the foundation of every club, finds its best and most natural expression in the common bond of music." (LOC.)

Kentucky native James Edward Chappell was the club's president in 1926. With a reputation as "one of the most brilliant Southern journalists of the era," as related in his club president's biography, he had been hired by the *Birmingham News* in 1908. When elected president of the club, Chappell was the president and general manager of the paper, a position he would hold for another two decades. (KCOB.)

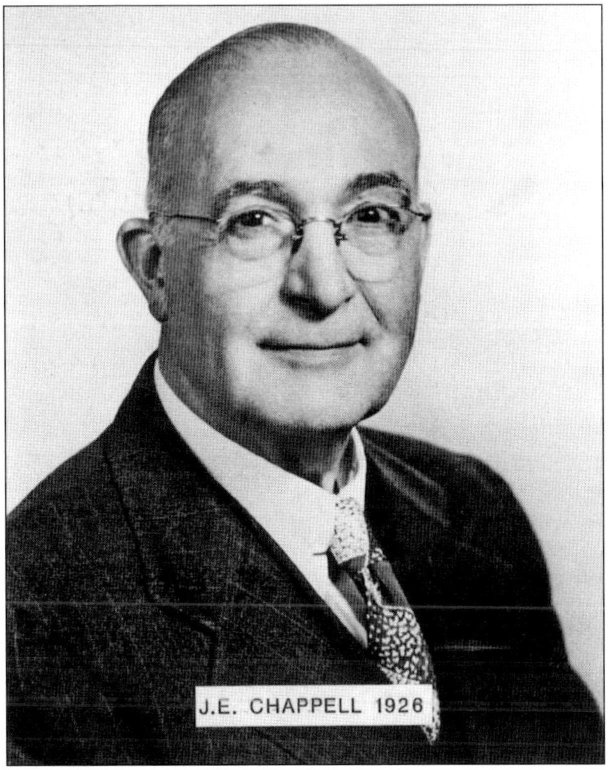

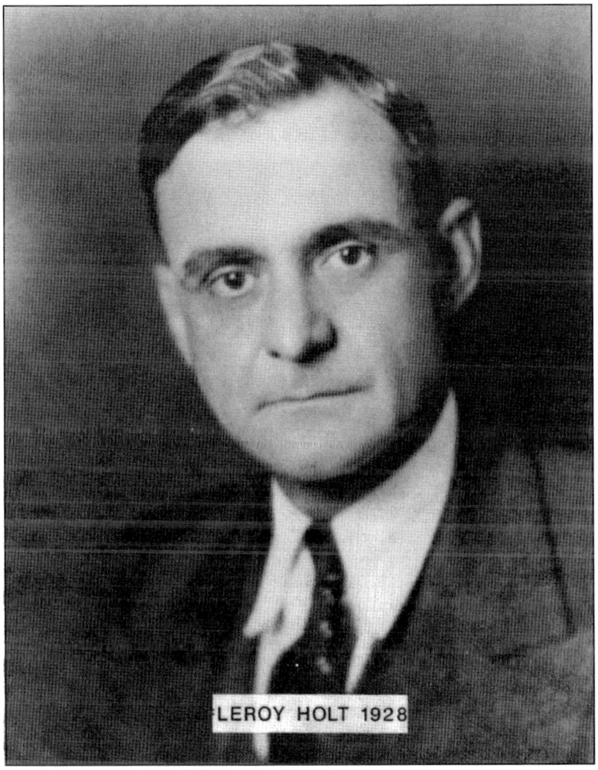

Harold McDermott and Leroy Holt became the club's 10th and 11th presidents respectively in 1927 and 1928. An officer with the Newcastle Coal Company and the Stith Coal Company, McDermott was one of the founders of the Crippled Children's Clinic and Hospital and became the organization's first president in 1929. When Holt (pictured) became the club's president in 1928, he was the purchasing agent for Tennessee Coal & Iron Company. (KCOB.)

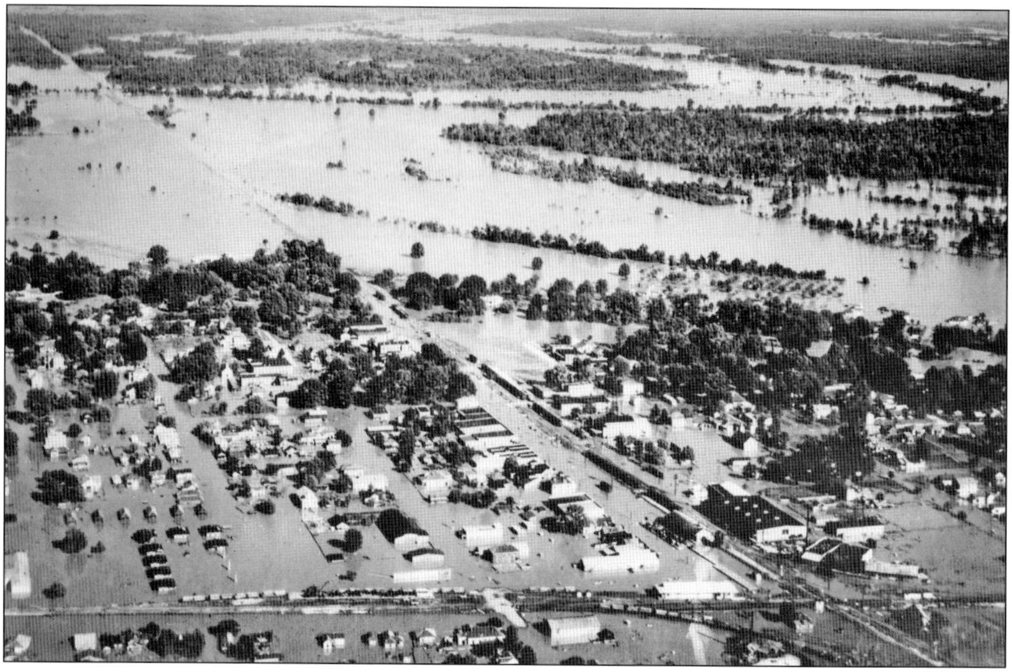

Catastrophically heavy rains in the winter of 1926–1927 led to what became known as the Great Mississippi Flood of 1927. It was the most destructive river flood in the history of the United States. Some 27,000 square miles along the Mississippi River were inundated, with over 700,000 people left homeless and more than 500 lives lost. The region—particularly Mississippi, Arkansas, and Louisiana—incurred $1 billion in damages. This was an incredible sum at a time when the entire federal budget was merely $3 billion. The Red Cross issued international pleas for assistance; the Kiwanis Club of Birmingham responded by donating over $1,700 to the relief effort—$100 from each member. (Both, US Army Corps of Engineers, Vicksburg District.)

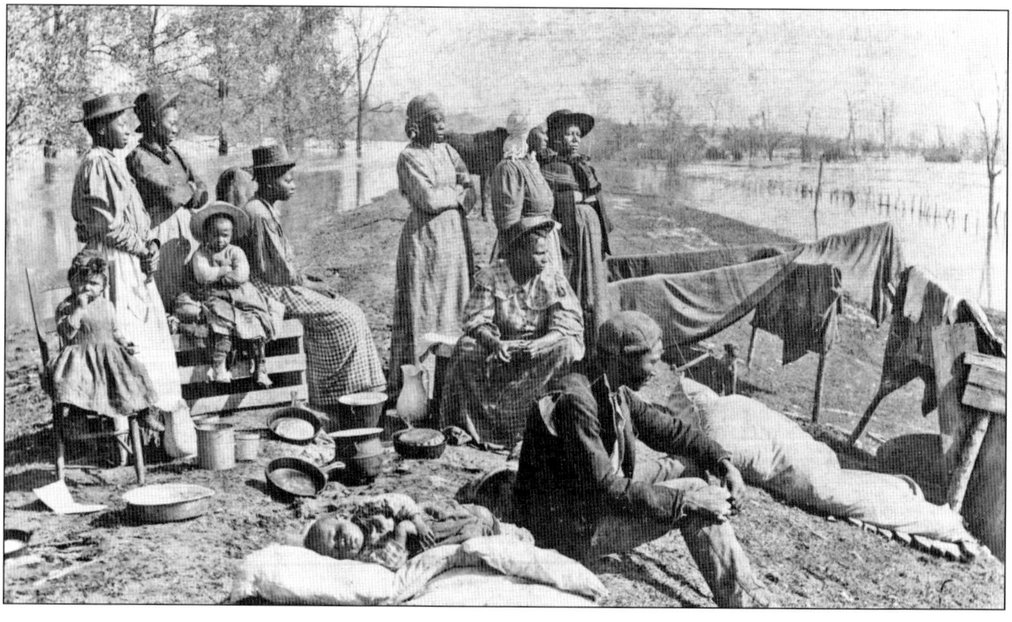

On January 11, 1927, the club met as guests of Alabama Power Company at the company's still-new (completed in 1925) corporate headquarters. The building was adorned with a 16-foot-high, gold-leafed statue of the Roman goddess Electra, much to the titillation of many an otherwise staid Birmingham businessman. As Alabama Power proudly pointed out to its guests, the building, designed under the architectural auspices of Birmingham's Warren-Knight & Davis firm, was built entirely of materials—steel, iron, brick, granite, and limestone—that came from within 60 miles of Birmingham. The building still stands on the corner of Sixth Avenue North and Eighteenth Street North. (Both, Alabama Power Company Archives.)

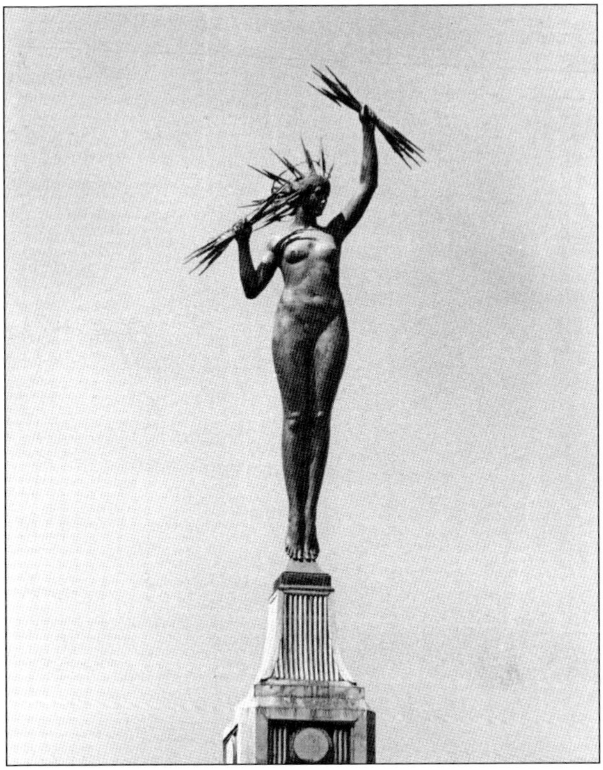

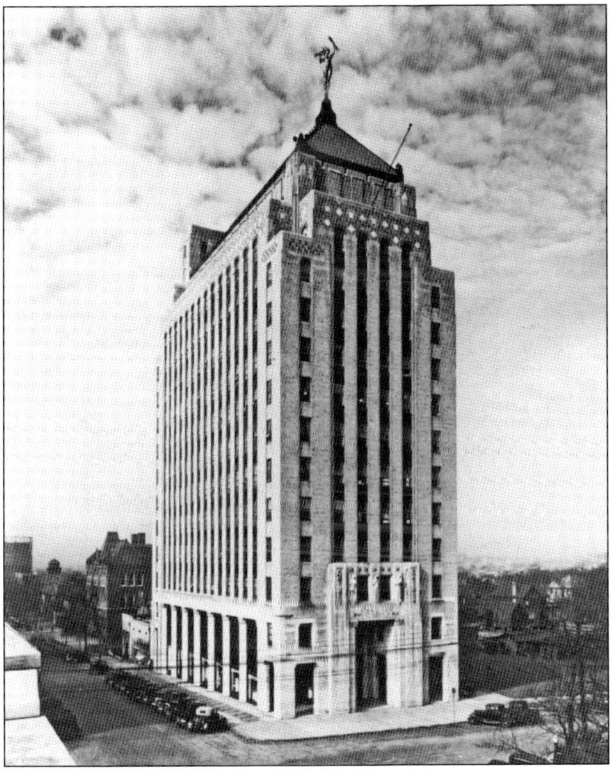

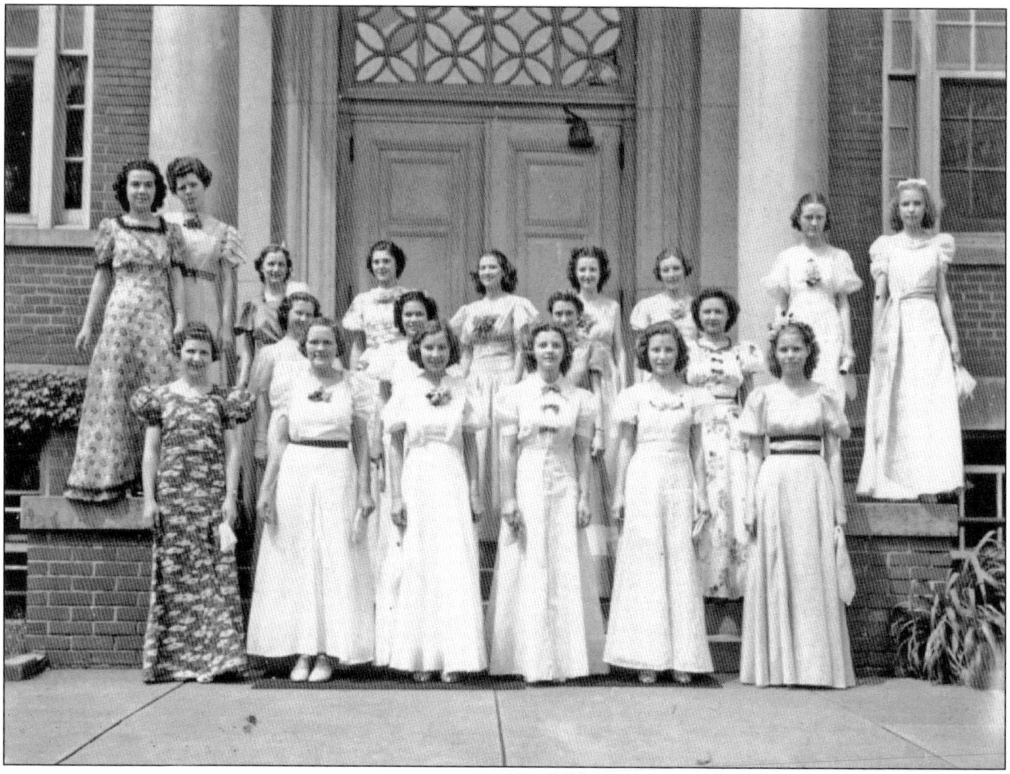

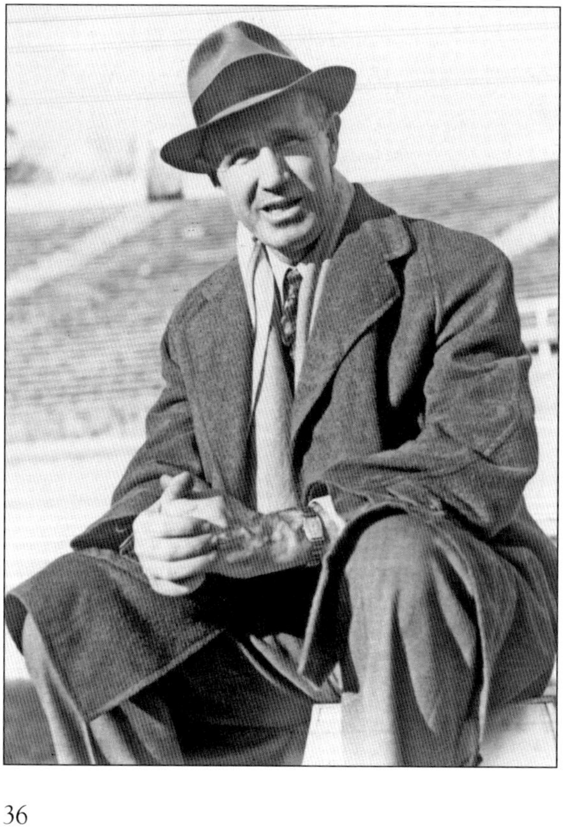

On February 9, 1928, the club took leave of Birmingham and, boarding a passenger train, embarked upon a one-hour journey south to Montevallo, home of the Alabama College, State College for Women, for a tour of the school, a luncheon, and entertainments provided by the college's students. Founded in 1896, the college ultimately went coed in 1956 and is today's University of Montevallo. (University of Montevallo.)

Legendary football coach Wallace C. Wade addressed the club on March 20, 1928. The University of Alabama had hired Wade away from Vanderbilt University, where he was an assistant coach, in 1923; Alabama's win over the University of Washington in the 1926 Rose Bowl changed the face of college football forever. When Wade spoke to the club, he had amassed a 39-7-3 record and claimed shares of three national championships in Tuscaloosa. (University of Alabama.)

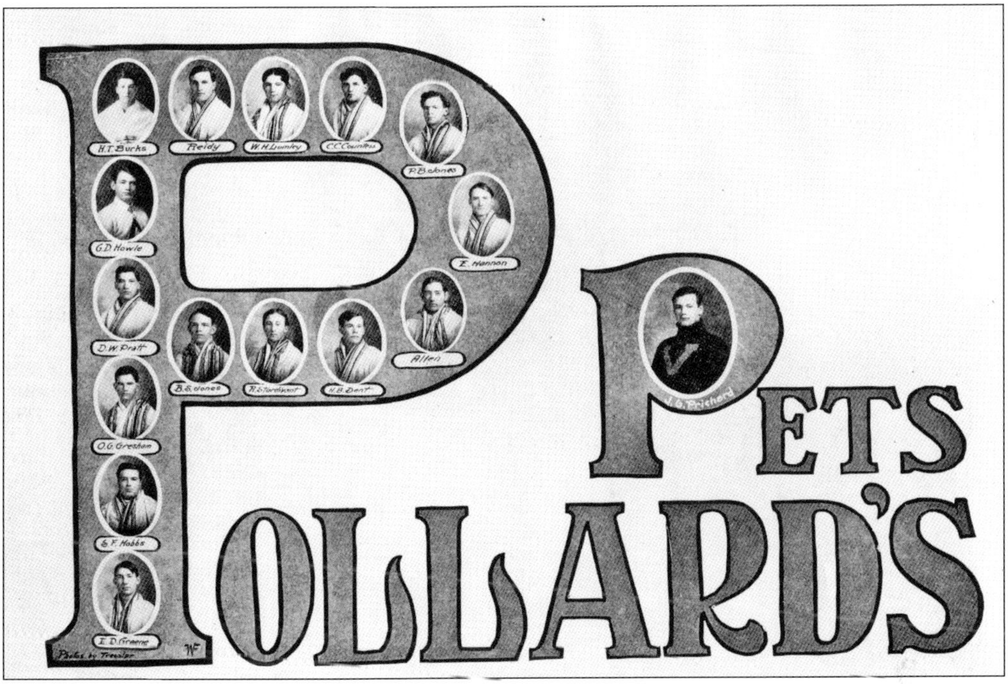

In the club's early years, its willingness to make bold resolutions regarding the pressing issues of the day was far more pronounced than today. The 21-year football hiatus between the University of Alabama (its 1907 team shown above) and Auburn was apparently one such issue. Accordingly, on May 1, 1928, the club resolved that the schools should resume the series that had last been played in 1907. (University of Alabama.)

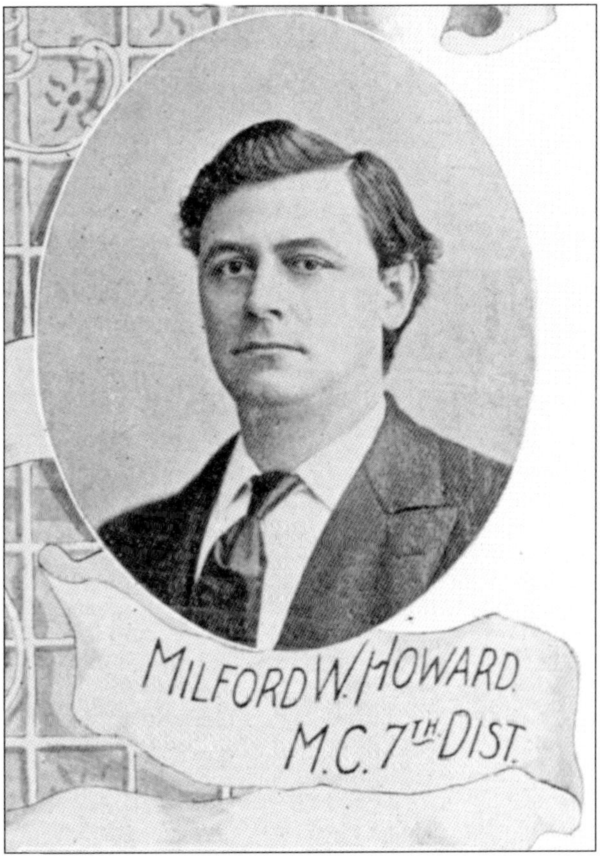

Milford W. Howard, who had formerly represented Alabama's Seventh District in the US House of Representatives, spoke to the club on September 4, 1928. Earlier that year, Howard had, remarkably, traveled to Italy to interview dictator Benito Mussolini and, in a talk entitled "Mussolini and Italy," expressed the unfortunate view that Mussolini's Fascism would "possibly form a working model for a storm-tossed world." (Collection of the US House of Representatives.)

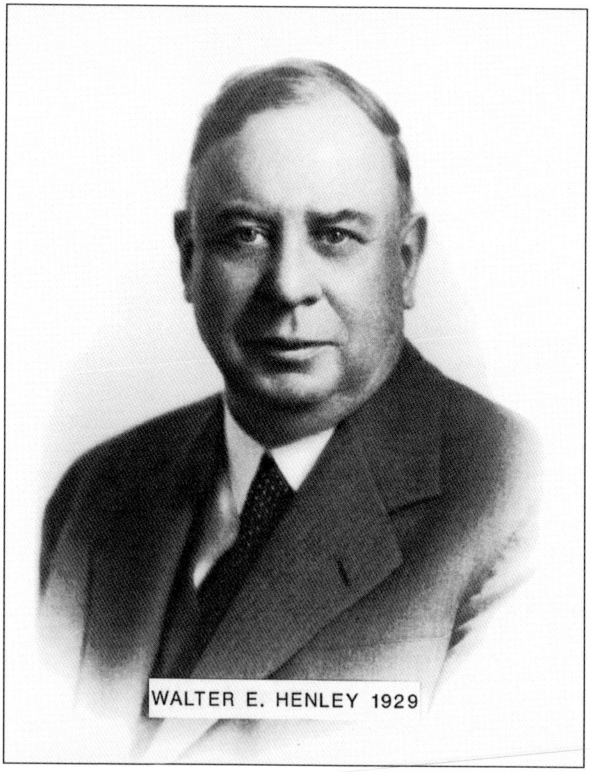

In 1929, Walter Henley became the club's president. Originally a developer of coal mines and the accompanying company town in Piper, Alabama, Henley had served on the three-man National Coal Commission during World War I. At the time he became the club's president, he was the president of the Birmingham Trust National Bank. (KCOB.)

As the 1920s closed, the club could look back with well-justified pride to one project in particular, a new building for the Boys' Club of Birmingham, to which Kiwanians contributed $37,000 in funds and labor. "The Kiwanis Club of Birmingham has decided to exemplify its motto 'We Build'," declared *Boys' Club Round Table* magazine. In the difficult decade to come, the building would serve an increasingly needy Birmingham. (BPLA.)

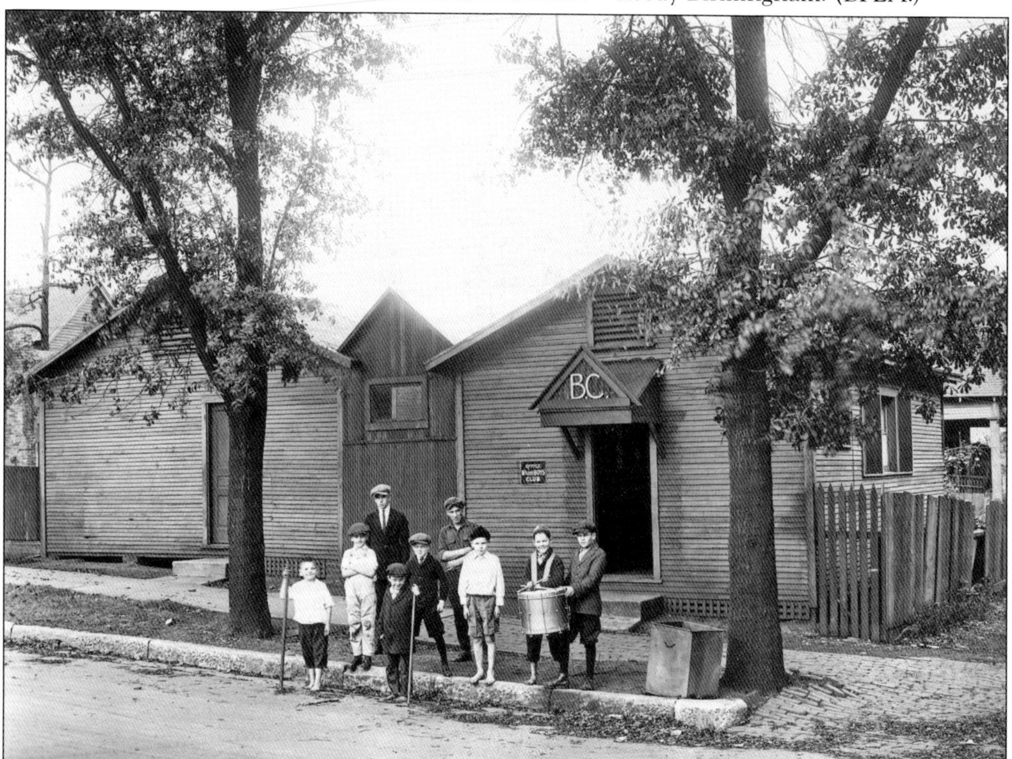

Two

THE GREAT DEPRESSION AND WORLD WAR II

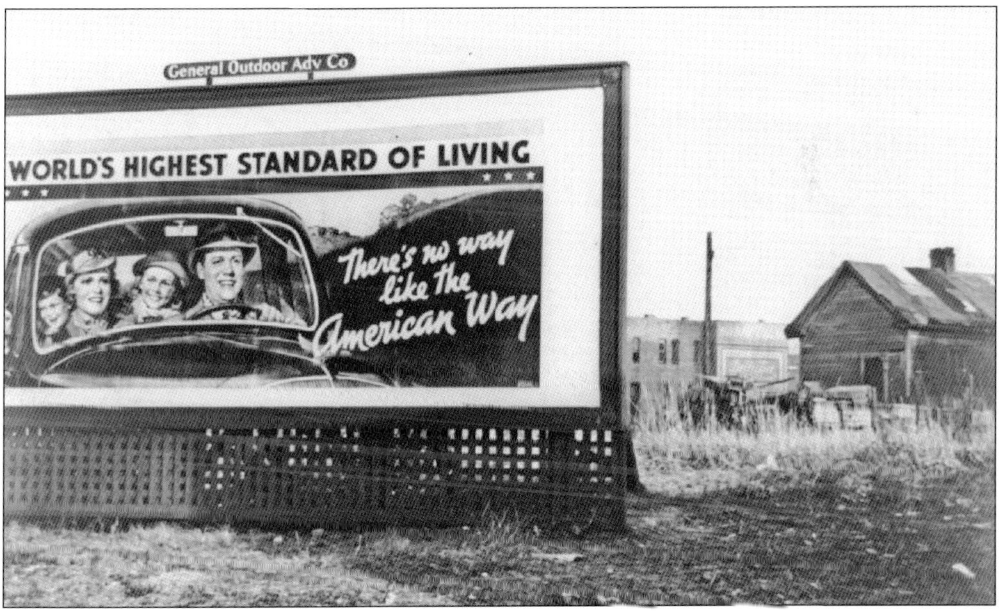

As this photograph of a billboard outside of Birmingham suggests, Birmingham during the 1930s was caught between clinging to the American Dream and struggling with the reality of what the federal government had observed to be "probably the hardest hit city in the nation" in the Great Depression. Full economic recovery would, sadly, take a world war to achieve. (LOC.)

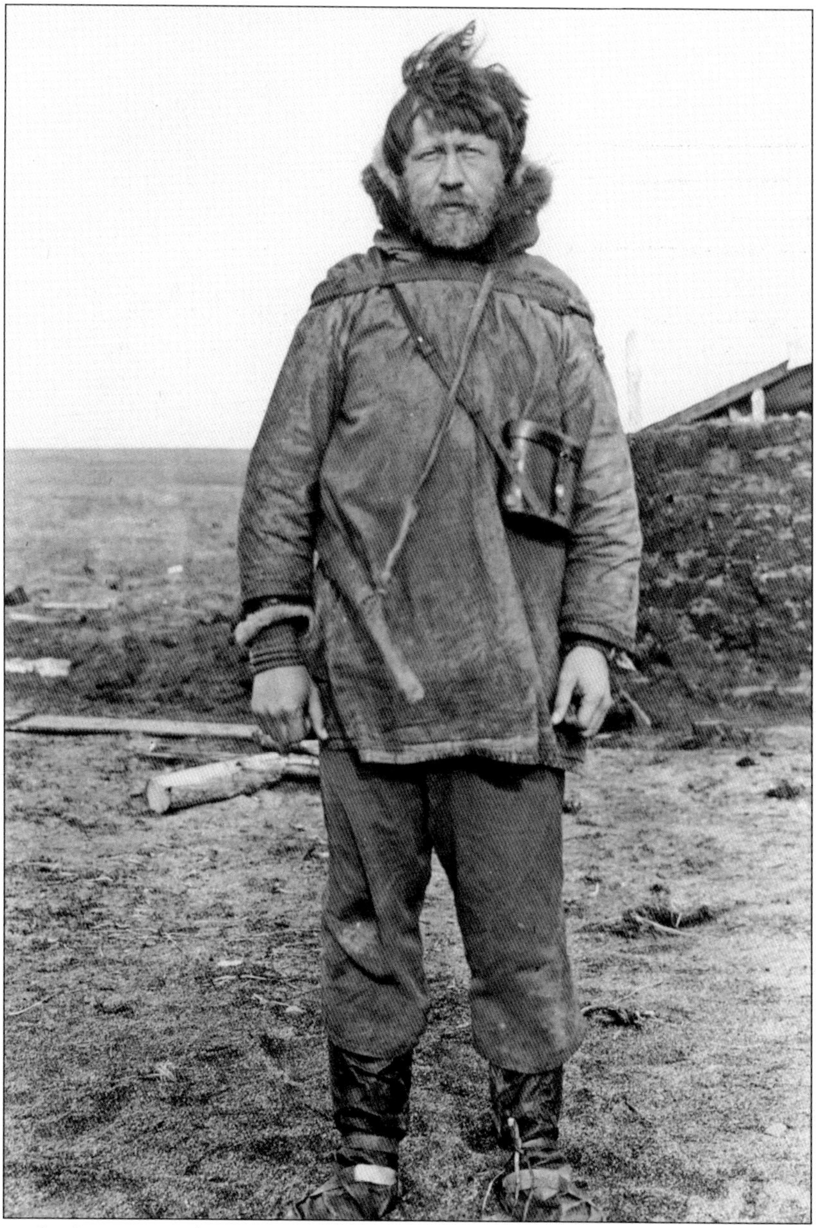

Vilhjalmur Stefansson spoke to the club on November 18, 1930. The Canadian-born Arctic explorer, cartographer, and ethnographer was one of the legendary figures of his age. He led the perilous (and deadly) Canadian Arctic Expedition (1913–1916), organized an ill-fated effort to colonize Russia's Wrangel Island for Great Britain, discovered such lands as Brock, Mackenzie King, Borden, Meighen, and Lougheed Islands, and surveyed the edge of the continental shelf. Later, Stefansson was the director of polar studies at Dartmouth College, helped the US Army develop its cold-weather warfare doctrine for World War II, and twice served as president of the Explorers Club. The author of numerous books about the Arctic, Stefansson was awarded the Hubbard Medal by the National Geographic Society and the Founders Gold Medal by the Royal Geographical Society in honor of his accomplishments in the northern latitudes. (Dartmouth College Library.)

James D. Porter, originally of Tennessee and a graduate of Vanderbilt University, became the club's president in 1930. At the time, Porter was the supervisor of southeastern operations for Chicago's Marshall Field & Company. Later he became a sales consultant working for Munsingwear. (KCOB.)

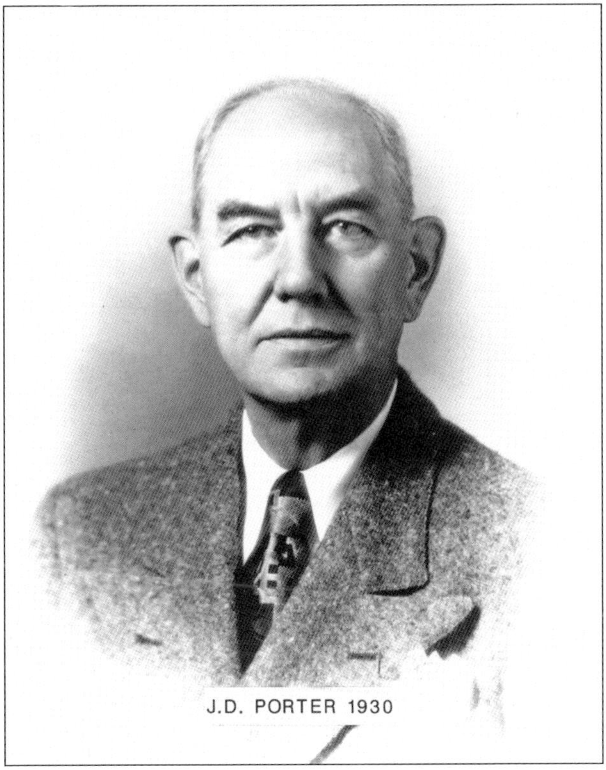

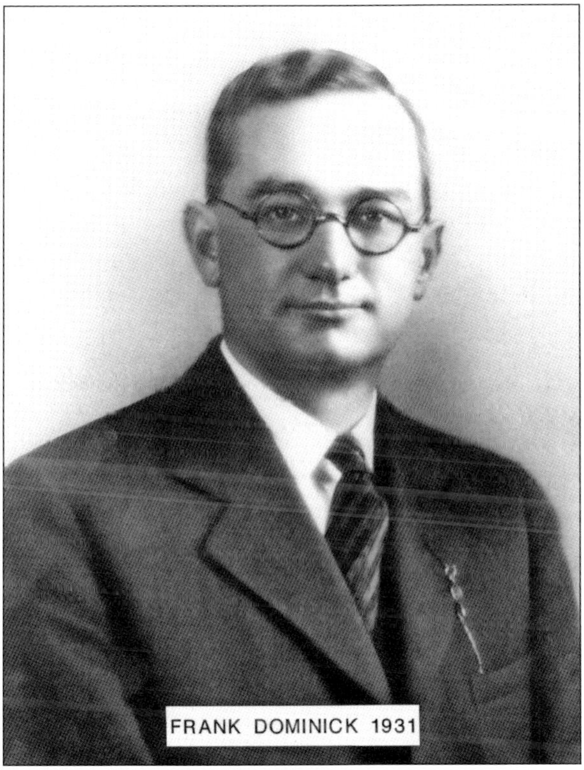

In 1931, Frank M. Dominick Jr. was elected the club's president. A native of Greensboro, Alabama, Dominick taught school in Centreville to earn the money to attend law school at the University of Alabama. He graduated in 1913 and, by the time he became the club's president, was a partner with Stokely, Scrivner, Dominick & Smith. (KCOB.)

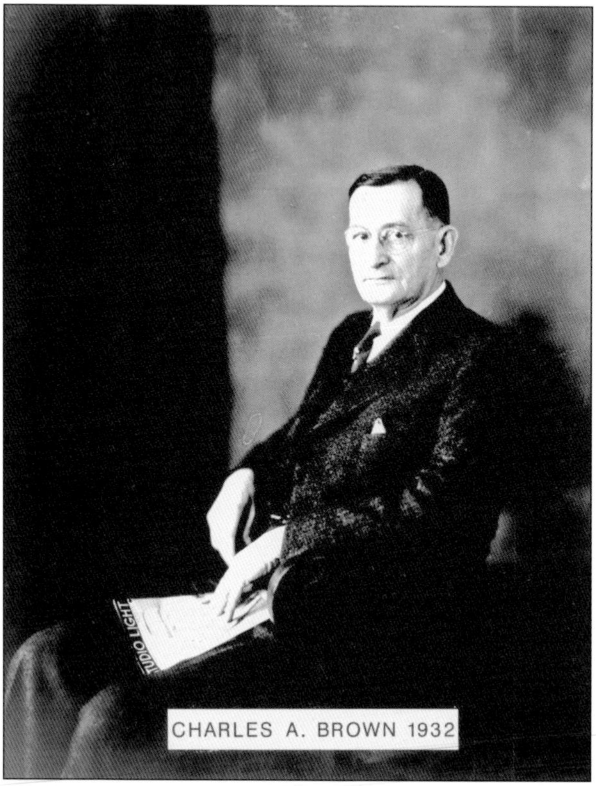

Charles A. Brown became the club's president in 1932. Brown was the associate superintendent of Birmingham's school system; he would also serve as president of the Alabama Education Association. During his tenure, the club began presenting the Charles A. Brown Football Trophy for the area's most outstanding high school football team. Bessemer High School earned the inaugural honors. (KCOB.)

US secretary of agriculture Henry Wallace spoke in Birmingham on December 16, 1933, in response to a request from the Kiwanis Club and the city's chamber of commerce. "The fact that people came here from all counties to hear Secretary Wallace speak attests to the intense interest that is felt in Alabama in the Roosevelt administration's plan for economic recovery in agriculture," declared the *Anniston Star*. (LOC.)

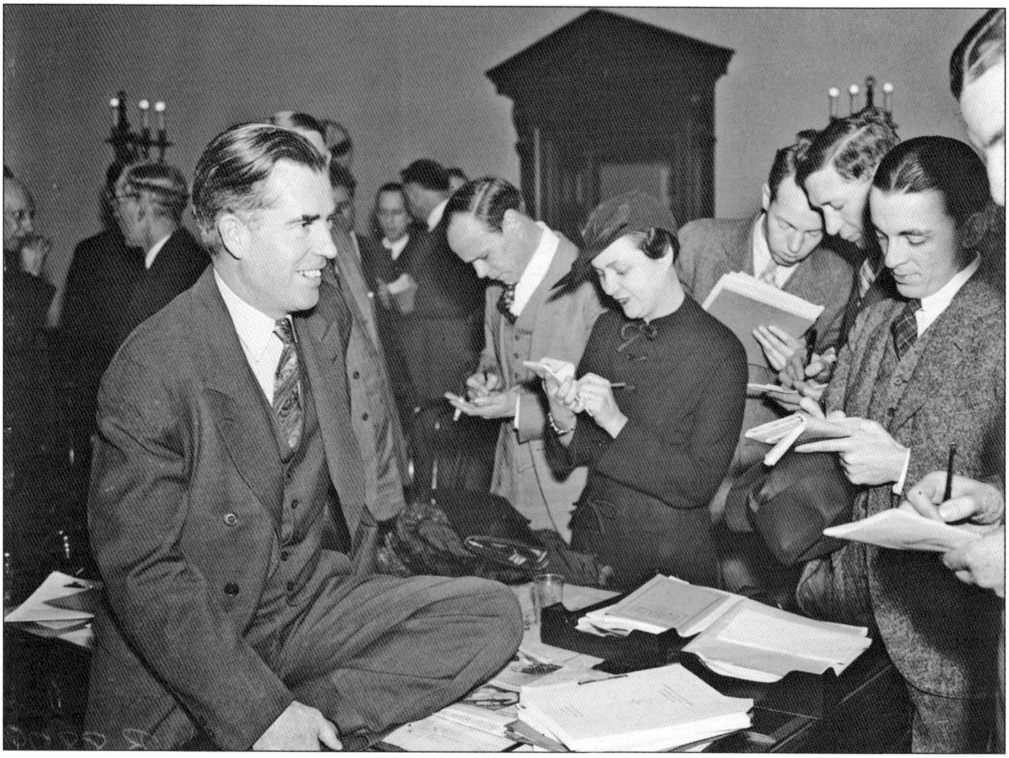

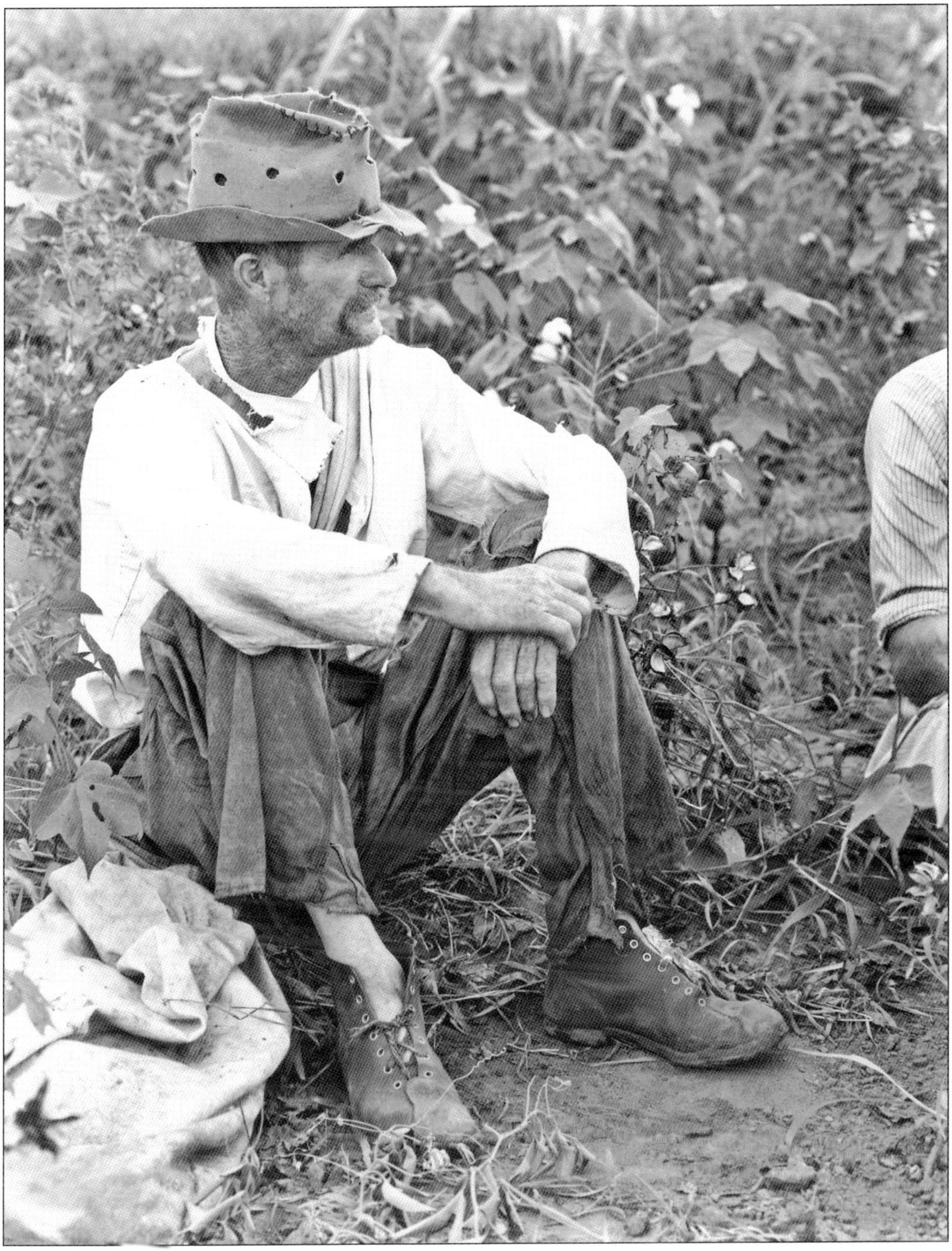

During the week of June 1–7, 1931, "whereas the Southern Farmer has been unable to finance himself because of the exceedingly low price of and overproduction of cotton, resulting in a greatly reduced purchasing power which as reflected itself in business throughout the entire South," the Kiwanis Club resolved to join with the Birmingham Chamber of Commerce and other civic groups in support of National Cotton Week. Members of the club pledged to buy and wear a cotton suit to their weekly luncheon at the Tutwiler Hotel as a symbolic show of support for the South's cotton farmers and their sharecroppers. One such man was the sharecropper Bud Fields, shown in this iconic photograph by Walker Evans taken in Hale County, Alabama. (LOC.)

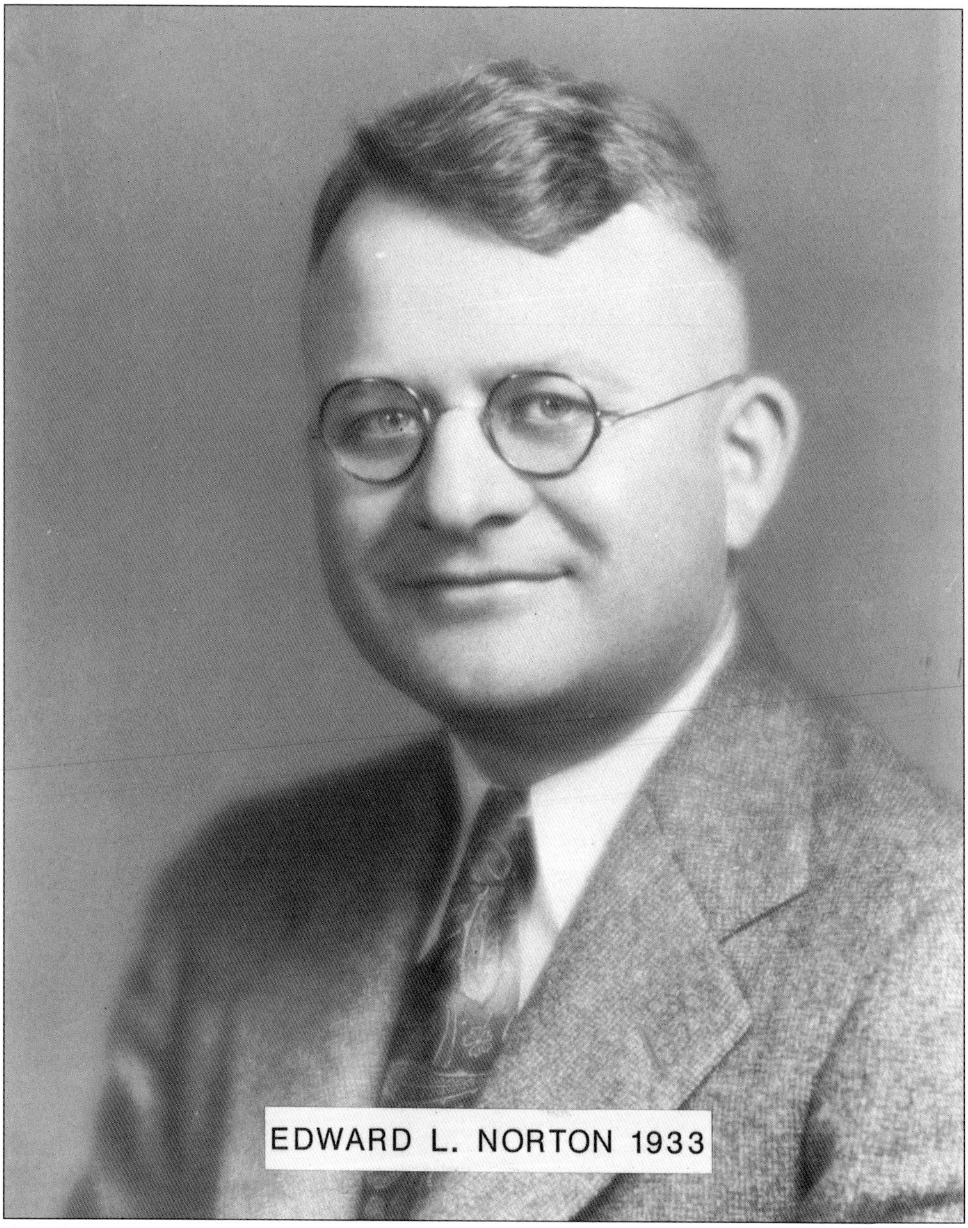

Edward L. Norton had a business career that beggars description. Born in Blountsville, Alabama, Norton was a graduate of Birmingham-Southern College and later earned a doctor of law from the University of Alabama. He began his business career as the personal secretary to R.S. Munger of the Munger Realty Company in 1915 before taking a leave of absence to serve in the US Navy during World War I. Returning to Birmingham, Norton was the executive vice president of Munger Realty Company and Munger Mortgage Company when he became the Kiwanis Club's president in 1933. Three years earlier, he had been president of the Birmingham Barons; later, Norton would serve as the chairman of the board of the Birmingham Branch of the Federal Reserve Bank of Atlanta, as the chairman of the board of directors of Royal Crown Cola Company, and as a member of the US Board of Governors for the Federal Reserve System in Washington, DC. (KCOB.)

William Morris Given grew up in Birmingham, attended Alabama Polytechnic Institute (Auburn), and, in 1907, secured a position as a clerk with the Young and Vann Supply Company. Given made a career at Young and Vann, eventually becoming the company's vice president. In 1934, he became president of the Kiwanis Club of Birmingham. (KCOB.)

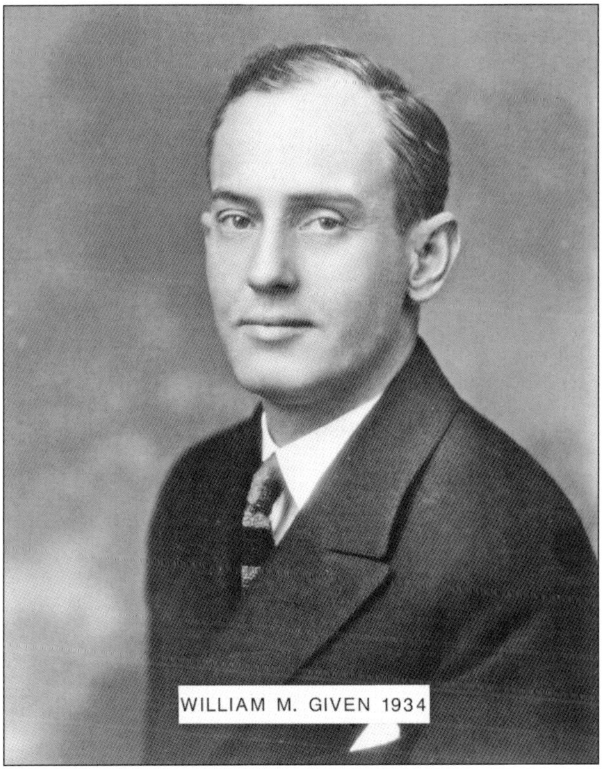

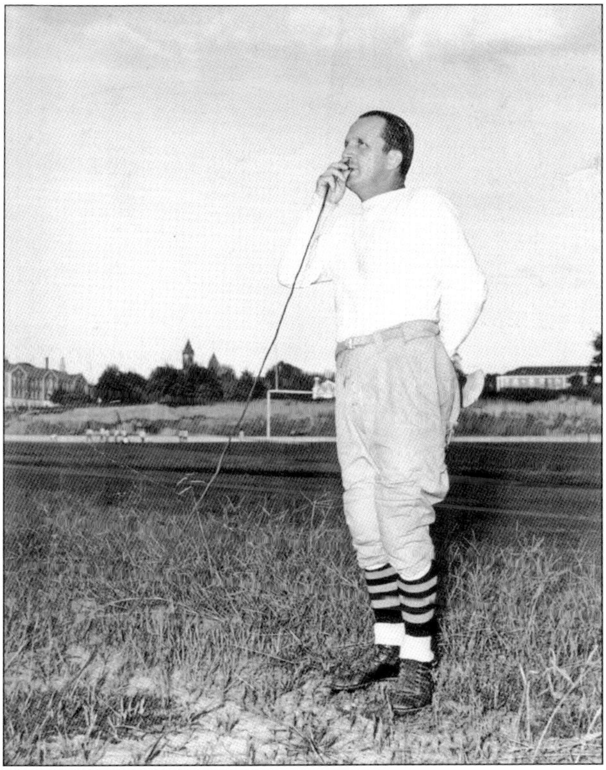

Football coach Jack Meagher addressed the club on May 22, 1934. At the time, he was Auburn's new football coach and destined for a 2-8 inaugural season. Better days were ahead for Meagher, however, and by the time World War II ended his coaching days at Auburn, he had led the school to its first two bowl games. (Auburn University.)

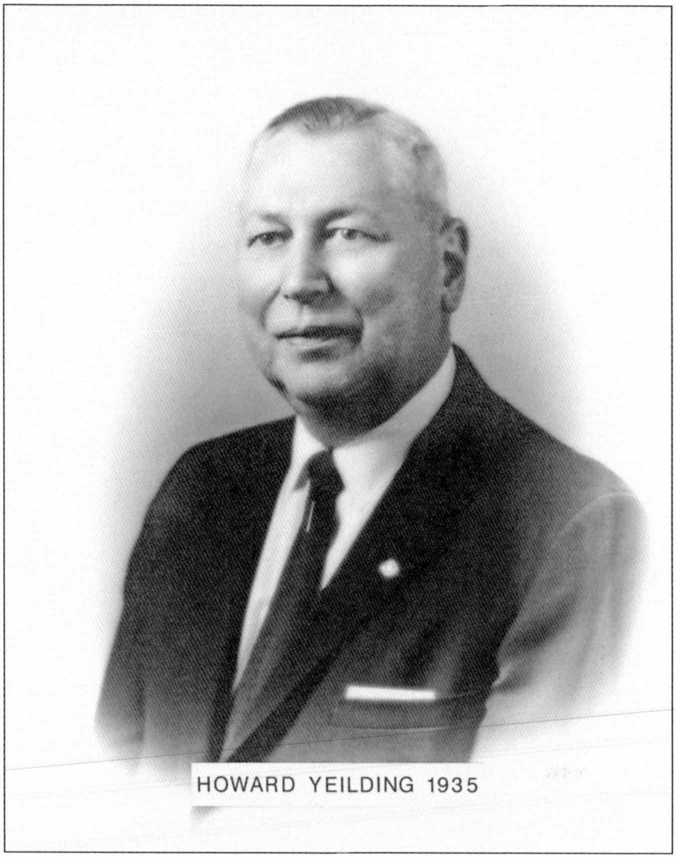

Howard Yeilding was elected the club's president in 1935. At the time, he was not only president of Yeilding Brothers Company, which ran a Birmingham department store, but was also the new chairman of the Jefferson County Personnel Board, a position he would hold from 1935 to 1946 and from 1952 to 1958. (KCOB.)

As the Great Depression wore on in Birmingham and throughout the United States, men such as the local miners pictured in this photograph counted themselves fortunate indeed. They had jobs, and they were likely grateful for them. By some counts, employment in the city dropped from 100,000 to barely 15,000 full-time workers. (LOC.)

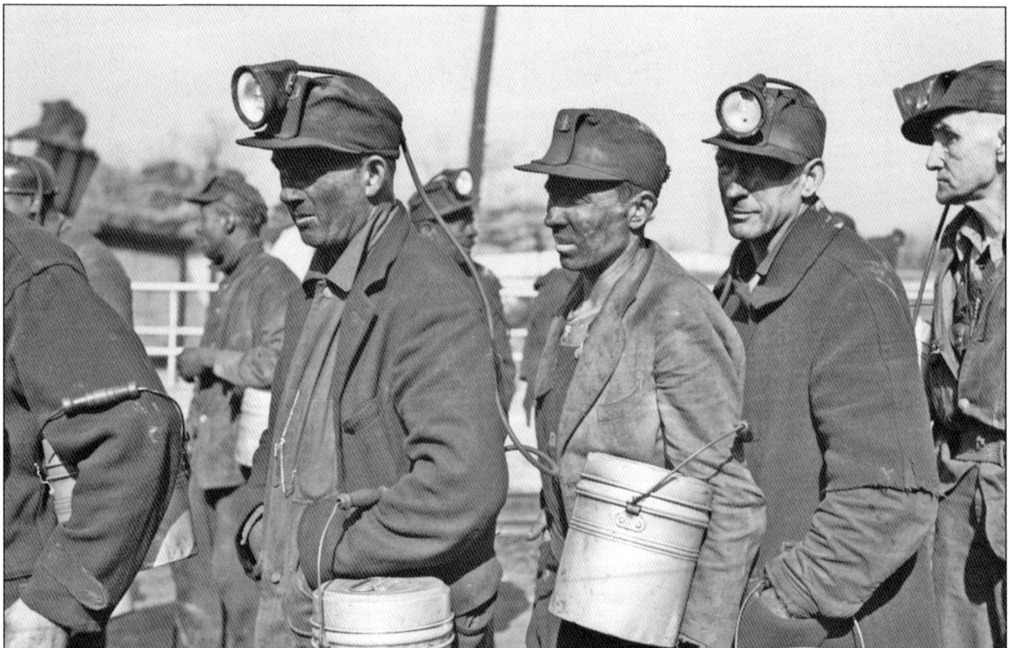

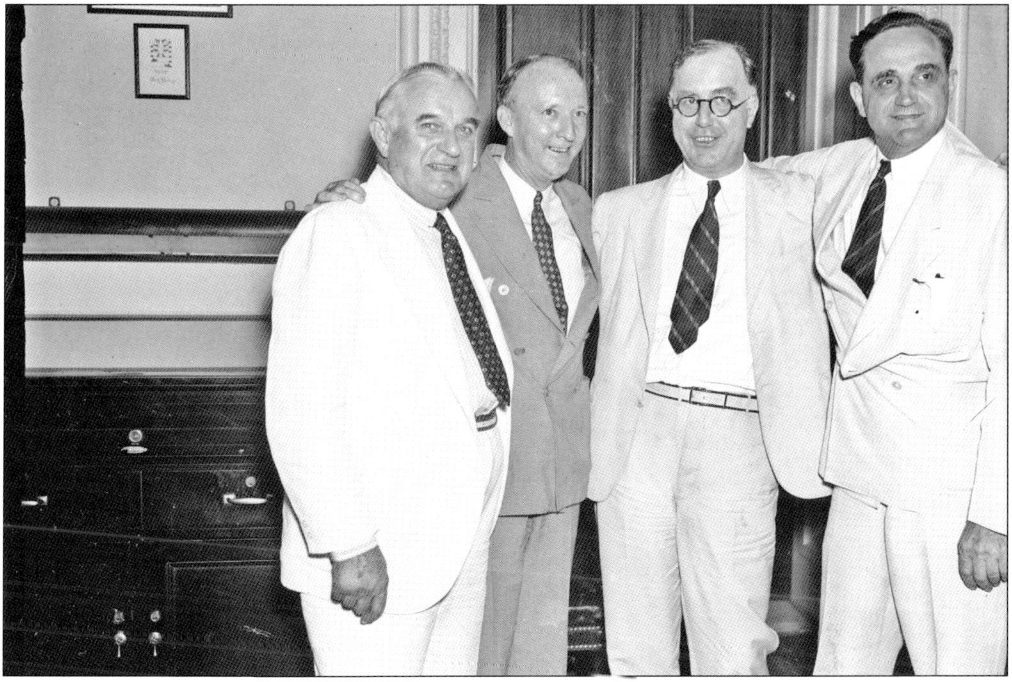

On September 10, 1935, US senator Hugo Black (second from left) addressed the club. The Alabama-born Black had taken office as the county prosecutor in Birmingham in 1917 during the same week the club held its first meeting; now, nearly two decades later, he was within two years of being elevated to the US Supreme Court. (LOC.)

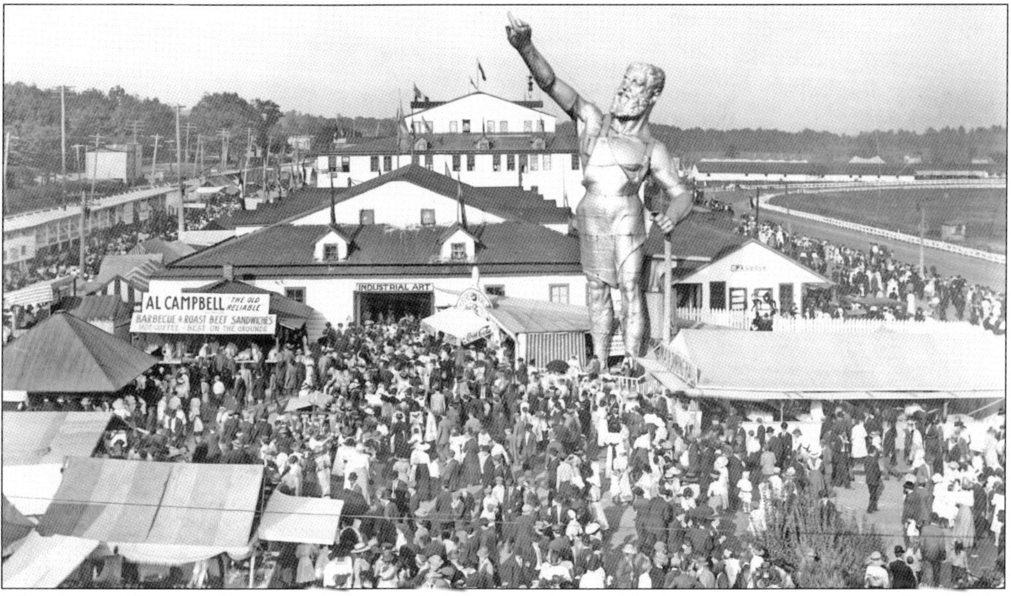

The City of Birmingham commissioned *Vulcan* as the world's largest cast-iron statue for the St. Louis World's Fair in 1904. Upon its return to Alabama, the 56-foot-tall statue was, as shown in this photograph, relegated to Birmingham's State Fairgrounds. In 1935, the Kiwanis Club, at the urging of members Mercer Barnett and Thomas Joy, sought a more suitable home for the Roman god of the forge. (BPLA.)

VULCAN BEING LIFTED TO TOP OF PEDESTAL

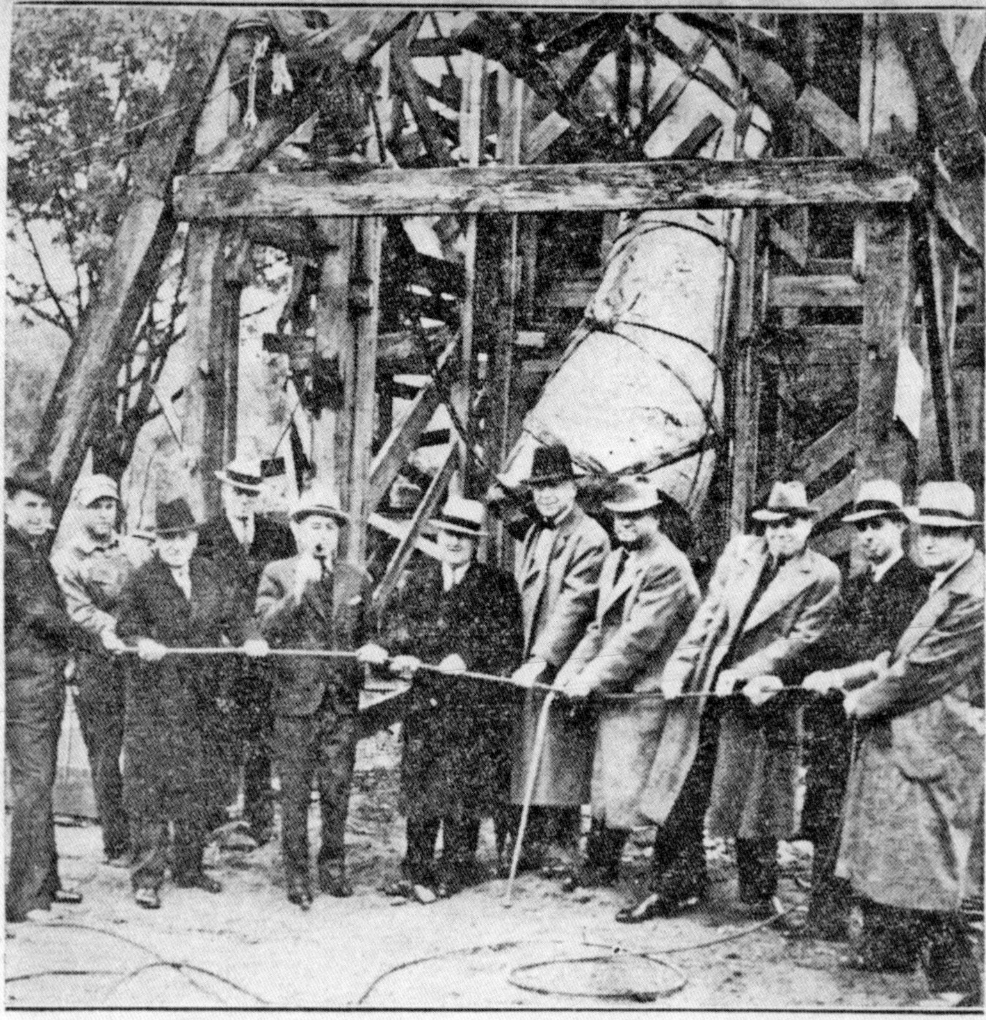

Shown above giving a tug on the wire cable just before the machinery was started that sent the nearly five-ton right leg and foot of Vulcan aloft to the top of his 123½-foot pedestal is a group of officials of the city, county and Park Board, the Kiwanis Club, and the Chamber of Commerce. Left to right they are, City Commissioner Robinson, Ed Weldon, a structural steel and iron worker; John H. Adams, Vernon Douglas, Tom H. Joy, T. L. Bissell, F. M. Jackson, City Commission President Jones, Thomas Bowron, City Commissioner Downs and Erskine Ramsay.

News 11-12

The Kiwanis Club convinced the Tennessee Coal & Iron Company to "sell" 4.45 acres of its Red Mountain land for $5 as a new home for *Vulcan* overlooking Birmingham. The club then successfully lobbied the New Deal's Works Progress Administration (whose Alabama efforts, fortunately, were headed by fellow Kiwanian Thad Holt) to provide the necessary funding and manpower for the construction project. In total, the project to move *Vulcan* from the Birmingham Fairgrounds to atop a new 123-foot-tall pedestal of local sandstone on Red Mountain cost nearly $50,000. The hoisting of *Vulcan*'s five-ton right leg and foot in November 1938 provided the photo opportunity depicted above in the *Birmingham News* for key leaders in the Vulcan Park effort, including Kiwanians Thomas Joy, T.L. Bissell, and Erskine Ramsay, as well as several leaders from Birmingham, Jefferson County, and the Birmingham Chamber of Commerce. (BPLA.)

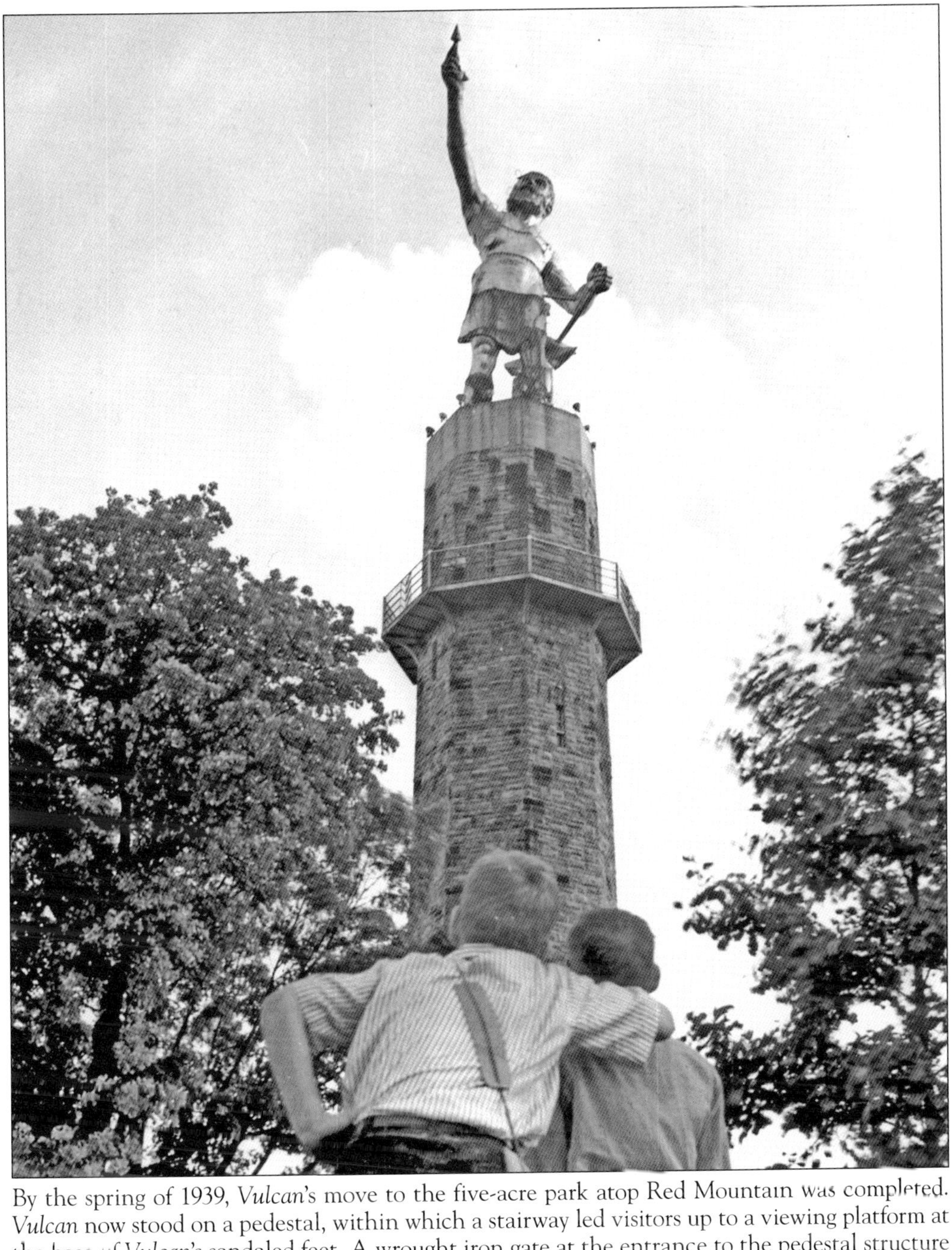

By the spring of 1939, *Vulcan*'s move to the five-acre park atop Red Mountain was completed. *Vulcan* now stood on a pedestal, within which a stairway led visitors up to a viewing platform at the base of *Vulcan*'s sandaled feet. A wrought iron gate at the entrance to the pedestal structure was emblazoned with the Kiwanis crest in recognition of the club's role in creating what would become Birmingham's iconic park. On the base of the pedestal, an inscription read, in part, "o'er and o'er nature hath flung her treasures with a generous hand and Birmingham sits enthroned," a clear reference to the great deposits and reserves of coal, iron, limestone, and timber that had fueled Birmingham's rise to prominence. The Kiwanis Club marked the occasion on May 9, 1939, with a 10-day series of celebrations and events, including the crowning of Evelyn Tully as the Queen of the Vulcan Dedication. (BPLA.)

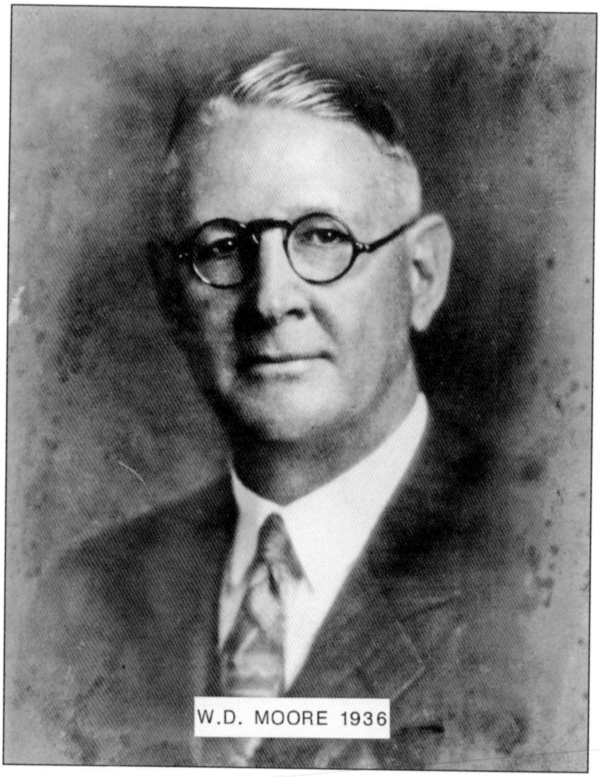

In 1936, Missouri native William D. Moore became the president of the club at a time when the club's 195 members were paying $30 annually in dues. A talented and inventive engineer, he was destined to serve for 22 years at the president of the American Cast Iron Pipe Company, also known as ACIPCO. Moore was respected internationally as a leader in the cast-iron pipe industry. (KCOB.)

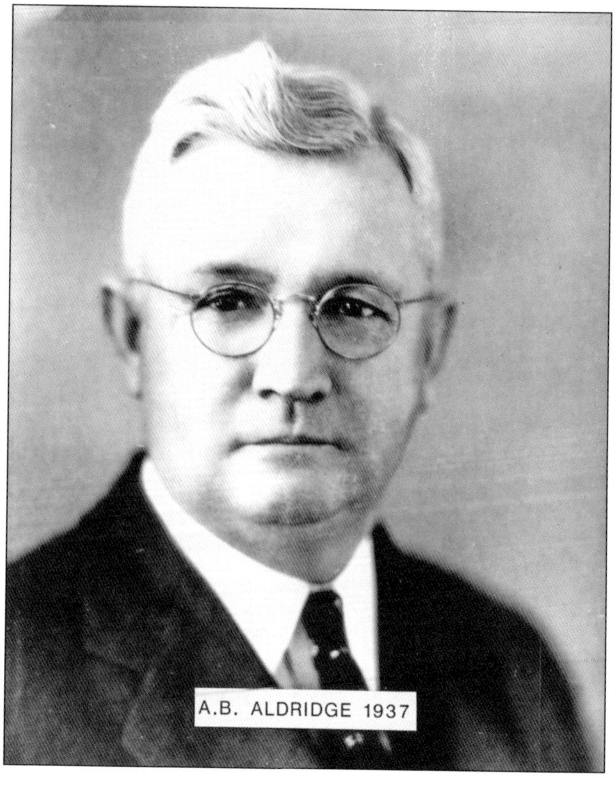

Abner B. Aldridge came to Birmingham to work in the coal industry, where he became the superintendent of the Sloss-Sheffield Steel and Iron Company's largest coal mine in Brookside. When Alabama Power needed coal for Gorgas Steam Plant, Aldridge founded the Winona Coal Company. Sadly, Aldridge took ill in the spring of 1937 and resigned from the club in April; he died four months later, on August 29, 1937. (KCOB.)

The club elected Alexander C. Montgomery as president in 1937 to fill the remainder of Abner Aldridge's term of office. Trained as an engineer, Montgomery designed and developed residential neighborhoods in Fairfield and Birmingham, preserved Arlington as Birmingham's iconic antebellum house museum, and served as the chairman of the Birmingham Water Works Board for 15 years. (KCOB.)

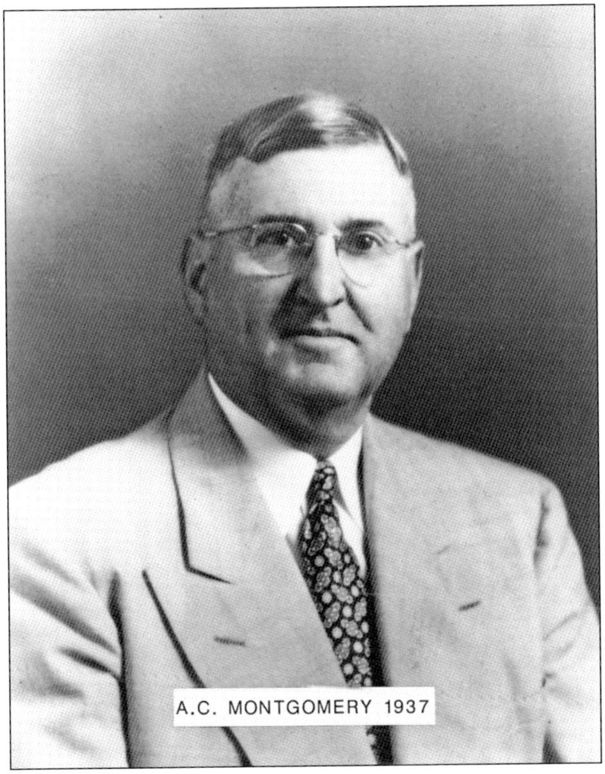

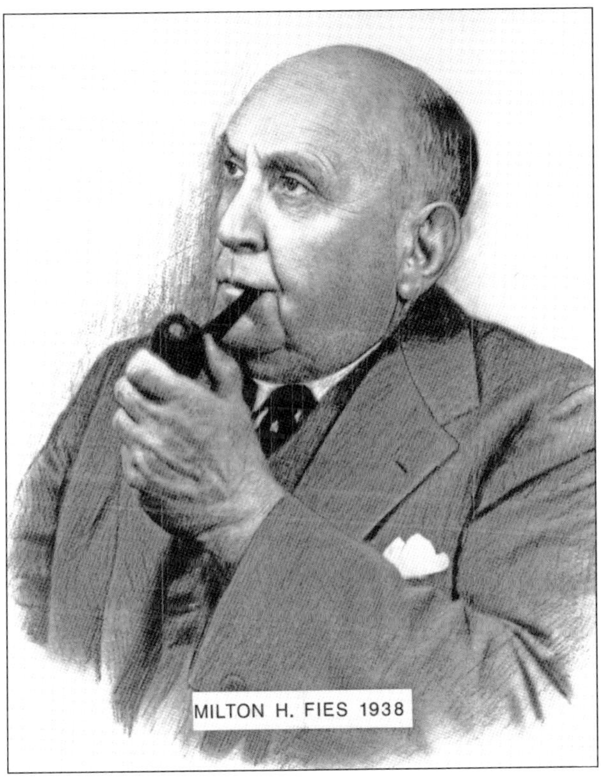

Milton H. Fies became the club's president in 1938. A Birmingham native born within two blocks of where the club met, Fies earned a degree in mining engineering from Columbia University. At the time of his election, he was the vice president in charge of operations for the DeBardeleben Coal Company. Later, he would become manager of coal operations for Alabama Power Company. (KCOB.)

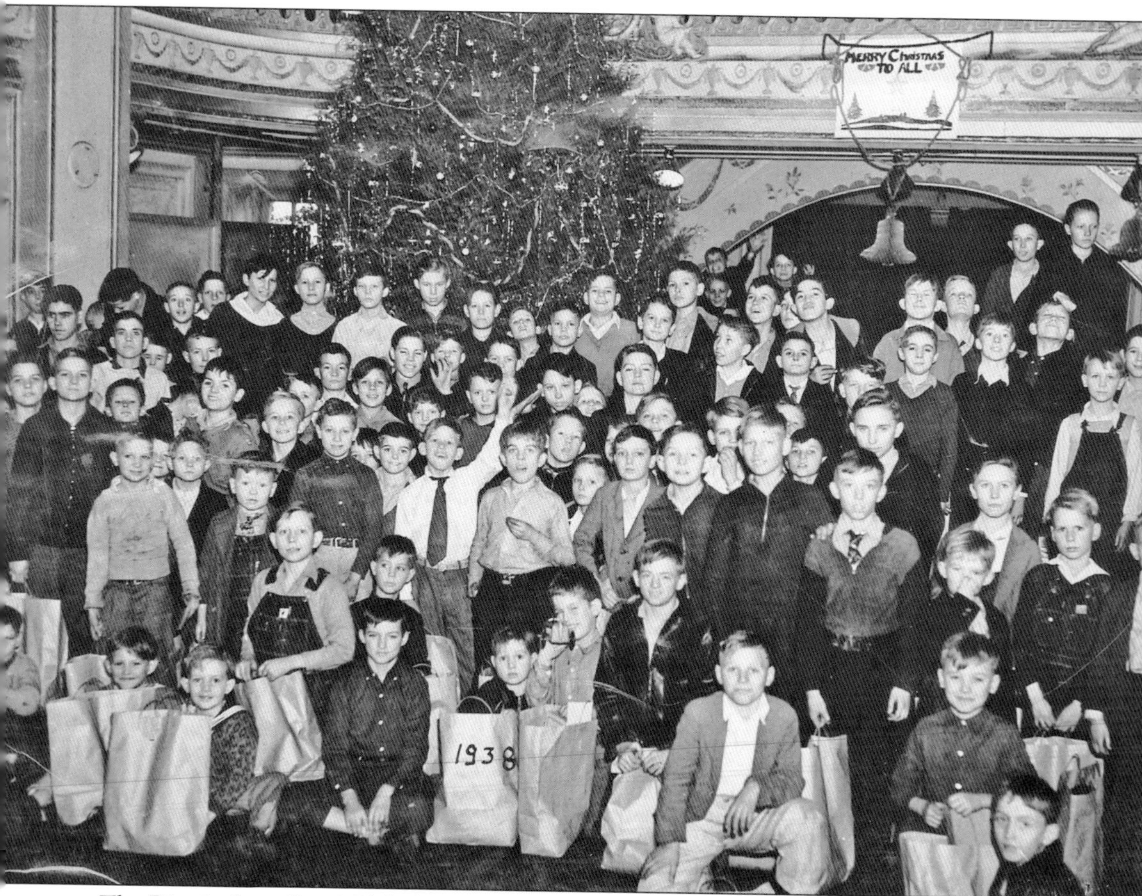

The Birmingham Boys' Club dated back to 1901, when it was formed as an organization to offer recreation, meals, and baths to orphaned boys living on the city's streets. Five years later, it became a founding member of the national Boys & Girls Clubs of America. Almost from the Kiwanis Club's inception, the Boys' Club was one of the club's favorite charities, as evident by the club's raising $37,000 for the Boys' Club for a vocational training building in the 1920s and the personal civic involvement of many Kiwanians in the Boys' Club's leadership. In the 1930s, when the Great Depression brought the economic hardships of such boys to a razor-sharp focus, the Kiwanians habitually sponsored Christmas parties for the Boys' Club, such as the one shown here in 1938, and its counterpart for the city's "colored" children. Such philanthropy, it should be noted, was in addition to the Kiwanians' sponsorship of "campships" for needy girls at Birmingham's Girl Scout Camp each summer. (BPLA.)

In 1939, John B. Newsome was elected the club's president. A Tennessee native and a veteran of World War I, Newsome was the founder of the Watts-Newsome Company, which was the Philco radio distributor for Alabama. In 1942, Newsome would be elected as a Democrat to a single term in the US House of Representatives, a singular honor for the club. (KCOB.)

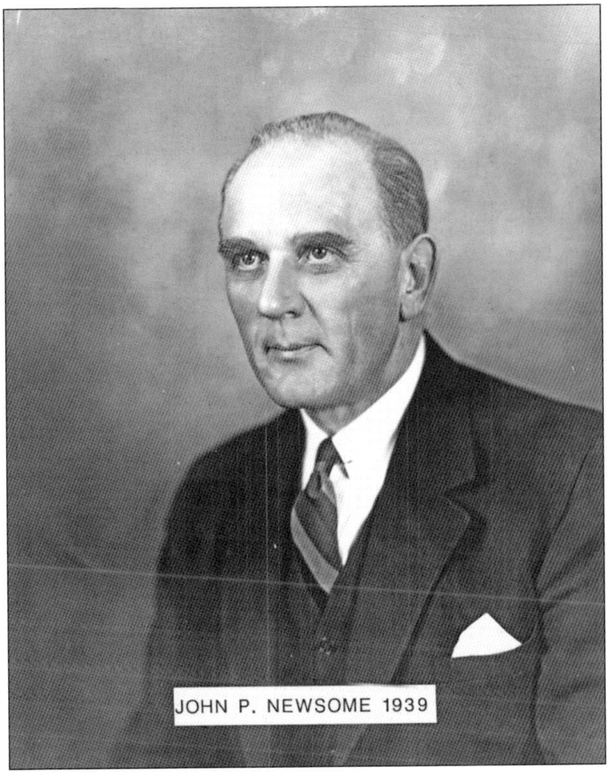

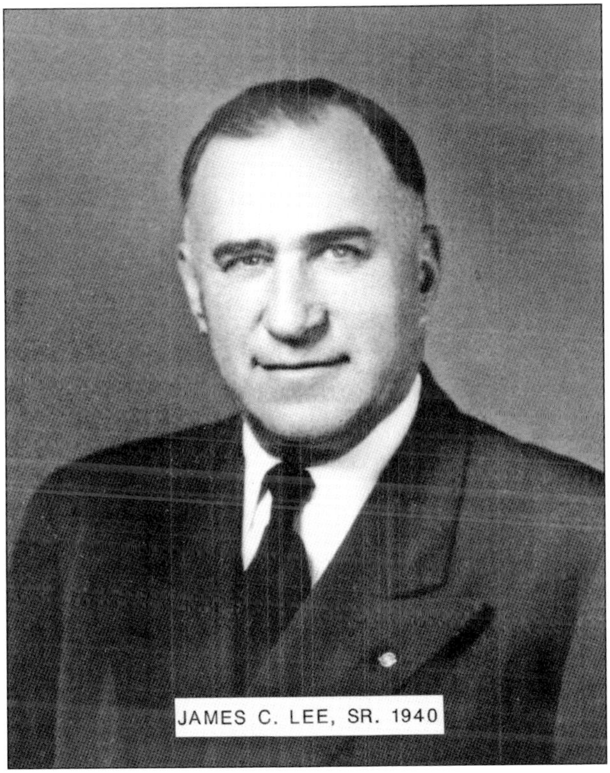

James C. Lee Sr. was elected the club's president in 1940. A veteran of World War I and a graduate of Auburn University, Lee ultimately went to work for his father, Sidney, who had founded the Alabama Grocery Company in 1901. The company would eventually become the Buffalo Rock Company, and Lee would take its helm upon his father's death. (KCOB.)

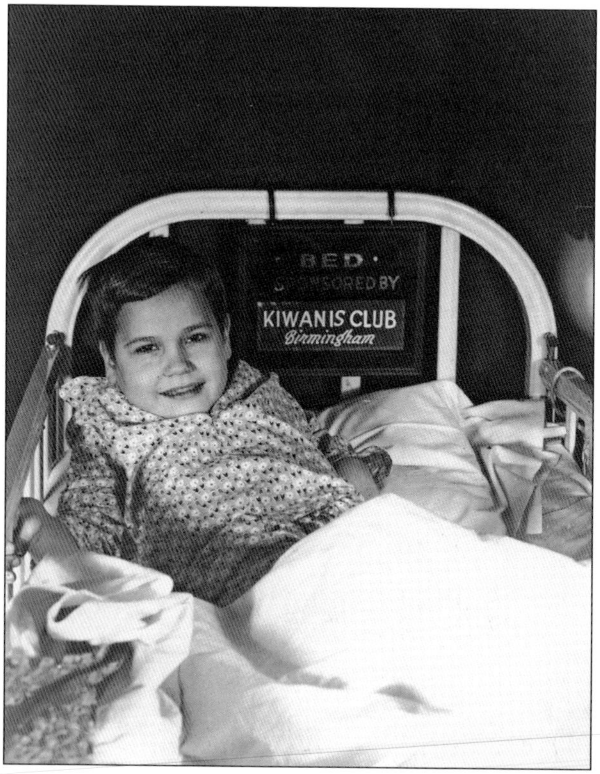

Birmingham's Crippled Children's Clinic opened its doors in 1929 to treat children stricken with polio. The demand for the clinic's services was so great that, in 1936, the clinic moved into a vacant hospital building. Once refurbished, the building provided 40 beds and other medical facilities for the clinic's children. In 1940, the Kiwanis Club began annually sponsoring one such bed. (KCOB.)

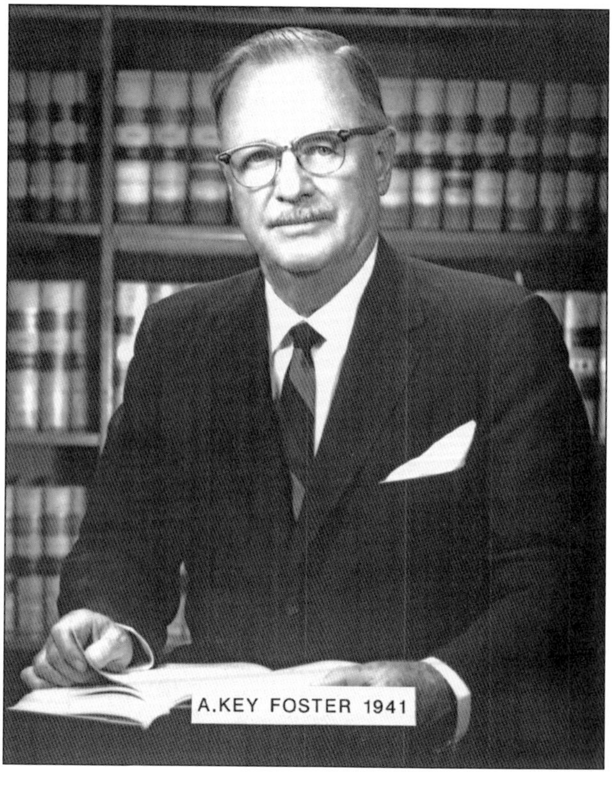

In 1941, Arthur Key Foster, known as "Key," became the club's president. He held degrees from the University of Alabama and Harvard University and, at the time of election, was an attorney with the Birmingham Trust and Savings Company. With America's entry into World War II, Foster would serve as the chairman of the Alabama War Chest, state chairman for Navy Day, and state treasurer for the USO. (KCOB.)

Kiwanis Club records show that the club's last official act of 1941, in the wake of the Japanese attack on Pearl Harbor, was to empty the club's savings account, draw from the club's checking account as necessary, and purchase three $1,000 defense bonds to support the American war effort. (LOC.)

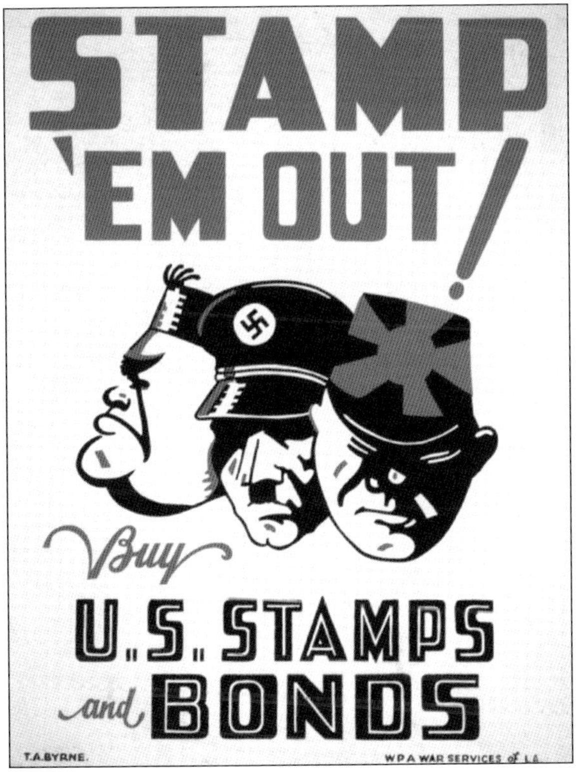

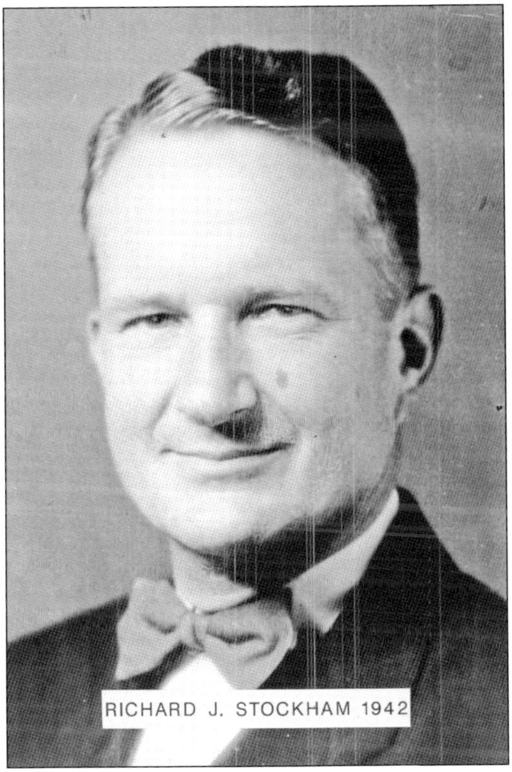

Richard J. Stockham became the club's president in 1942, even as the US Army called him to active duty as a lieutenant colonel in the Army's Ordnance Corps. Fortunately, Stockham, whose civic involvement included service on the boards of trustees of Samford University and Birmingham-Southern College and chairmanship of the board of stewards at Highlands Methodist Church, remained in Birmingham for his tour of duty. (KCOB.)

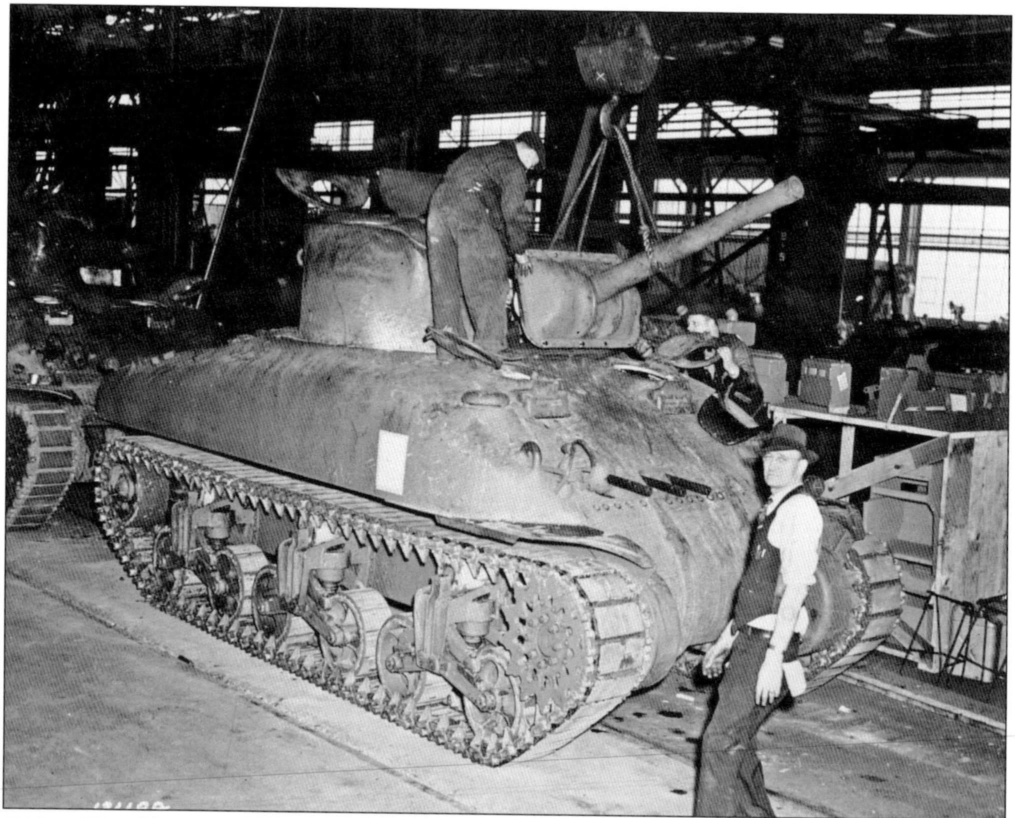

Richard Stockham spent his entire career at Stockham Valves & Fittings; he ultimately became the president of the company's board of directors. During World War II, Stockham Valves & Fittings earned three Army-Navy "E" production awards for the company's manufacture of shell casings, grenades, and armored plating for such tanks as the M4 Sherman shown here. (LOC.)

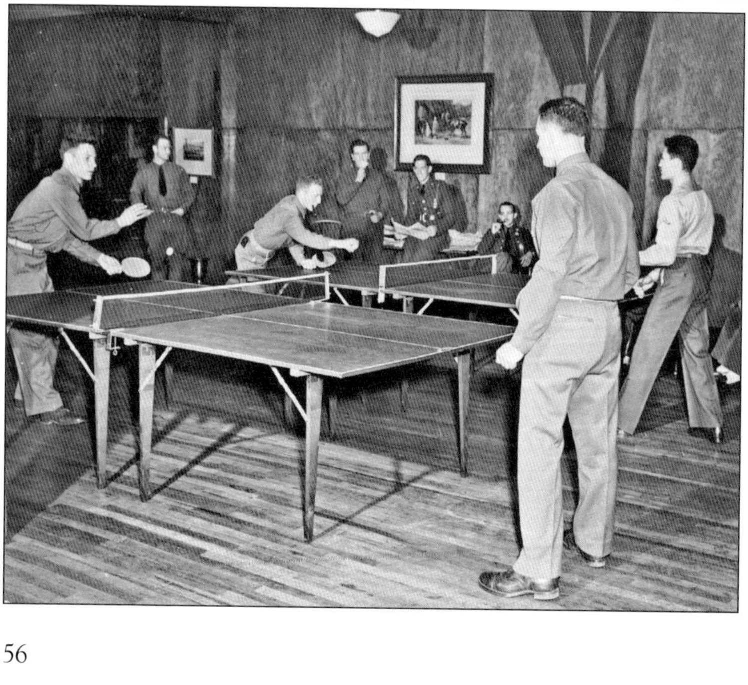

In 1942, the Kiwanis Club raised over $550 to furnish and equip the so-called Kiwanis Hut to provide for soldiers' recreation at Fort McClellan in nearby Anniston. During the war, Fort McClellan served primarily as a basic training camp for new recruits. By war's end, some 500,000 soldiers had passed through its gates. (ADAH.)

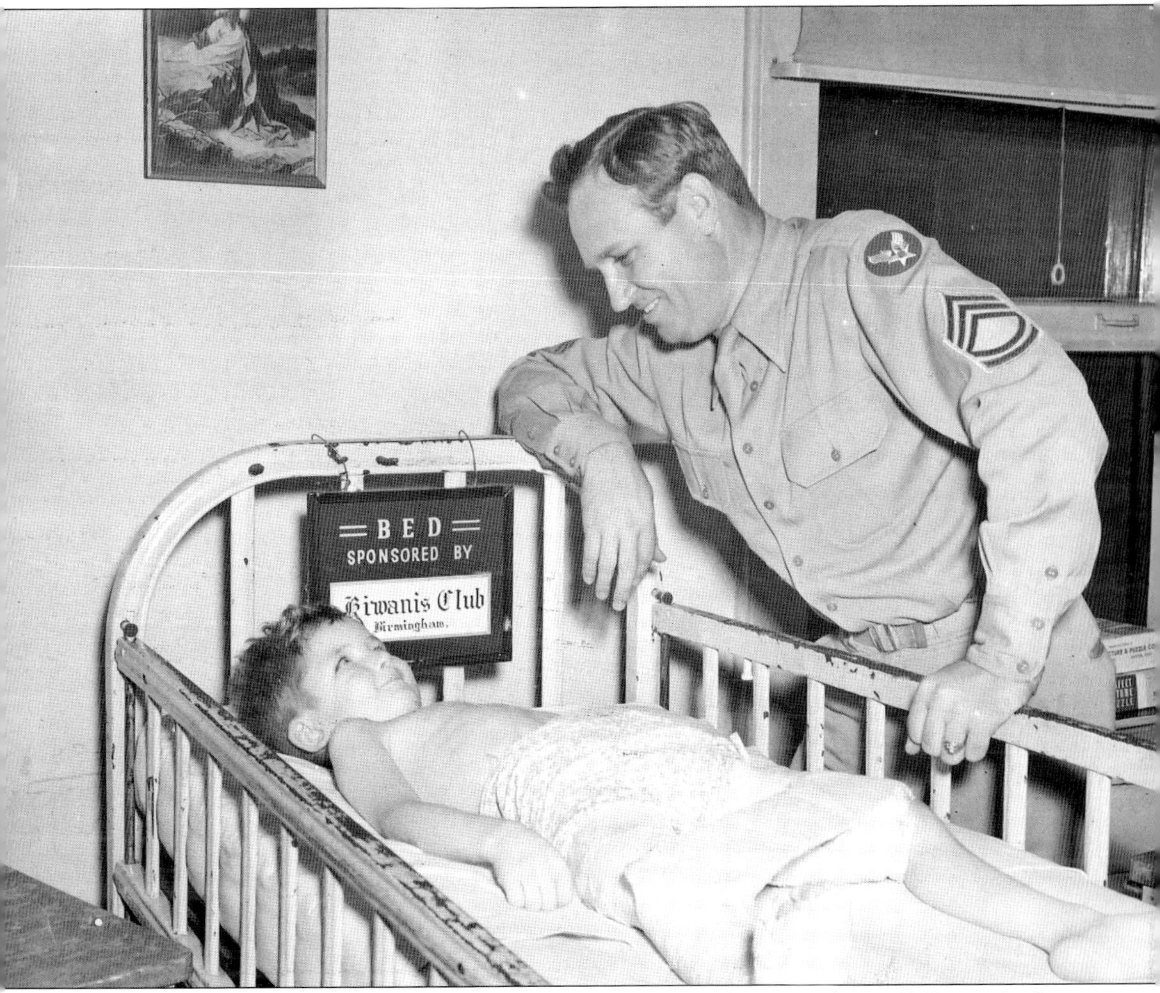

The Kiwanis Club sponsored a musical variety show in Birmingham on July 11, 1943, in which Army Air Forces personnel from the area showcased their talents. Legendary singing cowboy Gene Autry of the era's radio and movies headlined the show. Admission to the event was procurable through donations of war stamps and defense bonds as investments payable to Birmingham's Crippled Children's Clinic. During his visit to Birmingham, Autry (pictured) visited the clinic, where Kiwanis was among the local civic organizations that sponsored one of the beds for $365 a year. At the time, Autry had enlisted in the Army Air Forces, and the *Gene Autry Melody Ranch* radio show had become the *Sergeant Gene Autry* radio show. Previously licensed as a private pilot, Autry ultimately became a flight officer and served with the 91st Ferrying Squadron, based at Dallas's Love Field. (KCOB.)

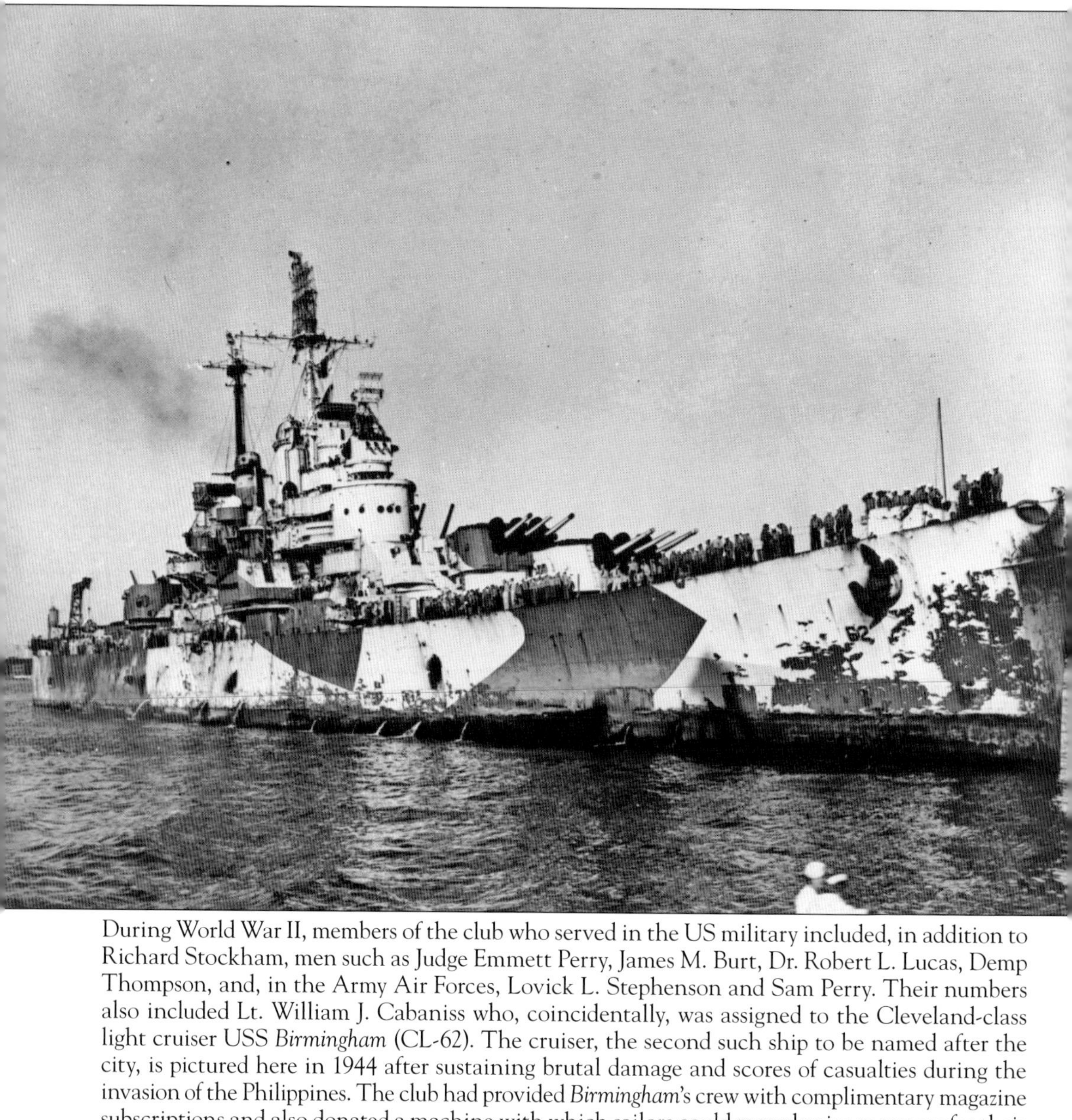

During World War II, members of the club who served in the US military included, in addition to Richard Stockham, men such as Judge Emmett Perry, James M. Burt, Dr. Robert L. Lucas, Demp Thompson, and, in the Army Air Forces, Lovick L. Stephenson and Sam Perry. Their numbers also included Lt. William J. Cabaniss who, coincidentally, was assigned to the Cleveland-class light cruiser USS *Birmingham* (CL-62). The cruiser, the second such ship to be named after the city, is pictured here in 1944 after sustaining brutal damage and scores of casualties during the invasion of the Philippines. The club had provided *Birmingham*'s crew with complimentary magazine subscriptions and also donated a machine with which sailors could record voice messages for their loved ones back home. Later in the war, *Birmingham* would survive a bloody kamikaze attack in the waters off Okinawa. (NARA.)

In 1943, George A. Mattison Jr. became the club's president. A graduate of Auburn University, Mattison was the president of several successful slag and aggregate companies. His history of civic involvement is too lengthy to list; suffice it to say that, according to *The Presidents of the Kiwanis Club of Birmingham*, "George always listed his hobbies as his family, the rehabilitation of underprivileged and crippled children, and football, in that order." (KCOB.)

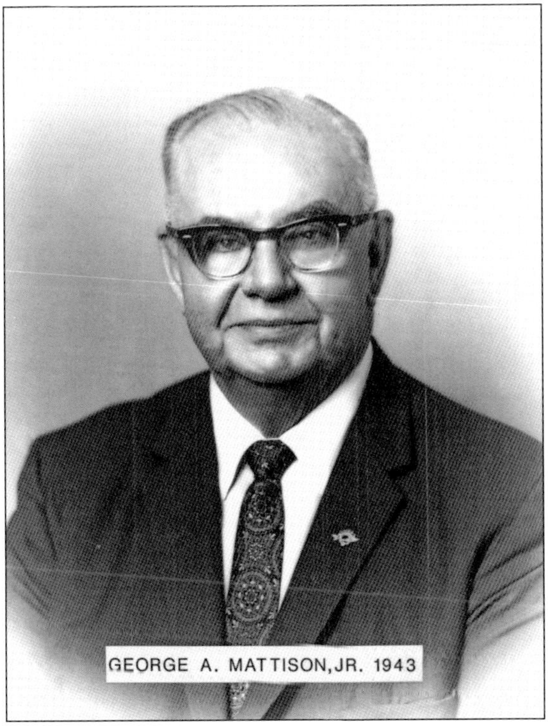

On Tuesday, April 6, 1943, Lord Halifax (pictured below in Washington, DC), Great Britain's ambassador to the United States, arrived in Birmingham for a two-day visit. On his first day, he addressed a joint luncheon of the Kiwanis and Rotary Clubs. "Our soldiers, who fought and died for us, won the last war, but we the people, who were to finish the job, lost the peace," he warned the clubs. (LOC.)

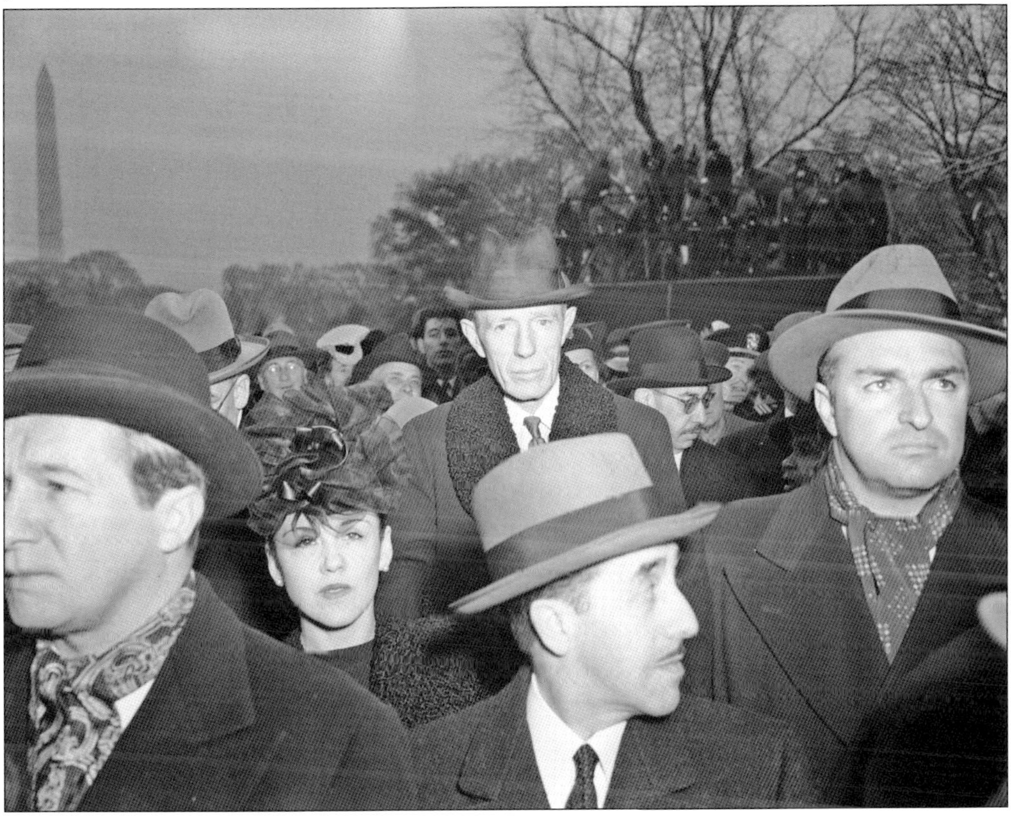

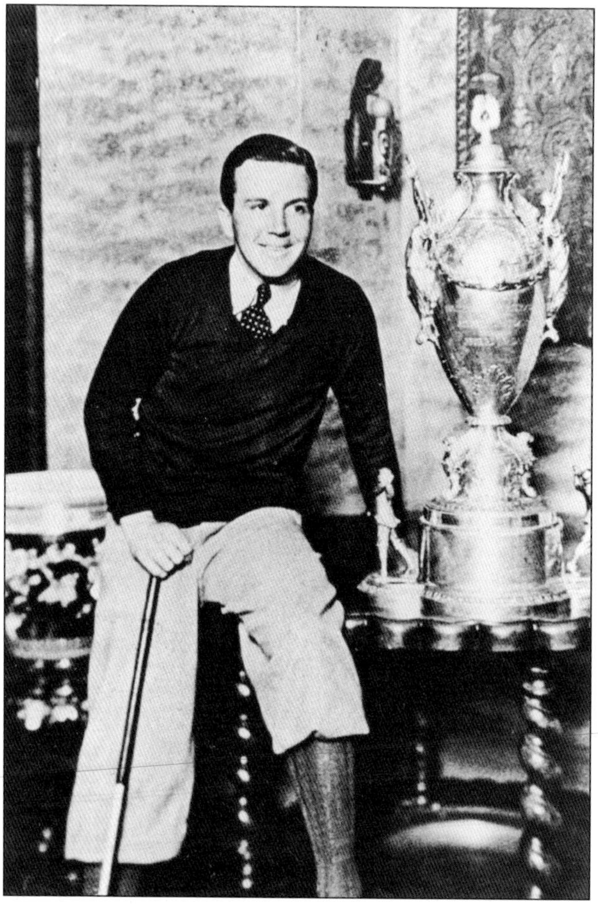

In January 1944, the ominous news reached Birmingham that the club's own Sam D. Perry, called to active duty with the Army Air Forces, had gone missing on a flight in the South Pacific. An insurance executive in Birmingham, Perry was a great golfer who had won the Southern Amateur golf championship in 1929, 1931, and 1941. Captain Perry's body was never found. (Alabama Golf Association.)

The Second World War invigorated Birmingham with both patriotism and economic growth. The B-29 Superfortress *We Dood It*, shown here, was among the 5,000 bombers flown into Birmingham for modifications at the Bechtel-McCone-Parsons plant adjacent to the Birmingham airport. At the plant, some 14,000 workers (40 percent of them women) worked to modify B-24 Liberators, B-29 Superfortresses, P-38 Lightnings, and A-20 Havocs with various design improvements. (ADAH.)

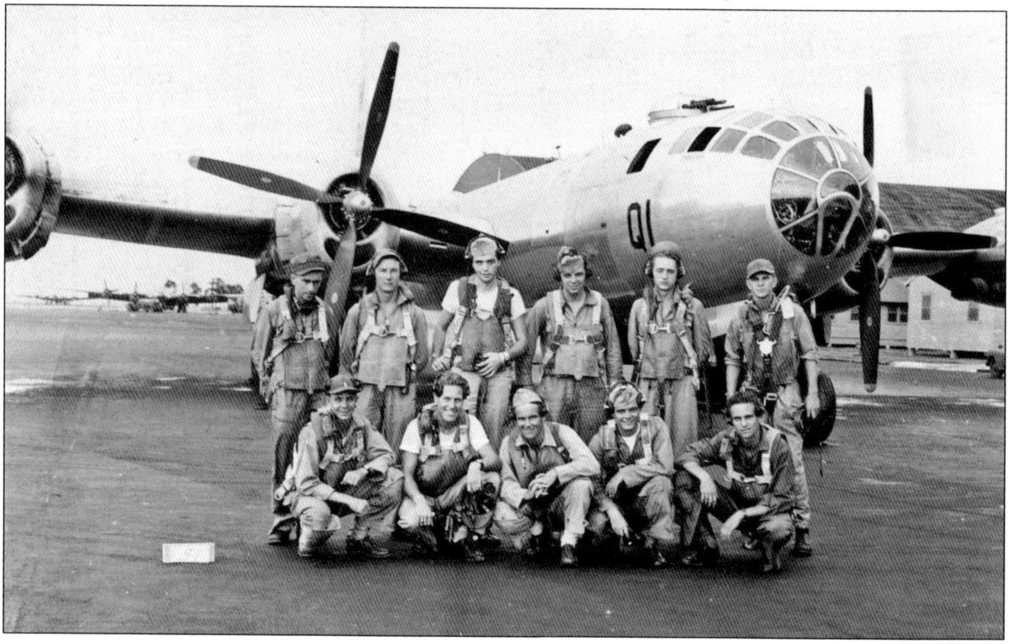

Ehney A. Camp Jr. graduated from the University of Alabama with a perfect straight-A record in 1928. Employed first by the investing firm of Ward, Sterne & Company, Camp ultimately became the executive vice president and treasurer of Liberty National Life Insurance Company. The Kiwanis Club elevated him to president in 1944 when president-elect Tom Bowron became too ill to take office. (KCOB.)

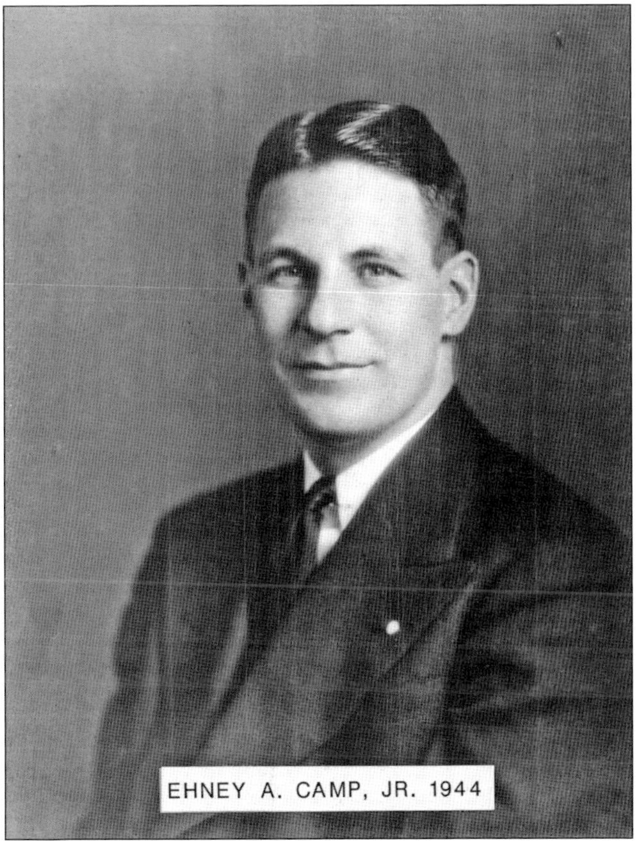

In 1944, the club donated $200 to furnish a "sun parlor" at Tuscaloosa's Northington Army General Hospital for patients such as these soldiers. Built during the war, the 160-acre facility was the only one of its kind in Alabama and tended to some 2,400 patients. On October 17, 1944, the Kiwanians hosted 20 of the men at their weekly luncheon. (ADAH.)

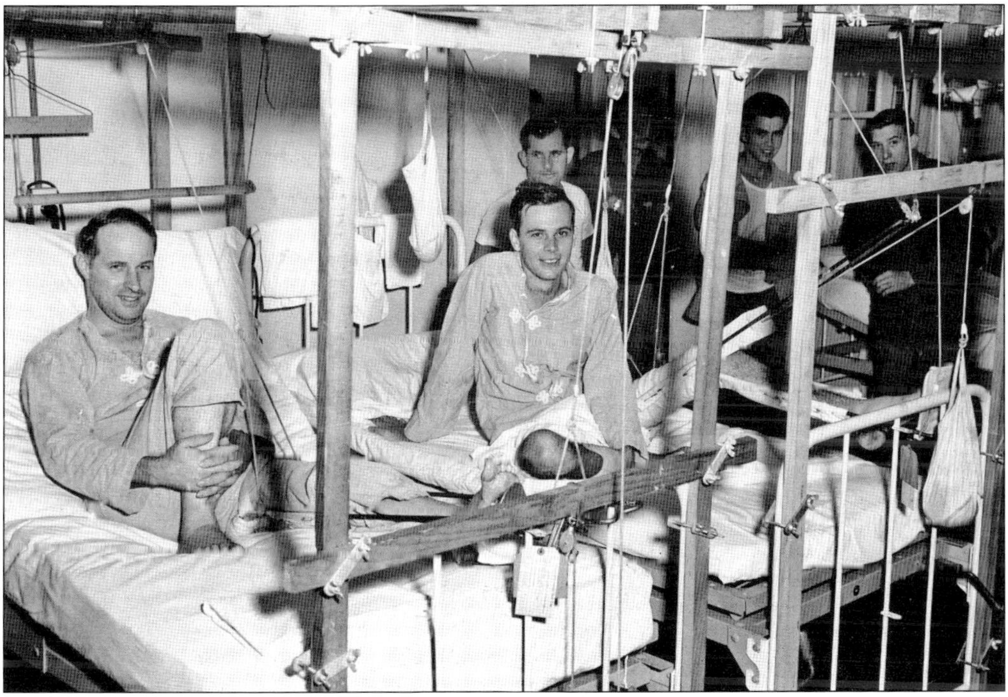

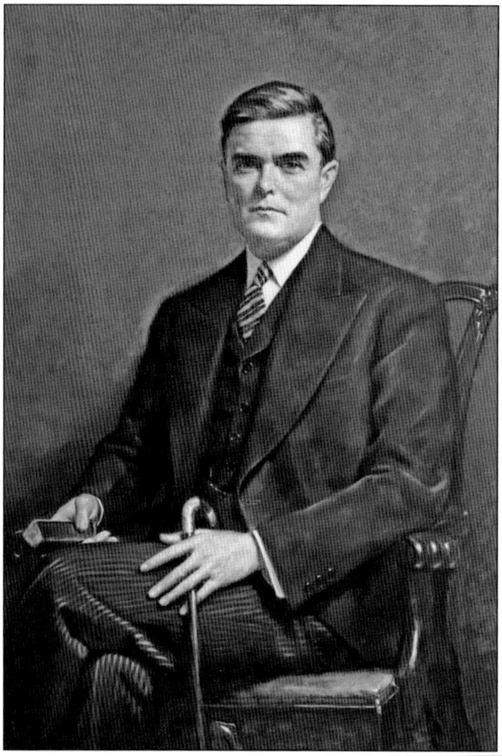

Back in 1938, the club had watched its own Frank Dixon be elected as Alabama's governor. On December 28, 1944, the former governor spoke to the club, calling for national unity. "Who is the president of the United States is of no interest to me. The only thing I am interested in and the only thing you are interested in is getting our boys back home." (ADAH.)

In January 1945, the Kiwanians mourned the loss of Sgt. Thomas Hendrick, son of club member Julius Hendrick. Enlisting in the Army after graduating from the McCallie School in Chattanooga in 1943, Hendrick was serving with the 178th Engineer Combat Battalion when he was killed by German artillery outside of Bastogne, Belgium, during the Battle of the Bulge. (NARA.)

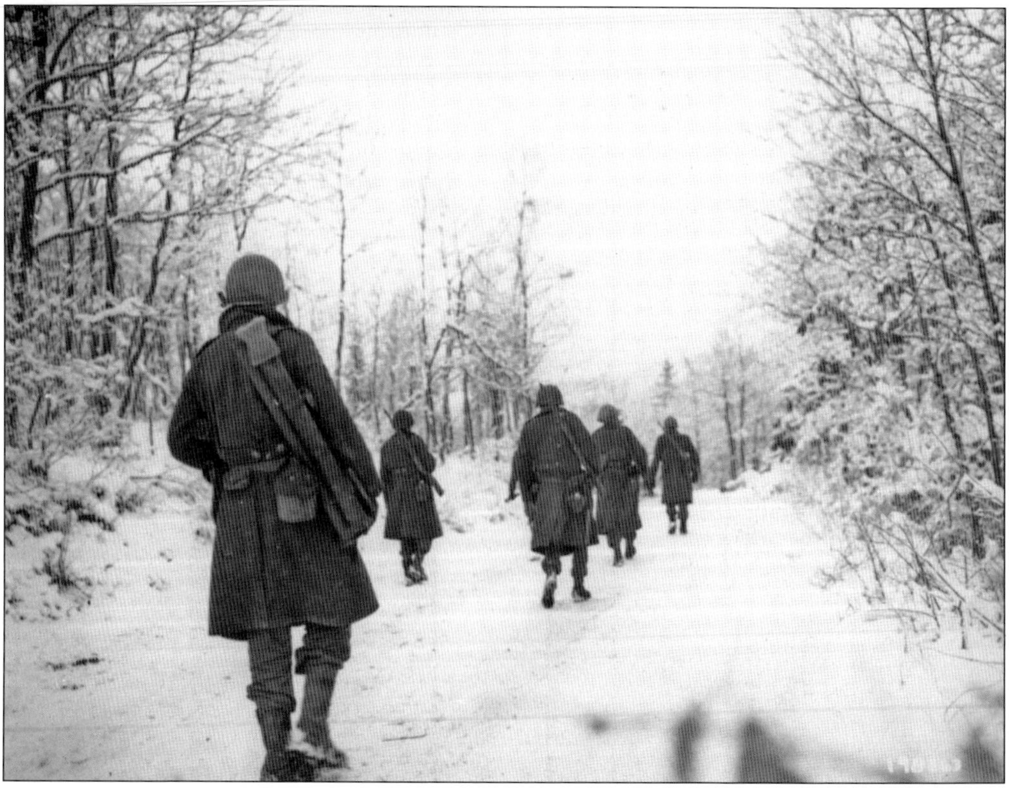

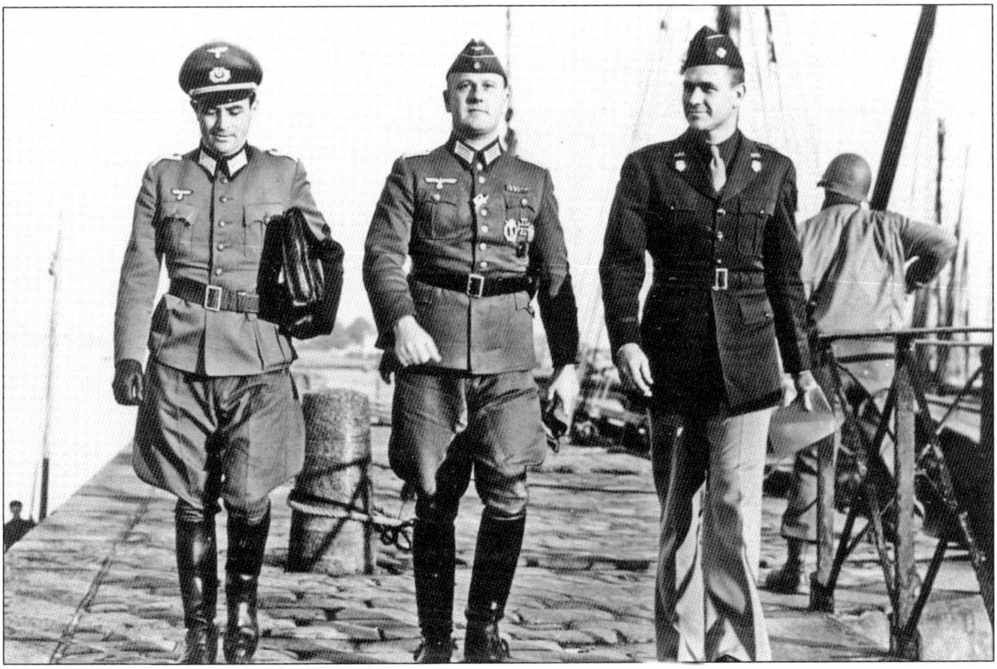

Sidelined by a football injury to his shoulder from his playing days at Howard College (now Samford University), A. Gerow Hodges (right in both photographs) was ineligible for military service. Nevertheless, he joined the American Red Cross and successfully negotiated the release of 149 Allied soldiers from the Germans. For his courageous actions, including more than a dozen trips behind enemy lines, he was awarded two Bronze Stars. Returning to Alabama after the war, Hodges would become executive vice president of Liberty National Life Insurance Company, chairman of the board of directors of Samford University, and, in 1972, the president of the Kiwanis Club. Hodges also became the namesake of the club's A. Gerow Hodges Service Award. (Both, NARA.)

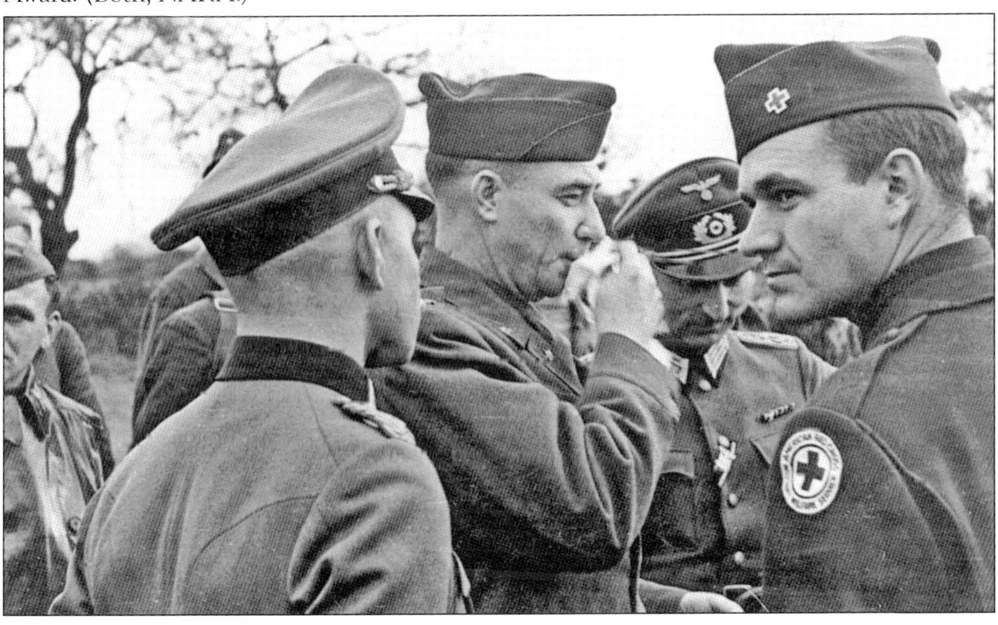

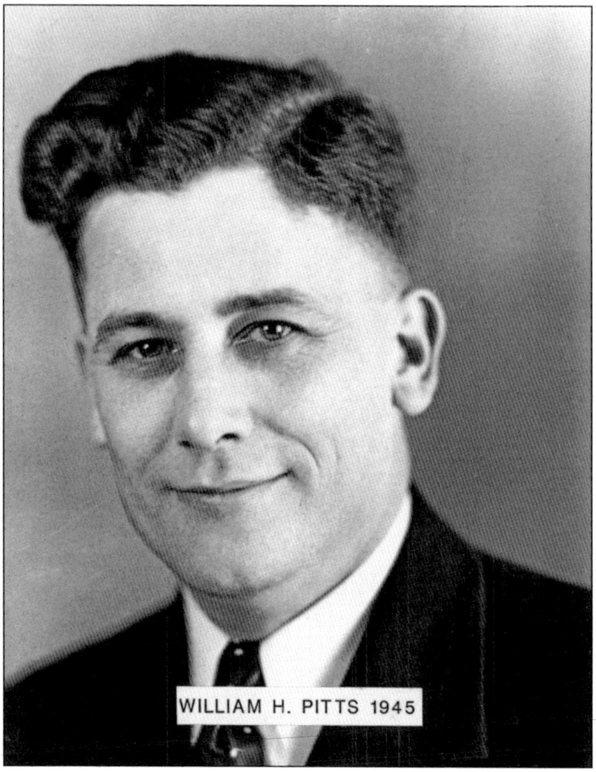

William H. Pitts, who was elected president of the club in 1945, had enlisted in the US Army at the age of 16 to serve in World War I. Actively involved in Birmingham's real estate market, Pitts was vice president of the Molton, Allen & Williams real estate company when he became the club's president. (KCOB.)

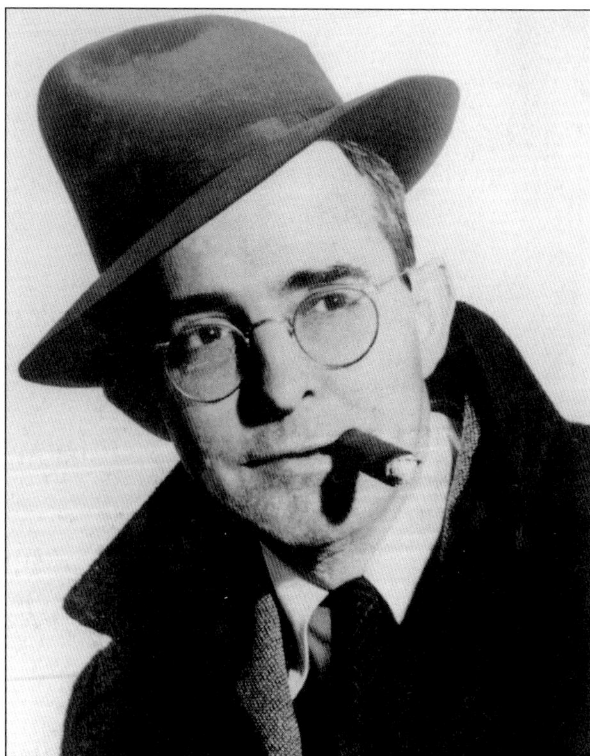

On February 20, 1945, the club honored longtime *Birmingham News* sportswriter Zipp Newman for his dedicated support of annual high school charity football games that benefitted the city's Crippled Children's Clinic. The Thanksgiving 1945 game raised $139,976, a figured that amazed featured guest speaker and famed New York City sportswriter Grantland Rice as "better than anything I ever heard of along this line." (Mrs. Walter F. Morris.)

Three

FORGING A NEW BIRMINGHAM

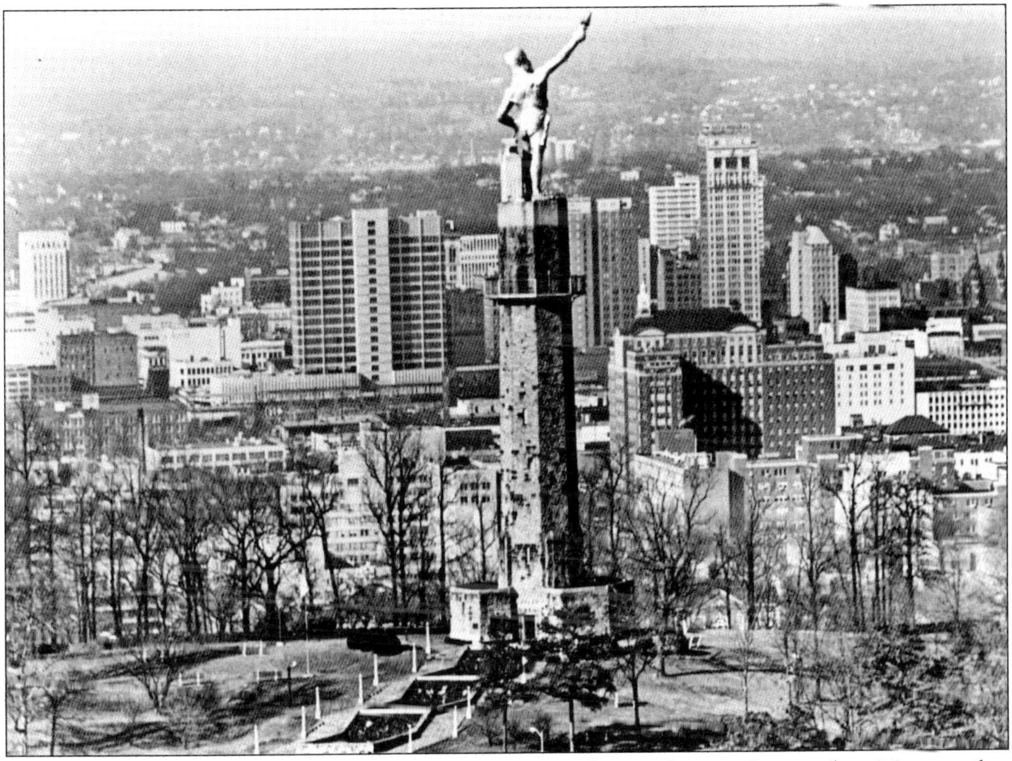

This 1965 photograph of *Vulcan* and downtown Birmingham to his north was taken 26 years after the Kiwanis Club, working with local government and the WPA, led efforts to place the statue atop Red Mountain. By this time, *Vulcan*'s forged spear had been replaced by a green neon torch that glowed red after a Birmingham traffic death. (BPLA.)

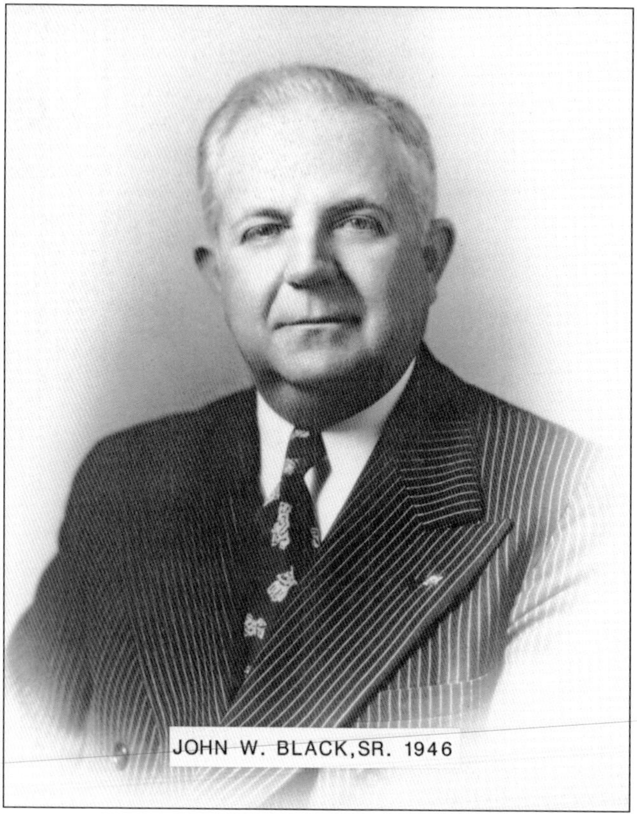

In 1946, John W. Black became the club's president. The founder of the Dixie-Drive-It-Yourself System and National Truck Rental, Black was particularly involved in supporting Birmingham's Girls' Club and was instrumental in raising $15,000 from the club for the construction of the Girls' Club's Minnie Mowry Recreational Center. (KCOB.)

The club held a special luncheon honoring longtime member Erskine Ramsay on March 18, 1947, broadcast live by radio station WAPI. In this photograph, taken in 1949, Ramsay is shown with shovel in hand breaking ground for the new auditorium at the Birmingham high school named after him and the site of the first Key Club sponsored by the club. (BPLA.)

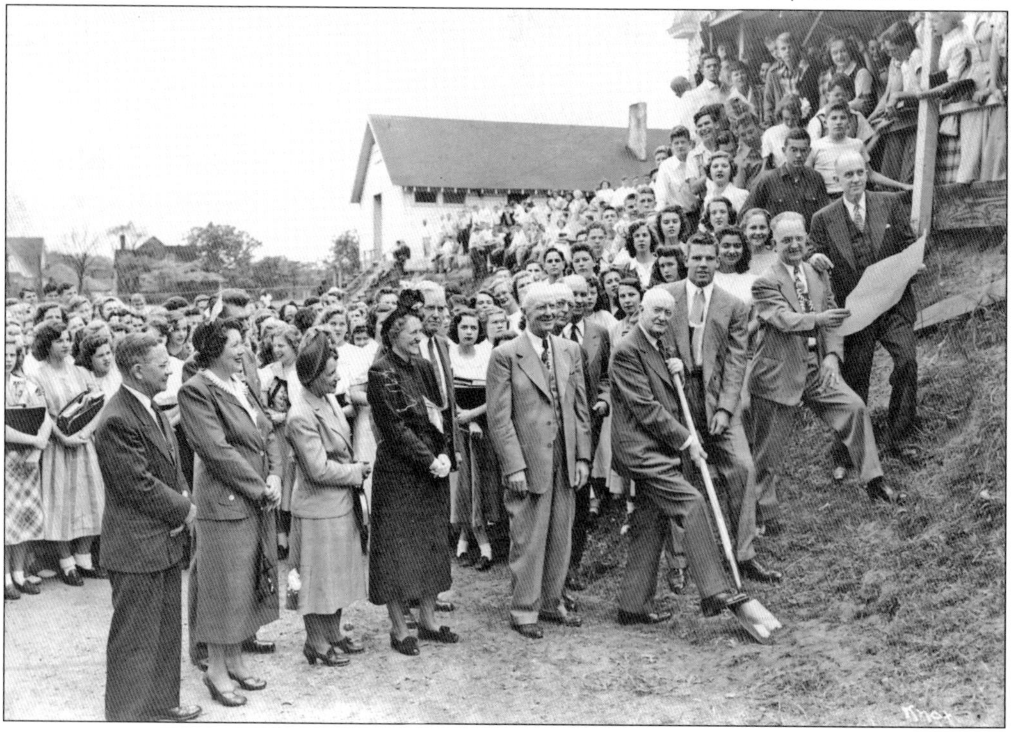

On November 27, 1947, Alexander M. Guerry, president of the University of the South, came to Birmingham, the self-proclaimed "Football Capital of the South," and warned that "the fact that many football coaches draw larger salaries than professors is evidence that colleges consider winning football teams more important than scholarship. This is a distortion of values, and today a sense of values is the most important in the world." (Sewanee.)

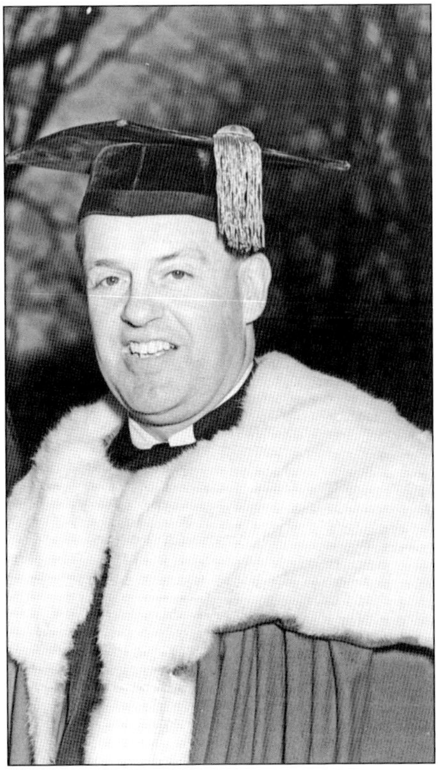

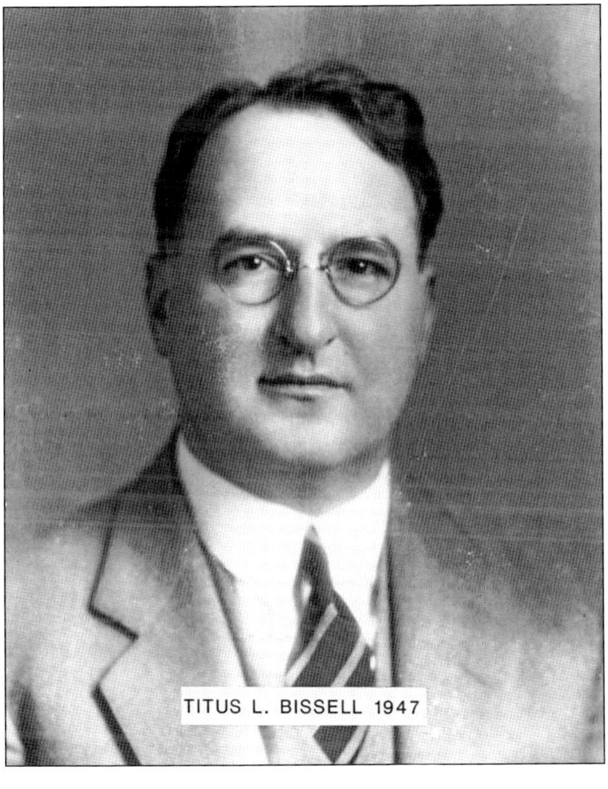

Titus L. Bissell, a native of Charleston, South Carolina, became the club's president in 1947. Educated as an engineer at Clemson University, he started his career with Westinghouse Electric Company. He came to Birmingham in 1916 and, seven years later, went to work for Alabama Power Company. When Bissell was elected president of the club, he was the manager of the company's Industrial Power Division. (KCOB.)

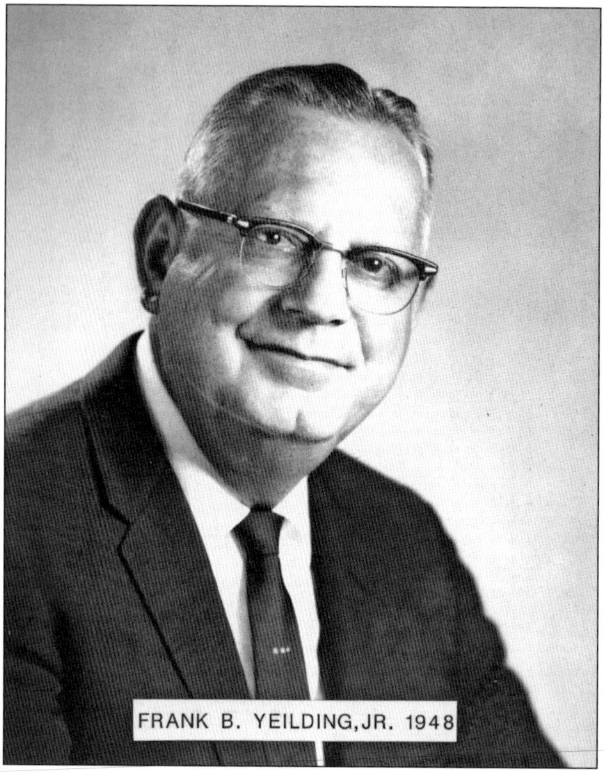

Frank B. Yeilding Jr. was the brother of Howard Yeilding, who had been the club's president in 1935; in 1948, he followed in his brother's footsteps at the helm of the club. A nationally recognized leader in the savings and loan industry, Yeilding was the head of the Jefferson Federal Savings and Loan Association. (KCOB.)

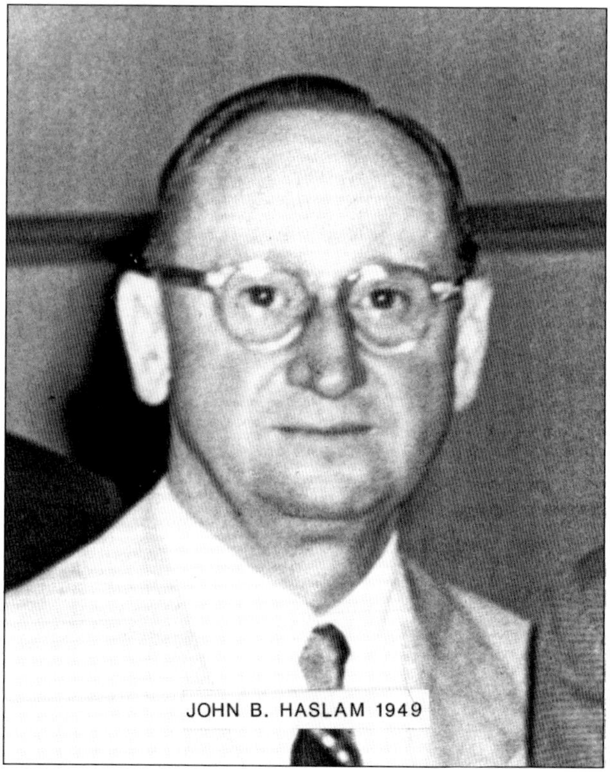

In 1949, Birmingham native John B. "J.B." Haslam was elected the club's president. A graduate of the Virginia Military Institute, Haslam earned early distinction as Alabama's youngest bank examiner. By the time he took the helm of the Kiwanis Club, Haslam was vice president of the Birmingham Trust and Savings Company. (KCOB.)

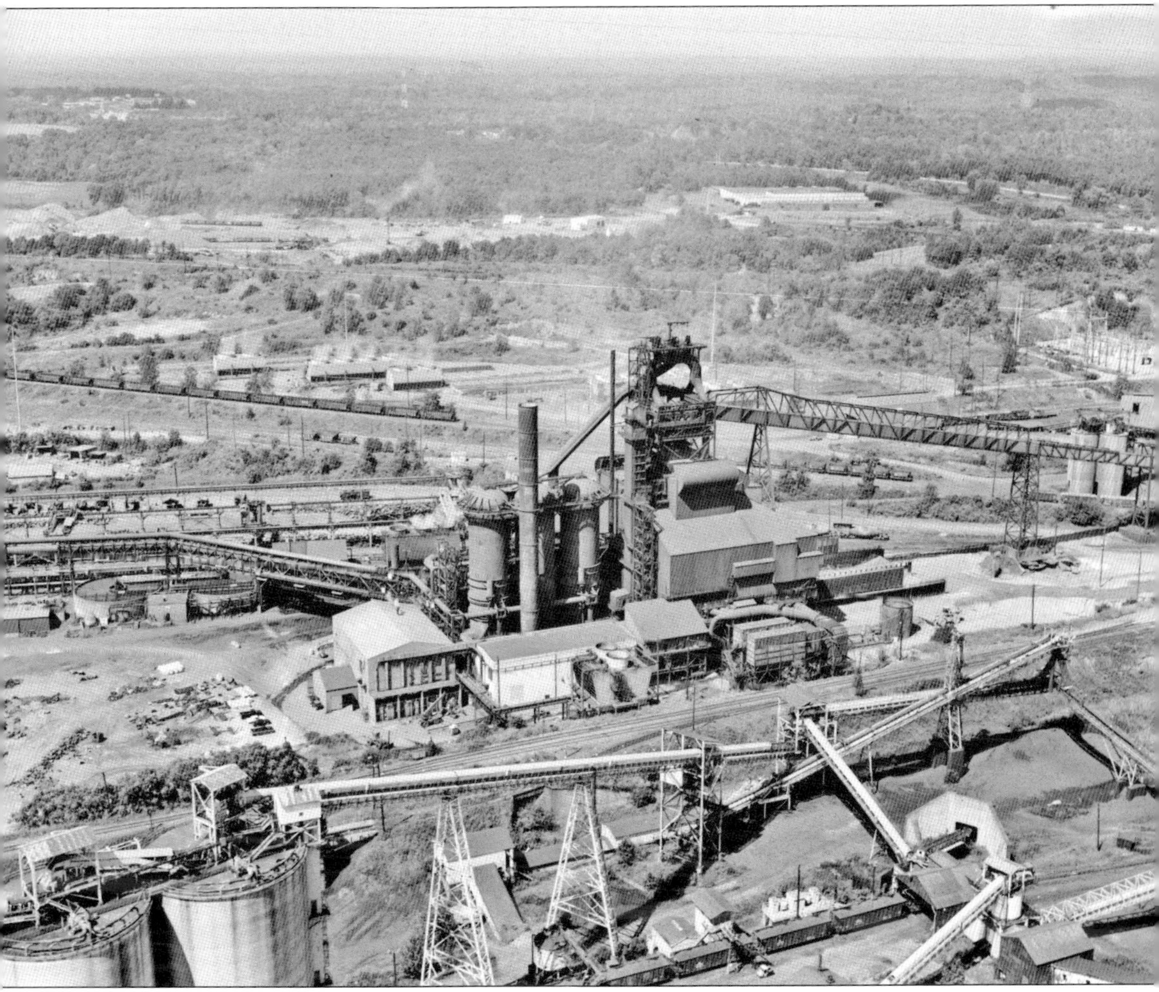

The club traveled off-site to tour the Tennessee Coal & Iron (TCI) Company's massive Fairfield steel works on February 9, 1949. At the time, TCI's mills, stretching across Birmingham's western suburbs, were the largest producer of primary steel in the Southeast and boasted a total annual capacity of three million tons of finished hot-rolled steel products, including rails, structural shapes, plates, reinforcing rods, bars, ingots, blooms, and billets for forging. During World War II, the plants supplied huge quantities of their products to southern manufacturers of defense items ranging from artillery shells to merchant ships. TCI employed as many as 28,000 persons at this time and contributed mightily to Birmingham's economic identity as the "Pittsburgh of the South." Although US Steel acquired TCI in 1907, the company retained its identity as TCI until 1964, when the Birmingham operations simply became a subsidiary. (LOC.)

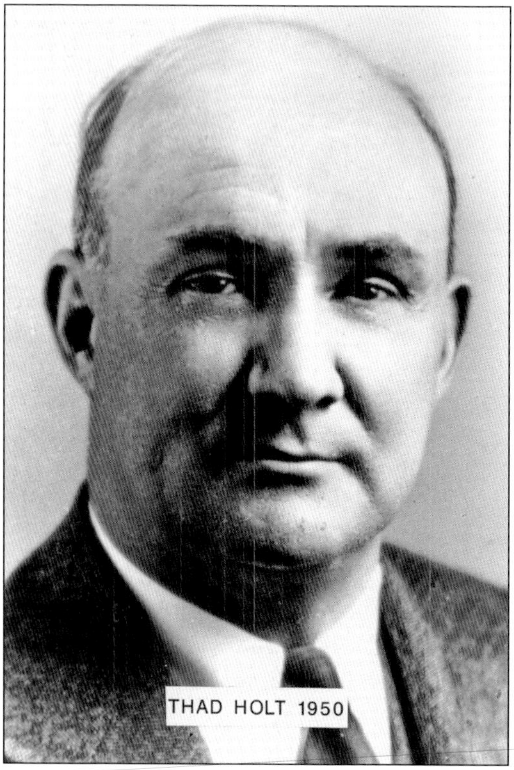

Thad G. Holt became president of the club in 1950. In the Great Depression, he was the Alabama state director of the New Deal's Works Progress Administration. Holt later ran WAPI radio and, procuring the state's first television license, launched WATV. Although Holt served as the chairman of the Birmingham Federal Reserve Bank, he viewed his greatest accomplishment as setting up Alabama's network of educational television stations. (KCOB.)

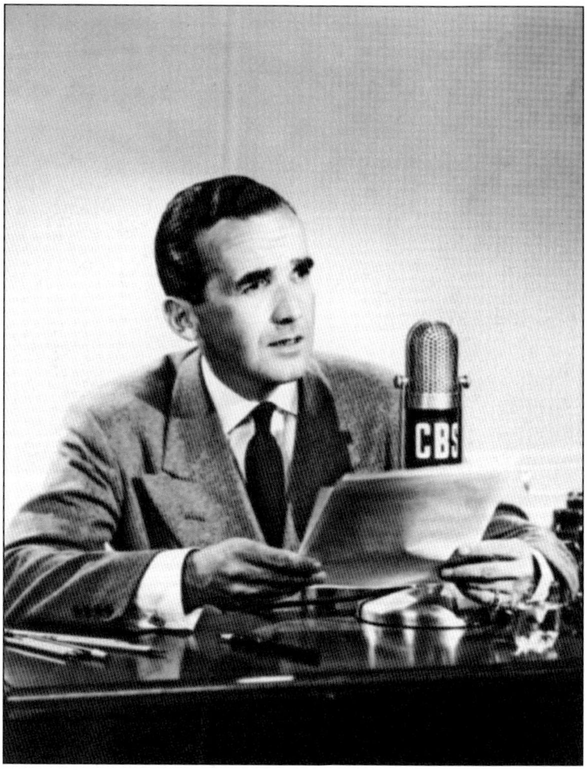

An annual Ladies Night was one of the all-male club's traditions. On December 4, 1950, at the dinner dance at Birmingham's Thomas Jefferson Hotel, the special guest speaker was legendary CBS radio broadcaster Edward R. Murrow, who had earned acclaim for his broadcasts from wartime London at the height of the German blitz and would later famously cross swords with Sen. Joe McCarthy during the Red Scare. (Tufts University.)

Orville W. Schanbacher, a native of St. Louis, Missouri, became the club's president in 1951. At the time, he was the president of Loveman, Joseph & Loeb. Schanbacher was well respected for his involvement in a myriad of civic organizations, ranging from the YMCA and the Red Cross to the Council on Foreign Relations. (KCOB.)

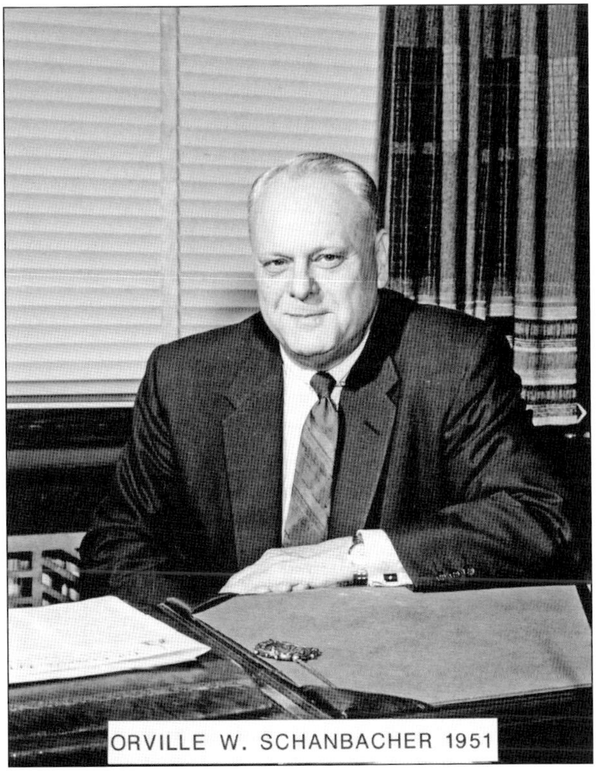

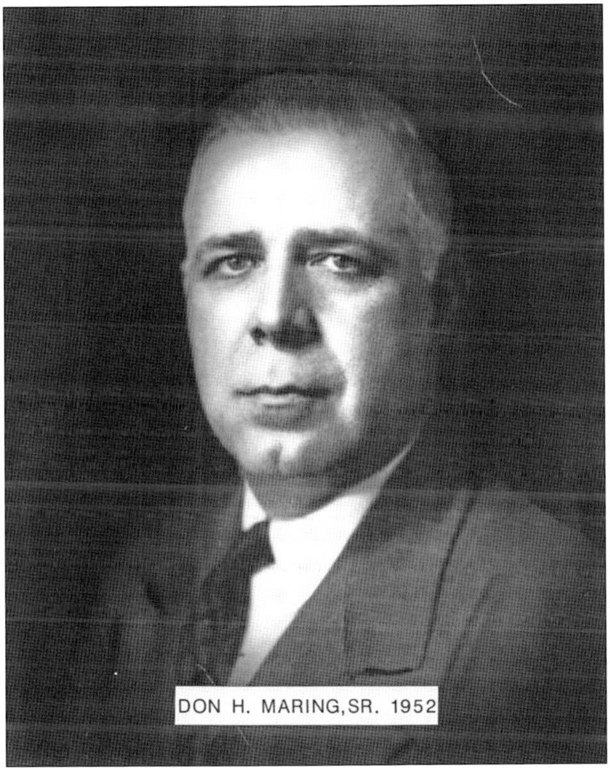

Don H. Maring was elected the club's president in 1952. He served in World War I, achieving the rank of major and earning the Legion of Honor from France. Employed first by Connors Steel and later in his father-in-law Sydney Bowie's Ford business, Maring served for two years (1948 and 1949) as the president of Birmingham's Community Chest. (KCOB.)

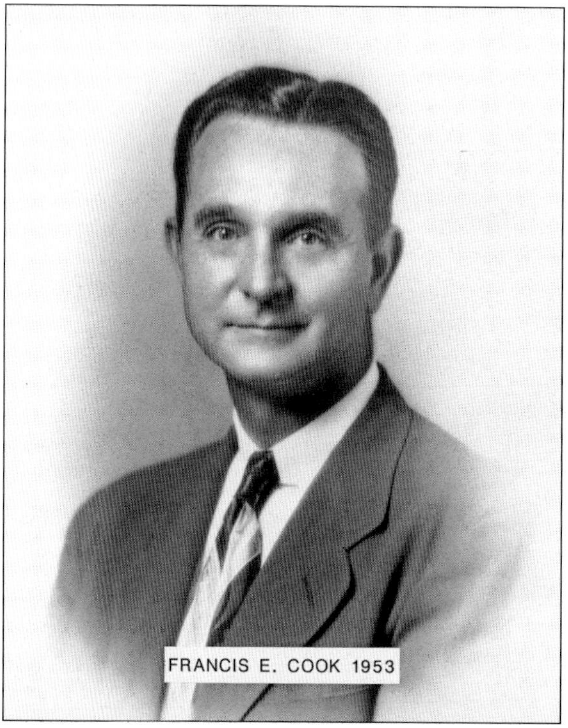

In 1953, Francis E. Cook became the club's president. Cook grew up in the Birmingham neighborhood of Ensley and later attended Georgia Tech. By the time the club's membership elected Cook president, he was a manager with Gulf Oil Company. Cook was also the president of the board of stewards for Highlands Methodist Church and a member of the board of directors of Carraway Methodist Hospital. (KCOB.)

The Birmingham Girls Club was founded in 1938 to provide a refuge for homeless young ladies and to help them develop important life skills. By the 1950s, a more youthful focus had evolved, but it still sought to provide a nurturing space for girls such as the ones below. Not surprisingly, the Girls Club was among the children's charities that benefited annually from the Kiwanians' generosity. (KCOB.)

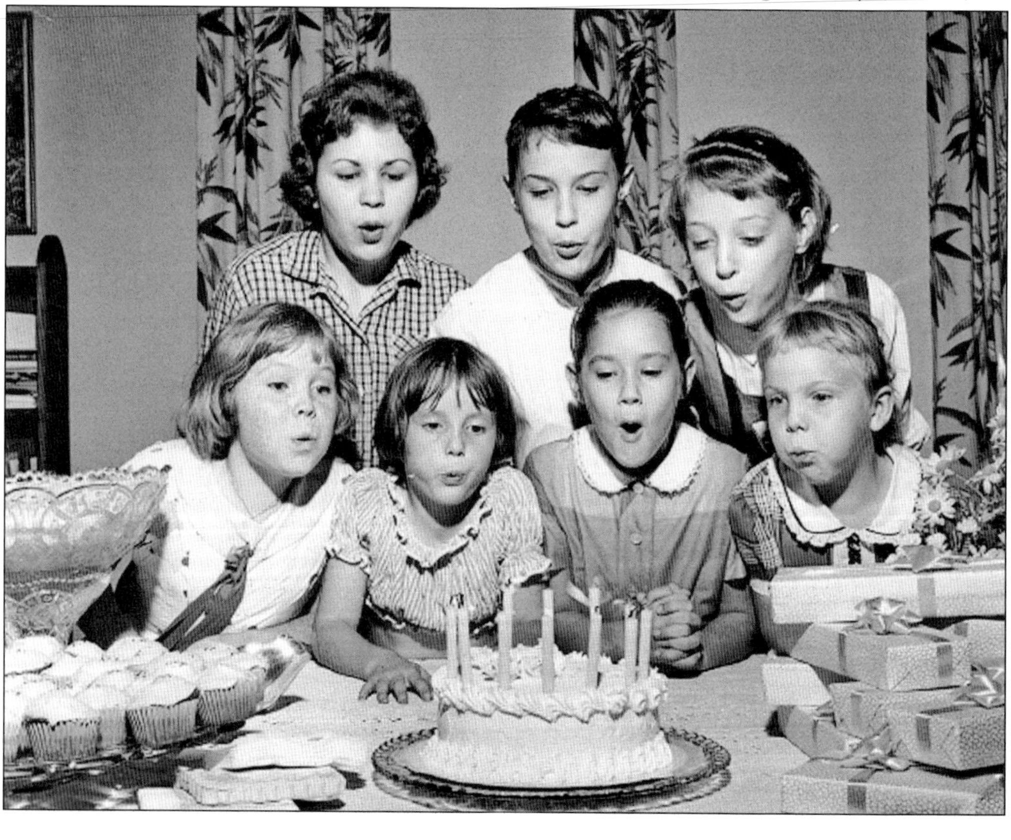

Clyde H. Porter was elected the club's president in 1954. A native of Birmingham and a graduate of the University of Alabama, he was the purchasing agent and assistant secretary for Alabama By-Products Company, a firm that owned tens of thousands of acres of coal lands surrounding Birmingham and a battery of coke ovens. (KCOB.)

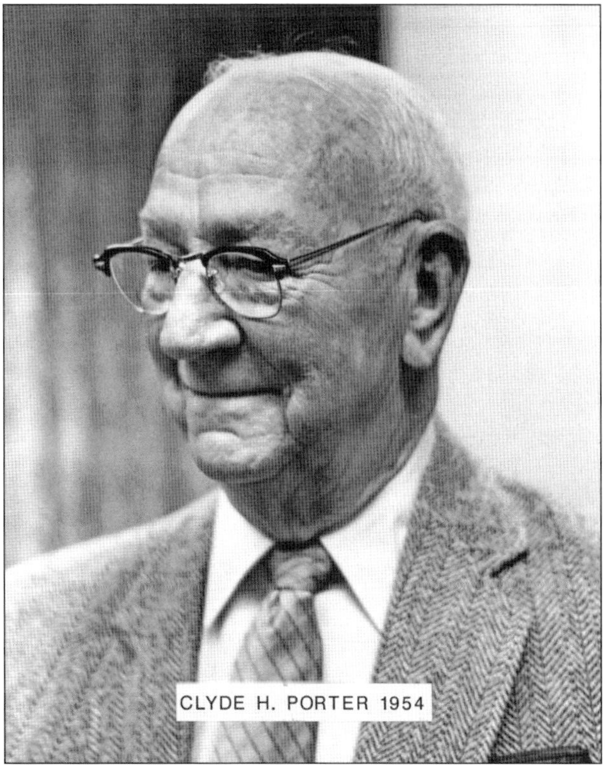

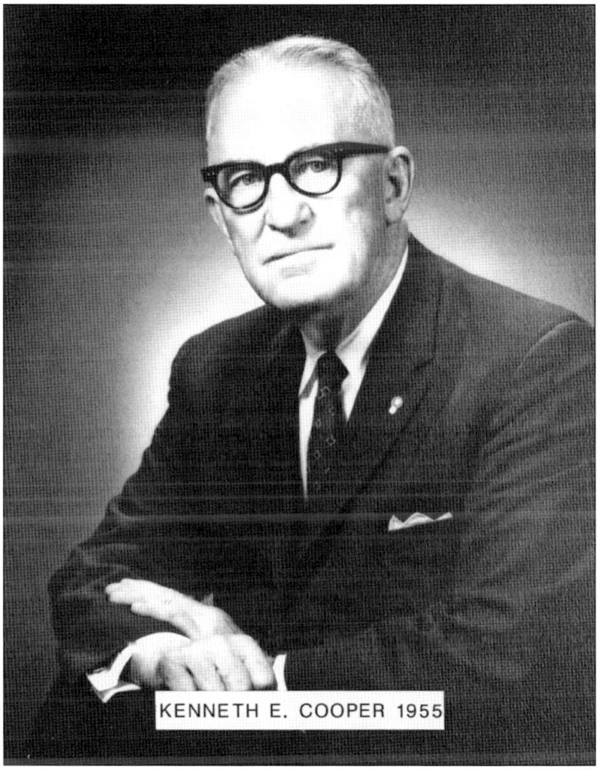

The club elected Arkansas-born Kenneth E. Cooper president in 1955. Admitted to the Alabama bar in 1916 after graduating from Southern University in Greensboro, Alabama, and studying law at the University of Alabama, Cooper was a partner in Cabaniss, Johnston, Gardner, and Clark. His civic leadership was evident with Alabama's Methodist Children's Home, Carraway Methodist Hospital, and the Methodist Home for Aging. (KCOB.)

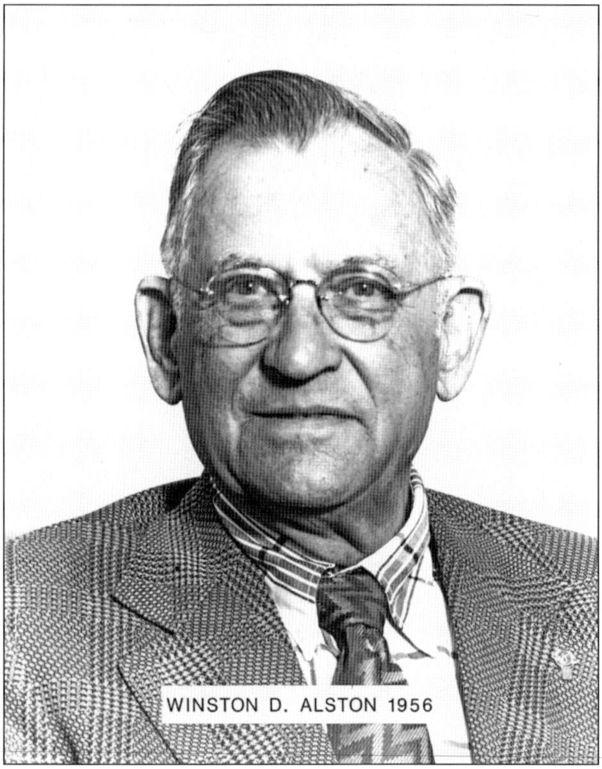

Winston Alston became the club's president in 1956. An executive with Southern Bell Telephone Company, he was educated in electrical engineering at Alabama Polytechnic Institute, graduating in 1928. Alston was reportedly known as "Mr. Kiwanis" to his friends and would ultimately count among his accomplishments his service as the Alabama district governor in 1960. (KCOB.)

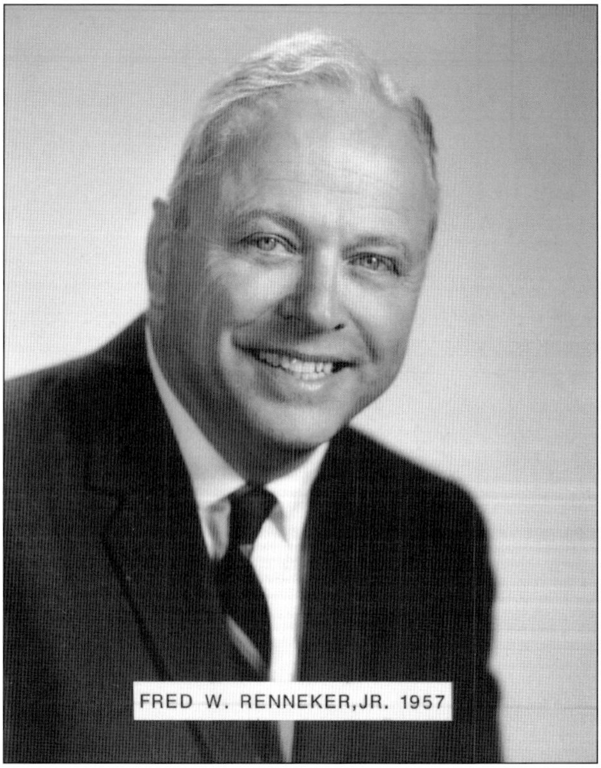

In 1957, Frederick W. Renneker Jr. became the club's president. Trained as an architect at Alabama Polytechnic Institute, Renneker headed a nationally known architecture firm ultimately known as Renneker, Tichansky & Associates. He was the driving force behind the establishment of the annual Kiwanis-Park Board Youth Tennis Tournament and, during his tenure, the club chartered its first Key Club, at Ramsay High School. (KCOB.)

To a large extent, the institutional growth of the nation's 4-H organization paralleled that of Kiwanis. Despite its urban base, the Birmingham Kiwanis had a long tradition of supporting 4-H clubs with annual donations and, in 1957, contributed $100 to sponsor a calf for a local youth to participate in 4-H's Dairy Calf Chain program. (KCOB.)

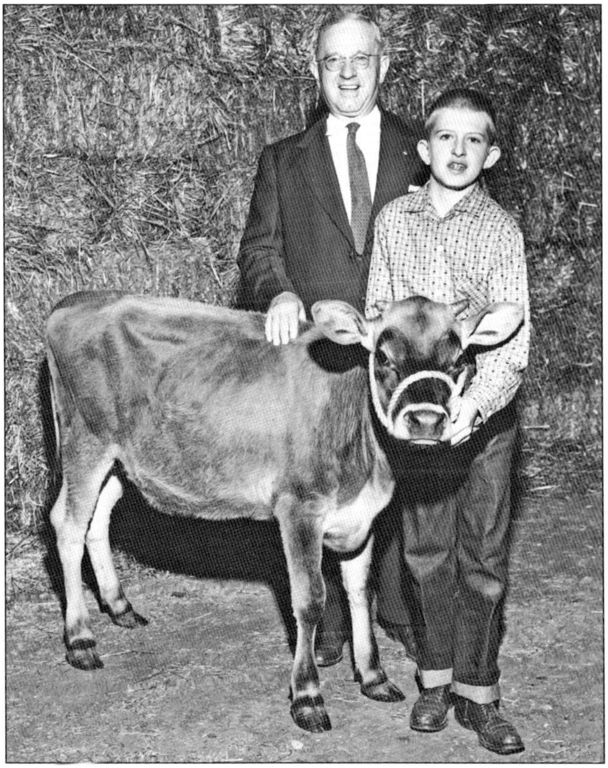

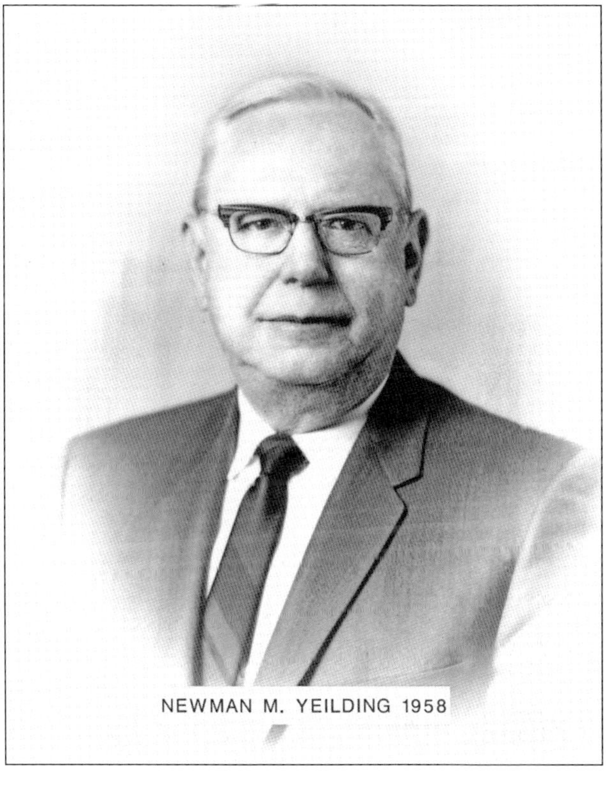

Newman M. "Red" Yeilding became the club's president in 1958. A 1922 graduate of Birmingham-Southern College, Yeilding was employed by the college from 1926 to 1965 as its bursar, treasurer, and financial vice president. Yeilding had the distinction of serving as the club's president in the same manner as his brothers Howard (1935) and Frank Jr. (1948). During his tenure, the club officially incorporated. (KCOB.)

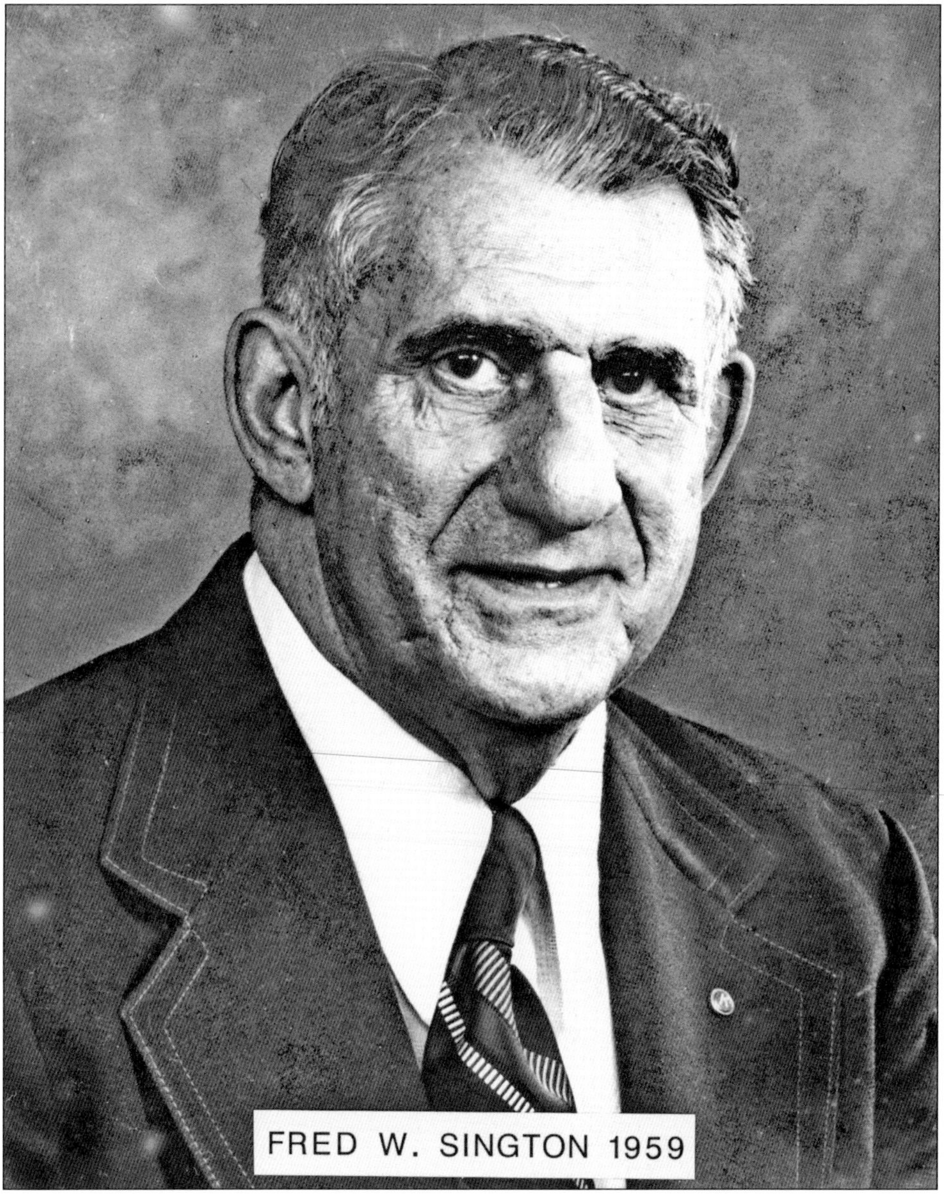

Frederick W. Sington served as the club's president in 1959. A man of remarkable athletic talents and civic drive, he was known as "Mr. Birmingham," according to *The Presidents of the Kiwanis Club of Birmingham*, "for his multi-year leadership in virtually all aspects of community life." A Phi Beta Kappa at the University of Alabama, Sington earned All-American honors in college playing both football and baseball in 1929, 1930, and 1931. He played for the Washington Senators and the Brooklyn Dodgers from 1934 to 1938, worked off-season as a football official for the Southeastern Conference from 1935 to 1955, and was a line coach for Duke University's football team. During World War II, Sington was commissioned in the Navy and served as an athletic officer and coach for the Norman Naval Air Station Zoomers in Norman, Oklahoma. Back in Alabama, he worked in recruiting Bear Bryant to return to Alabama to coach and also founded the Sington Sporting Goods Company. In 1990, the club elected to rename the Charles A. Brown Football Trophy as the Fred W. Sington Trophy. (KCOB.)

In 1960, Robert M. Montgomery became the club's president. A graduate of Birmingham-Southern College, he served in the FBI during World War II. Afterwards, Montgomery reentered the family real estate business of Montgomery Real Estate & Insurance Company. During his term, the club started a bowling team, led by Bill Ireland. It also donated $1,200 to equip the Kiwanis Hut at the new Boys Club Camp outside of Birmingham. (KCOB.)

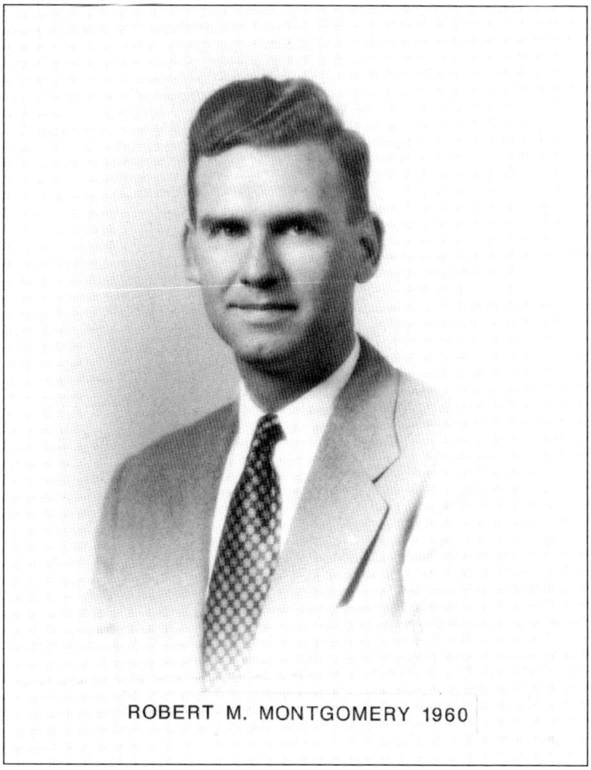

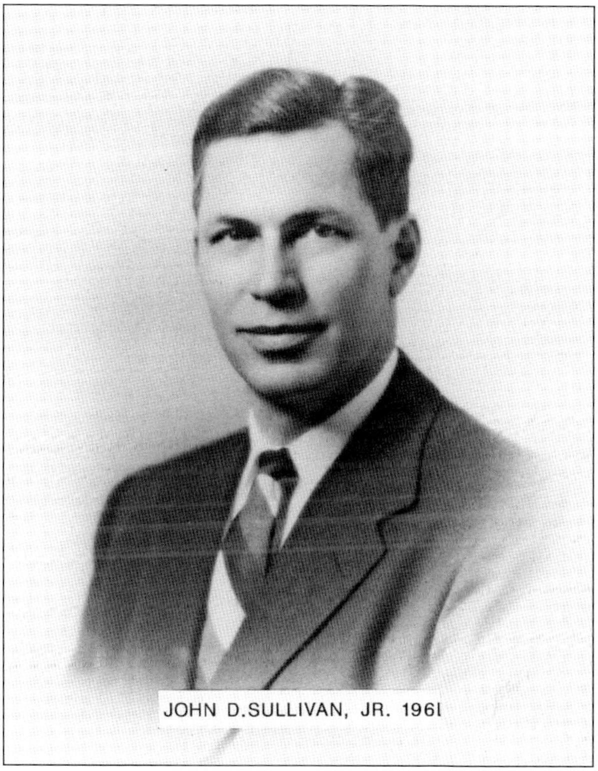

John Sullivan served as the club's president in 1961. His career included 15 years with the B.F. Goodrich Rubber Company and then time with Philco appliance distributor Watts-Newsome Company. Later, Sullivan headed distributorships for Philco-Ford in Birmingham and worked for the company in Detroit, Miami, and Atlanta. During his term, the club sponsored its first Circle K Club at Birmingham-Southern College. (KCOB.)

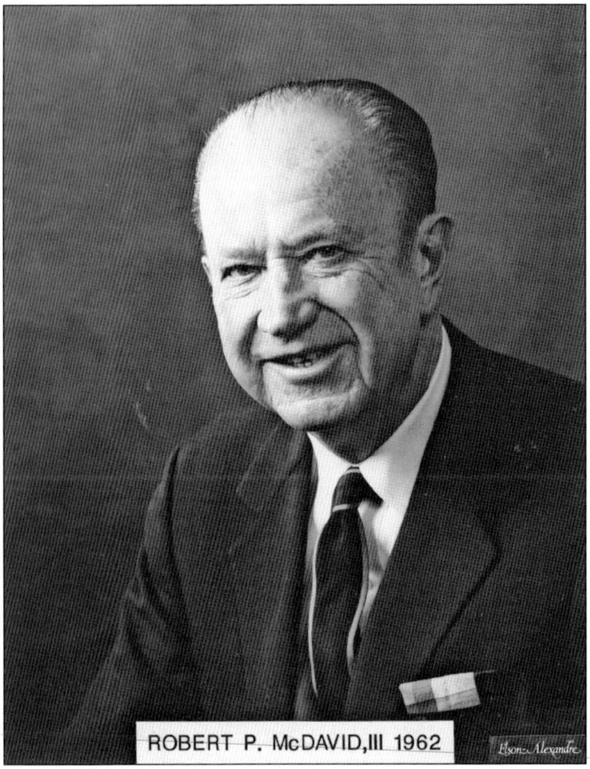

Robert P. McDavid III became the club's president in 1962. A veteran of World War II in North Africa and Italy, he was the president of the family business R.P. McDavid Company, Inc., a longtime distributor of RCA appliances and electronics. Active in civic life, McDavid's work included service as the president of the University of Alabama National Alumni Association. (KCOB.)

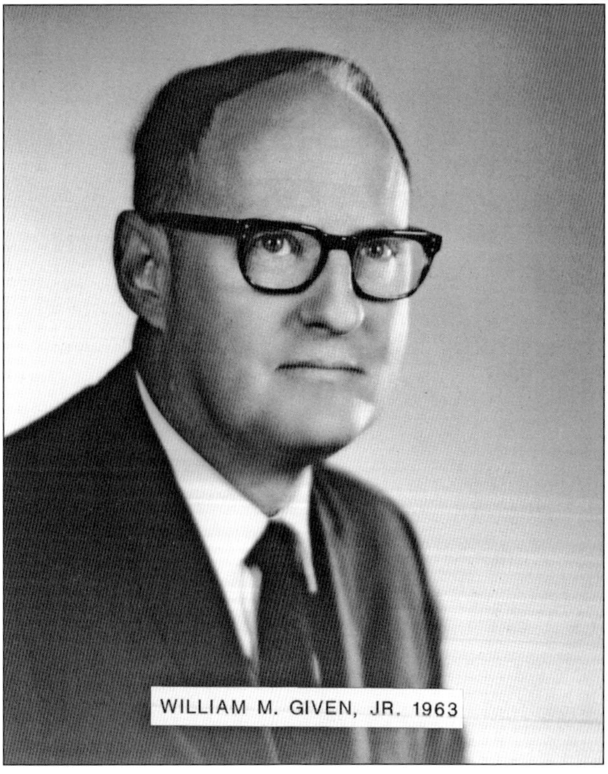

In 1963, William M. Given Jr. served as the club's president. A graduate of the University of the South, he held a master of business administration from Harvard University. Given owned the McVoy-Hausman Company and founded DeVault Ultra Precision, Inc., in Huntsville, Alabama. For three terms, he served as the mayor of the Birmingham suburb of Mountain Brook. (KCOB.)

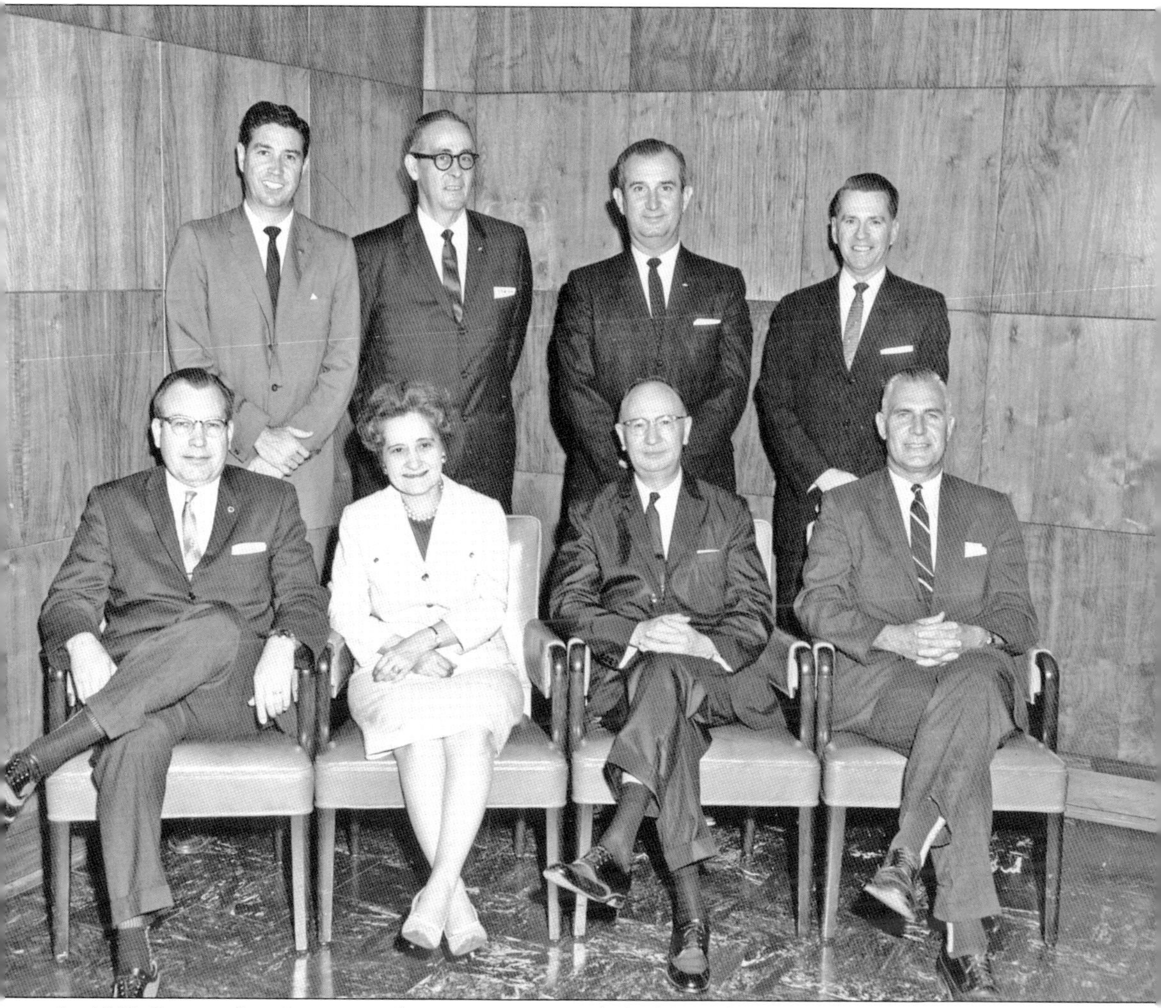

In 1963, Birmingham's system of city government shifted from being run by a three-person city commission (which included Bull Conner overseeing the city's police department) to a nine-person council. Tellingly, two of the nine members of the new council, Dr. John Bryan and M. Edwin Wiggins, were Kiwanians generally viewed to represent the hope of progressive change in Birmingham during this challenging era. Wiggins (first row, third from left) was the former treasurer of Alabama Power Company. Bryan (not pictured) was the executive vice president of the chamber of commerce and a former superintendent of the Jefferson County school system. Unfortunately, the city commission's petulant resistance to relinquishing power threw city government into turmoil and left it ill-prepared to effectively address and respond to the coming civil rights demonstrations in the spring of 1963. (BPLA.)

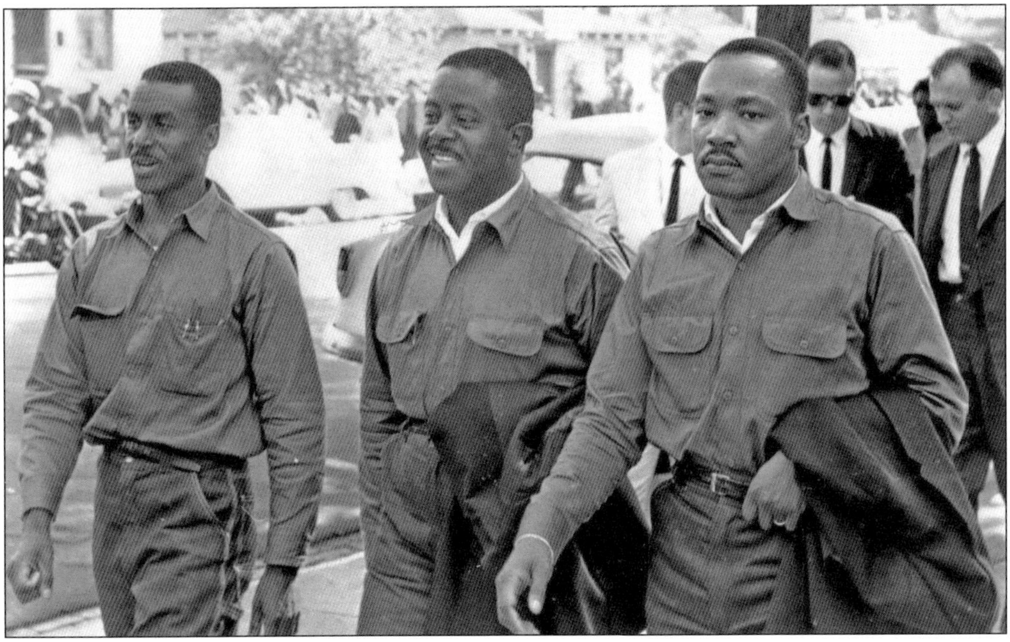

The spring of 1963 brought the world's attention to Birmingham, as civil rights demonstrations erupted downtown and were met with violent reaction by Bull Connor's police force. Atlanta's James Sibley, chairman of the Trust Company of Georgia, which effectively controlled Coca-Cola, spoke to the club on May 7, 1963, at a time when "the sound of anti-segregation demonstration [was] echoing in the street." Speaking to the Kiwanians, Sibley argued "for patience and forbearance," according to an article in the *Birmingham Post-Herald*. Even as Sibley spoke, police had blocked off the streets around the Tutwiler Hotel in an attempt to control the unfolding demonstrations. During this time, the Kiwanians struggled to reconcile support for their moderate brethren on the city council with Bull Connor's behavior and the bombing of the Sixteenth Street Baptist Church. (Both, BPLA.)

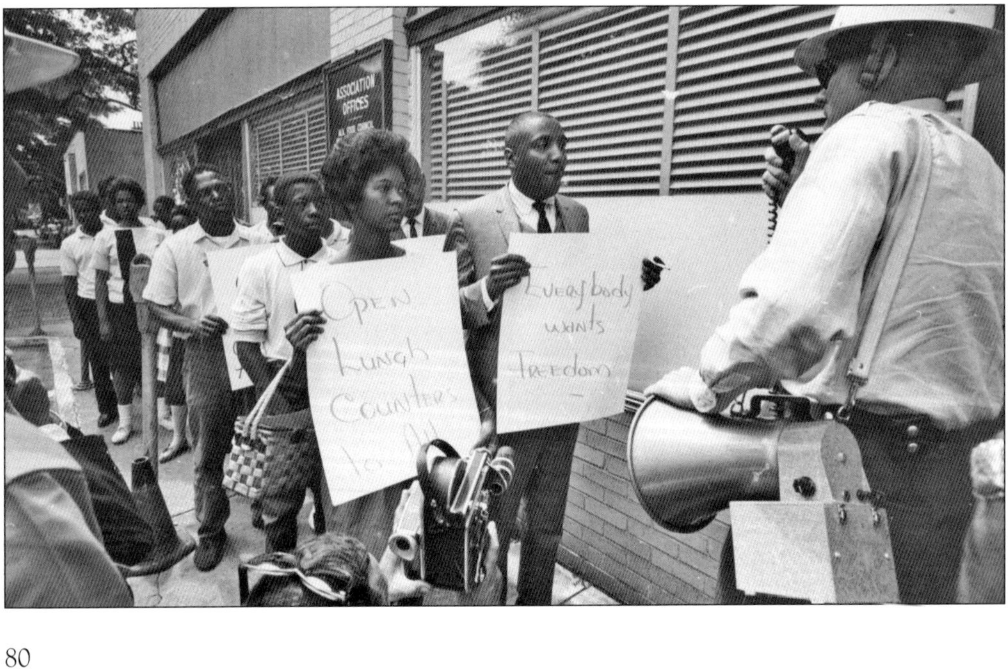

Robert E. Luckie Jr. was elected the club's president for 1964. Service as a press officer with the US Pacific Fleet during World War II and as the advertising manager for the *Birmingham News* positioned him well to launch Robert Luckie & Company, Inc., a nationally recognized advertising agency based in Birmingham. (KCOB.)

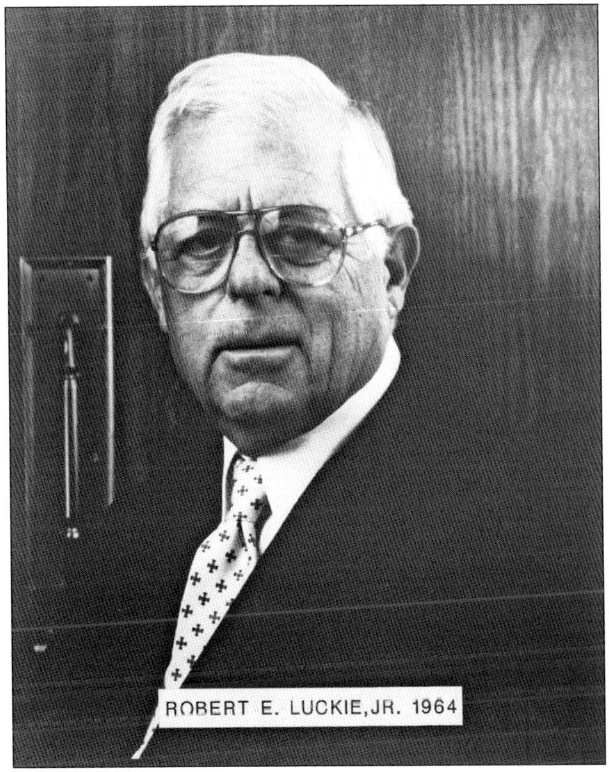

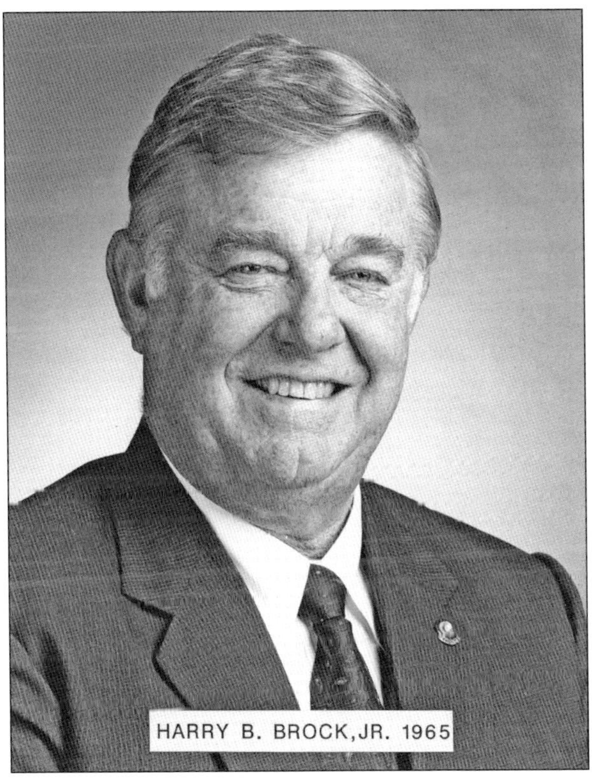

In 1965, Harry B. Brock Jr. became the club's president. Pursuing a career in banking, he ultimately founded Central Bank & Trust Company of Birmingham, a precursor of Compass Bank, now part of BBVA Compass. A club history notes his contributions to "his community and his church" as "too numerous to list," but his vision in working to establish and fund the Kiwanis Foundation was particularly noteworthy. (KCOB.)

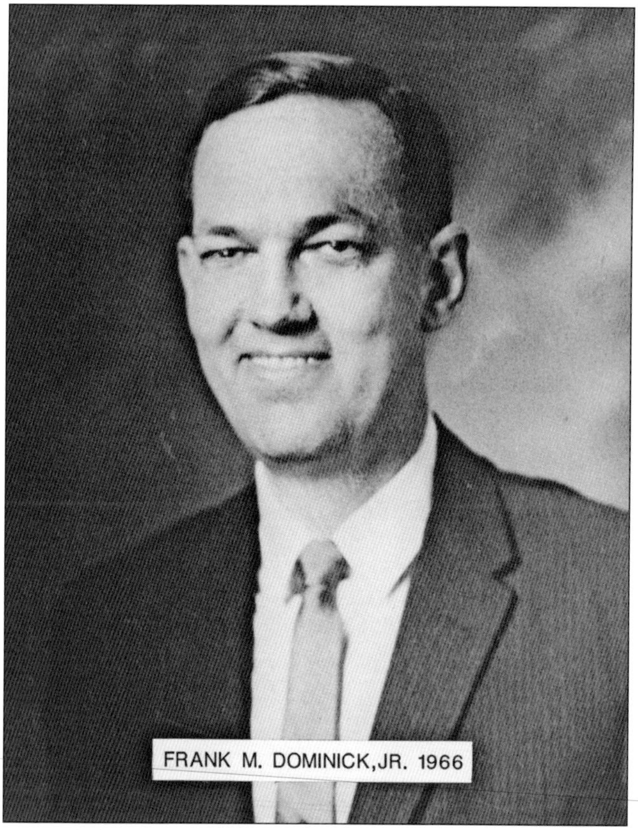

Following in the footsteps of his father, who was the club's president in 1931, Frank M. Dominick Jr. became the club's president in 1966. Like his father, Dominick was an attorney and eventually became the senior member of the firm Dominick, Fletcher & Yeilding. Among other civic leadership positions, Dominick also served as the chairman of the board of trustees of Birmingham-Southern College. (KCOB.)

In 1966, the club continued its long-standing tradition of awarding the Charles A. Brown Football Trophy. Below, the trophy is being presented to Alvin Bresler (right) and an unidentified teammate from Shades Valley High School. Bresler would ultimately play for Auburn University and become a successful high school football coach himself. (IUPUI.)

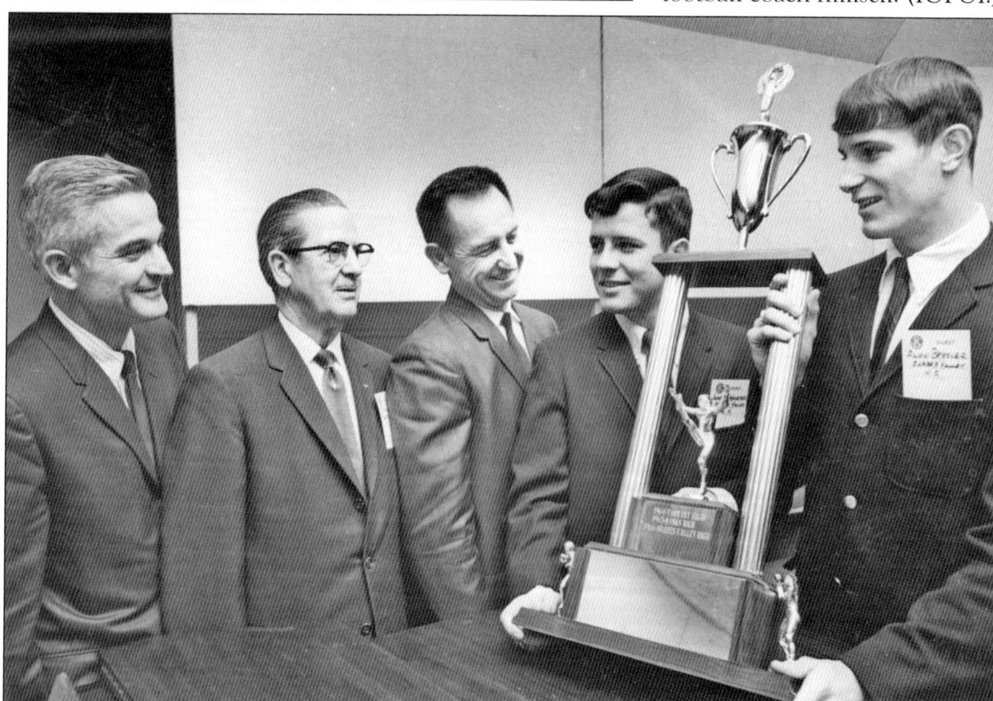

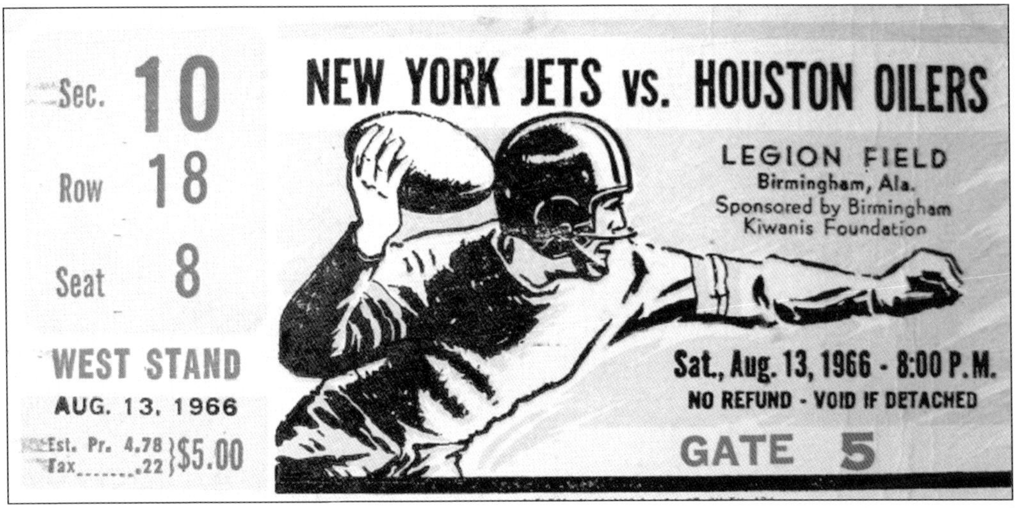

On August 13, 1966, the club, encouraged by former president Harry Brock, sponsored a professional football exhibition game at Birmingham's Legion Field between the AFL's New York Jets and the NFL's Houston Oilers. Played on a muggy night in front of a crowd mostly rooting for the Jets (who were led by former University of Alabama quarterback Joe Namath), the game was won by the Jets, who bested the George Blanda–led Oilers 16-10. (KCOB.)

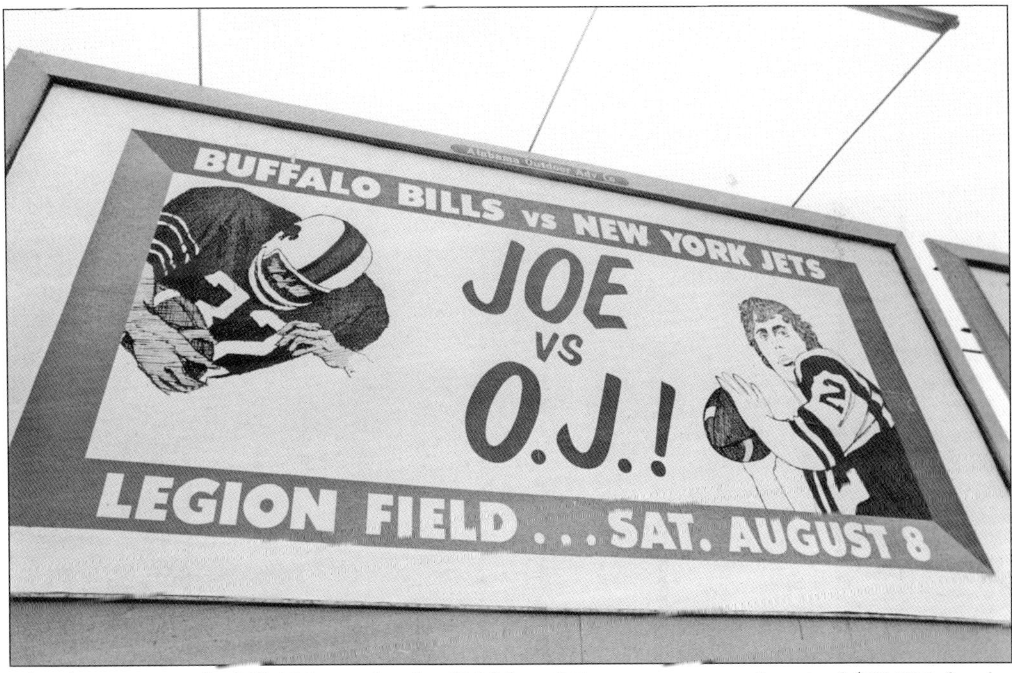

Thanks to a crowd of 57,000 people, the 1966 Jets-Oilers game not only raised $65,000 for the Kiwanis Club's nascent charitable foundation but also, for a time, encouraged the unrealized prospects of an NFL franchise for Birmingham. The success also inspired the club to sponsor future games. Jets-Chiefs in 1967, Jets-Falcons in 1968, Chiefs-Oakland Raiders in 1969, and, in 1970, the Jets versus the Buffalo Bills. (IUPUI.)

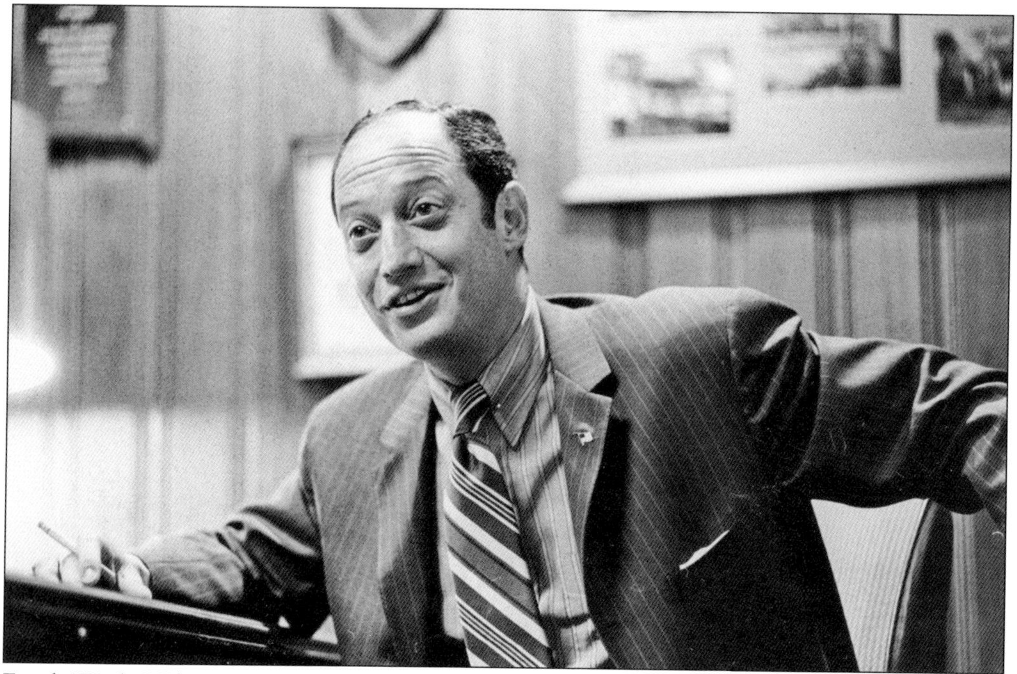

Frank "Tucky" Thomas Jr. (above) and Harold Blach Jr. (below) led the Kiwanians' organization for 1970's Jets-Bills game. The two men faced a daunting task; after the impressive success of the first three games, 1969's game between the Chiefs and Raiders (under new head coach John Madden) at Legion Field had only drawn 19,000 fans and, in the end, lost the club $50,000. In many people's eyes, the poor crowd for the Chiefs and the Raiders (both, ironically, destined for a rematch in 1969's AFL championship game) reinforced the importance of the fans seeing homegrown superstars like Joe Namath at the game. (Both, IUPUI.)

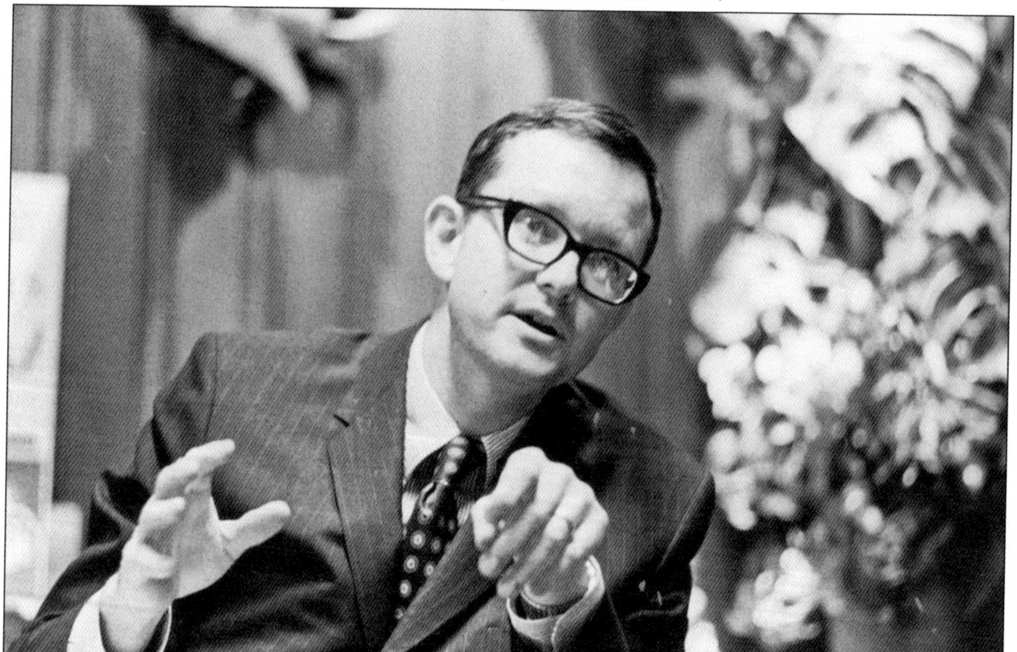

Jets coach Weeb Ewbank (right) arrived in Birmingham for the 1970 game to be greeted by Frank Thomas Jr. (left). Ewbank has the distinction of being the only coach to win the NFL Championship, the AFL Championship, and a Super Bowl. Thomas no doubt appreciated these accomplishments more than most; his father was the University of Alabama great Frank Thomas. (IUPUI.)

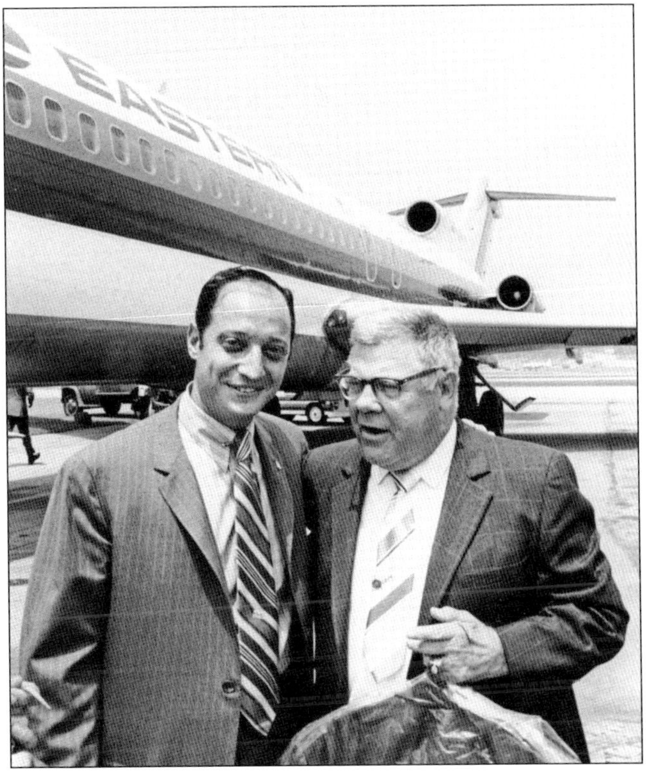

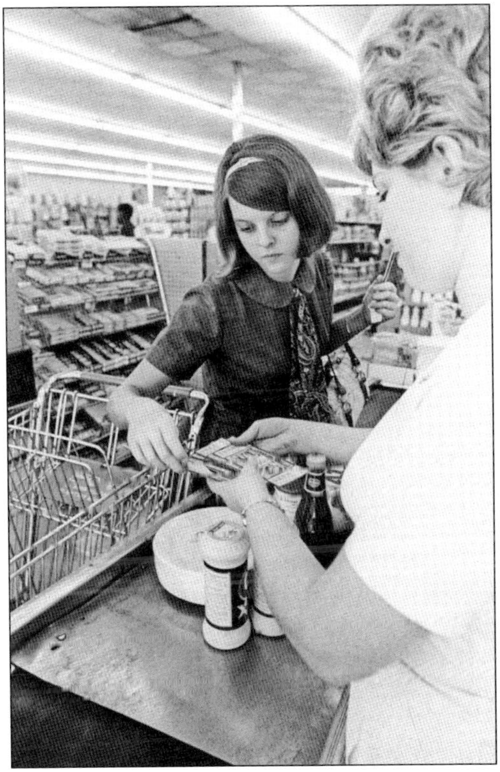

To entice the Jets and Bills to Birmingham for the 1970 game, the club guaranteed each team $35,000. It also covered the game expenses, which totaled $45,000. Therefore, assuring an adequate number of ticket sales was critical to the club, but the securing of 51 corporate sponsors for $1,000 each certainly aided the effort. Particularly helpful was the purchase of 5,000 tickets by Bruno's supermarkets, owned by Kiwanian Joe Bruno. (IUPUI.)

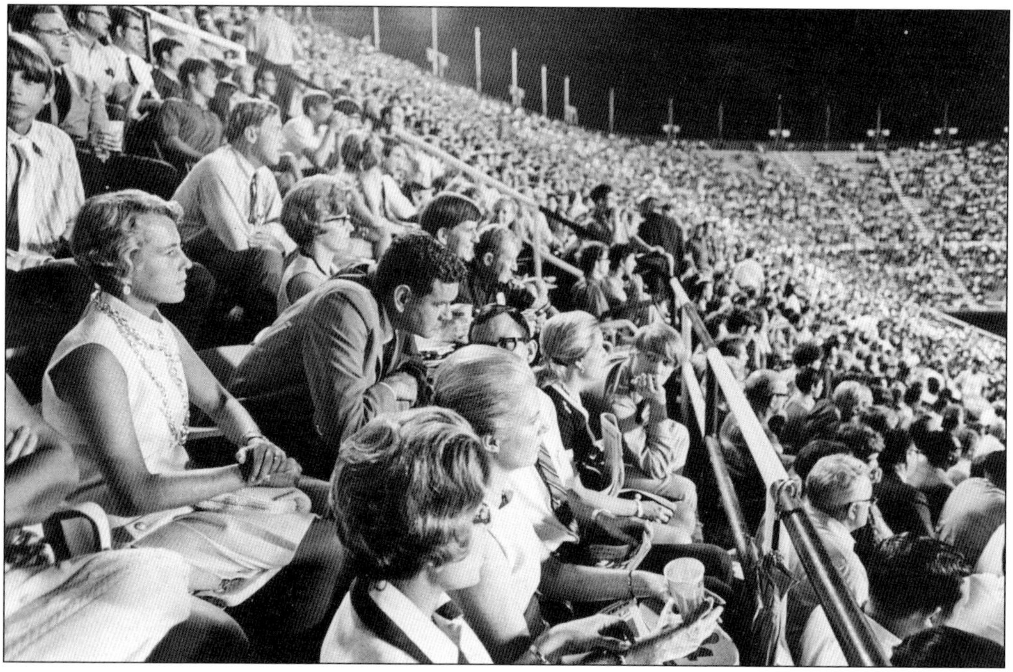

When the day of the big game arrived on August 8, 1970, a troublesome NFL players strike had been resolved and Legion Field's new artificial Poly-Turf was firmly in place. Equally importantly, some 48,000 fans were in the stands, despite the fact that Joe Namath was, unfortunately, absent from the Jets roster. Nursing old injuries and expressing doubts about his ability and desire to play in the coming season, he would not join the Jets for another nine days at their summer training camp in New York. Namath's absence left the role of Jets quarterback in the hands of the trio of Al Woodall, Babe Parilli, and Phil Theosiledes. (Both, IUPUI.)

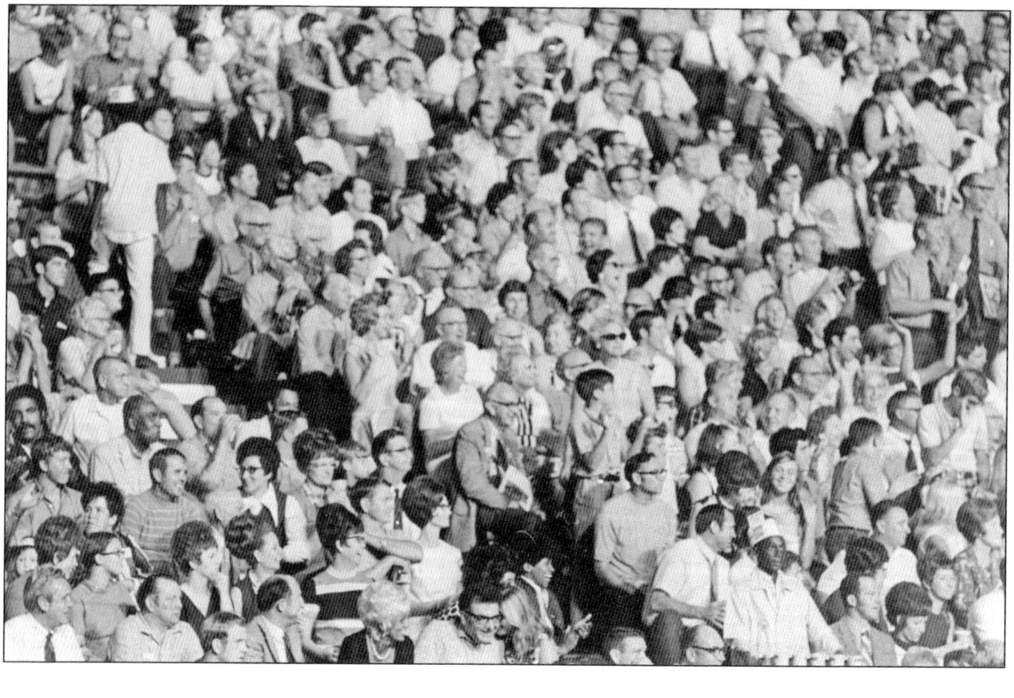

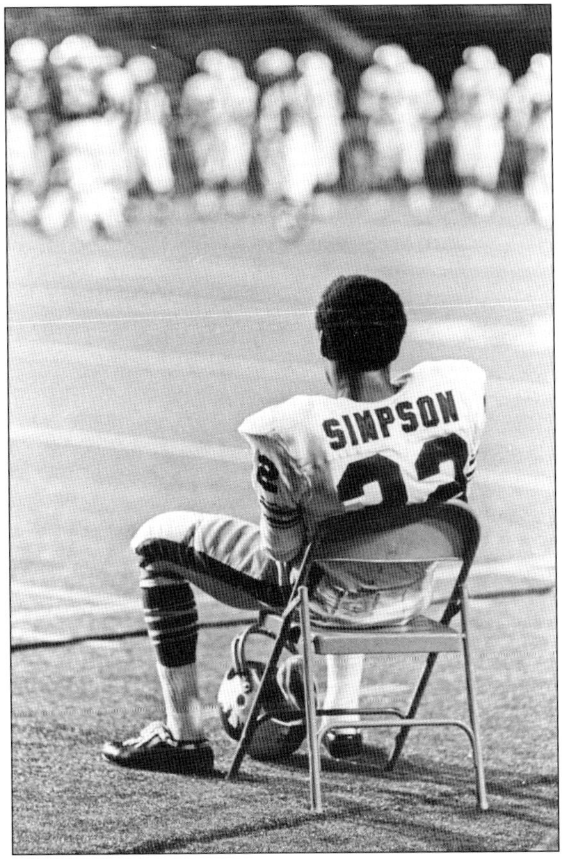

Despite Joe Namath's absence from the Jets roster, the fans in Birmingham were still excited to have a glimpse at running back O.J. Simpson in action. Simpson had played his college ball at the University of Southern California, where he won the Heisman Trophy in 1968. He was the number one pick in the 1969 AFL-NFL Common Draft and was signed by the Bills (who were nursing a 1-12-1 record from their 1968 campaign) for a record $650,000 contract. But Bills head coach John Rauch was hesitant to build his offense around just one running back, and Simpson endured a mediocre rookie season in 1969. His experience in Birmingham against the Jets would, unfortunately, prove no different. (Both, IUPUI.)

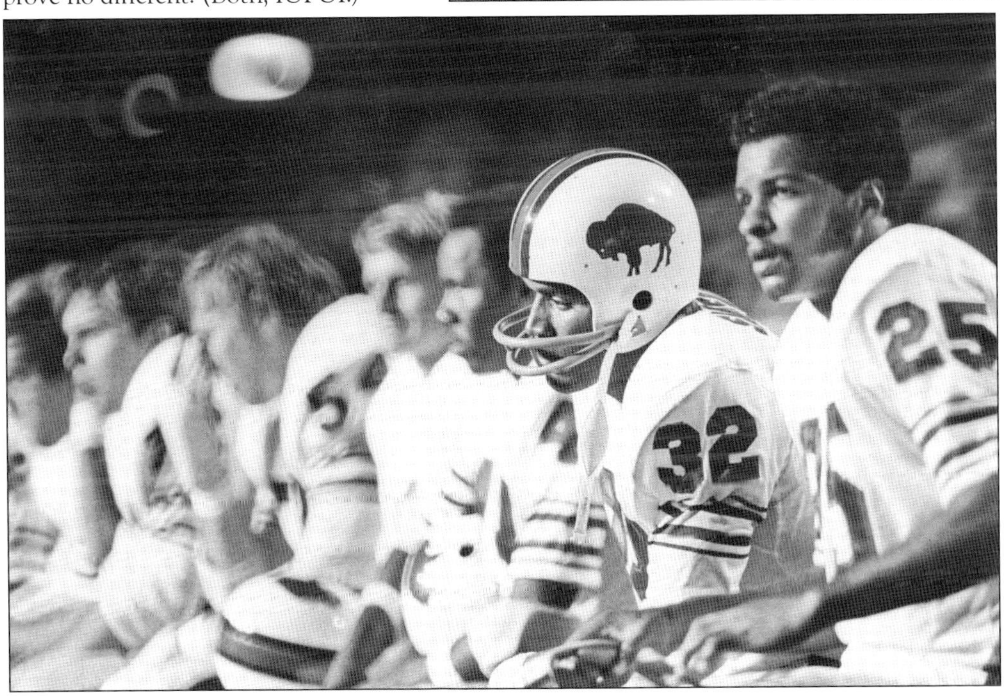

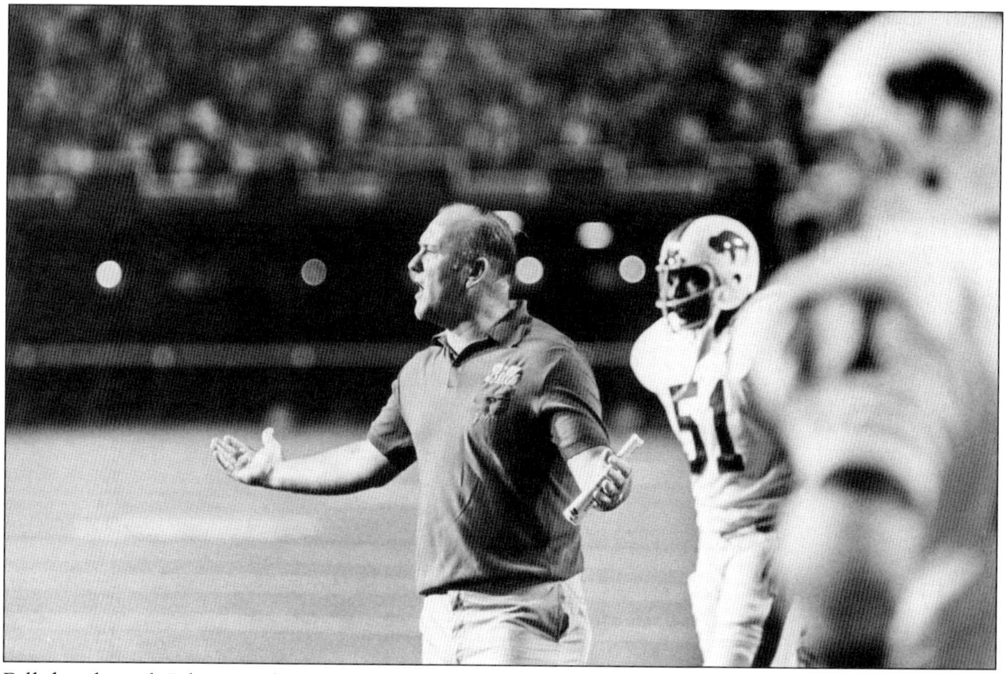

Bills head coach John Rauch was a familiar figure to many fans in Birmingham for the Bills-Jets game. In the 1940s, he had been a starting quarterback for all four of his years at the University of Georgia. Two years earlier, Rauch had coached the Oakland Raiders in Super Bowl II but, complaining of Raiders owner Al Davis, had taken a job with the Buffalo Bills in 1969. (IUPUI.)

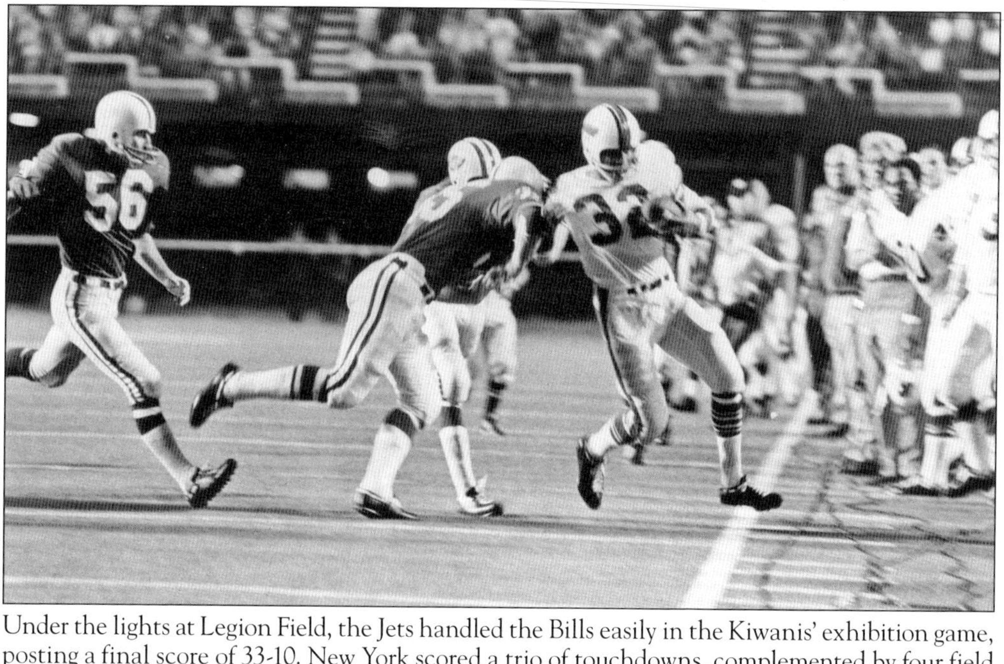

Under the lights at Legion Field, the Jets handled the Bills easily in the Kiwanis' exhibition game, posting a final score of 33-10. New York scored a trio of touchdowns, complemented by four field goals kicked by Jim Turner. The Bills' only touchdown came from a fumble recovery by 282-pound defensive tackle Bill Costen, who, as reported by the *Anniston Star*, "stumbled face first into the endzone" from the Jets' six-yard line for the score. (IUPUI.)

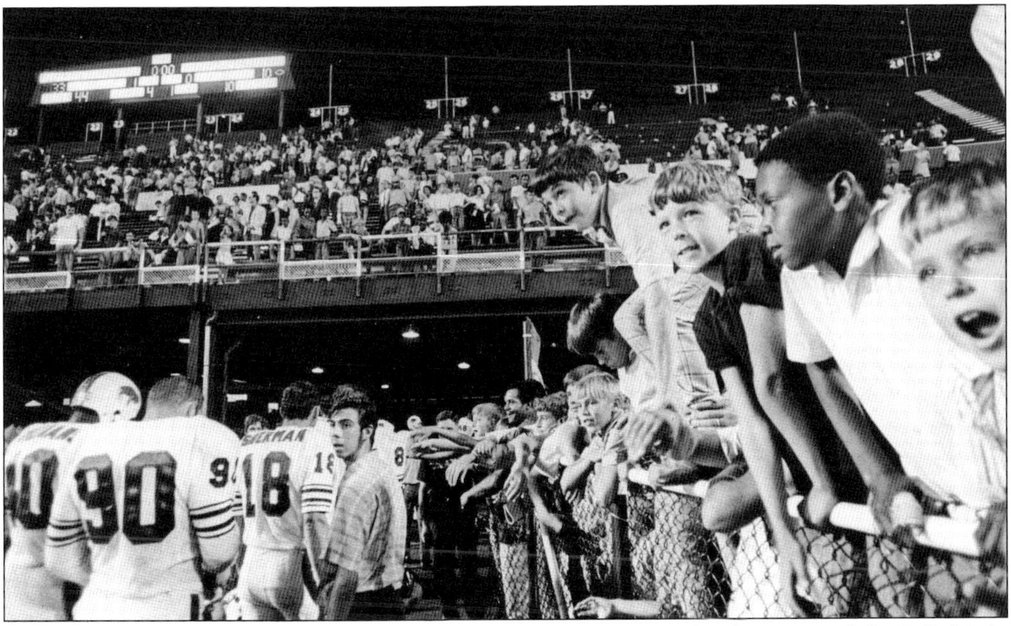

Although the local fans were no doubt disappointed by Joe Namath's absence, and the Bills likely hoped they would soon forget their thrashing at the hands of the Jets, the Kiwanians were thrilled with their $50,000 proceeds from the 1970 game. The club donated its earnings to Operation Drug Alert to establish a drug abuse center and clinic at the University of Alabama Medical Center in Birmingham. (IUPUI.)

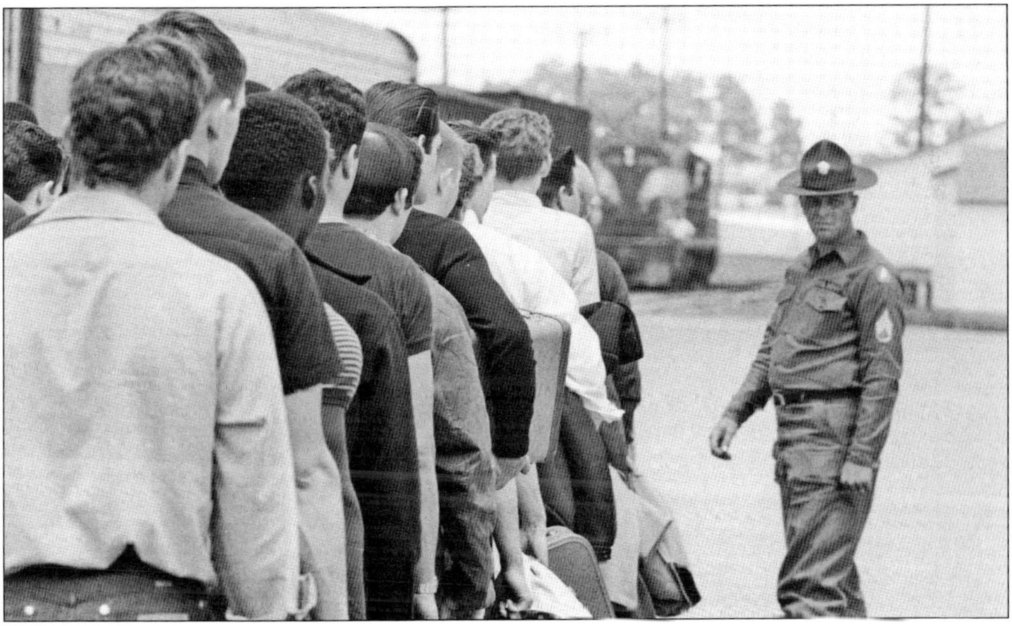

In the 1960s, club records indicate that the club adopted a unit of the 1st Infantry Division. At the time, the division was deployed to Vietnam, and the Kiwanians were concerned about "contradict[ing] the effects of draft card burning, etc." on American servicemen deployed overseas. In the years to come, a number of future Kiwanians would look back with pride on their own service in Vietnam at the time. (LOC.)

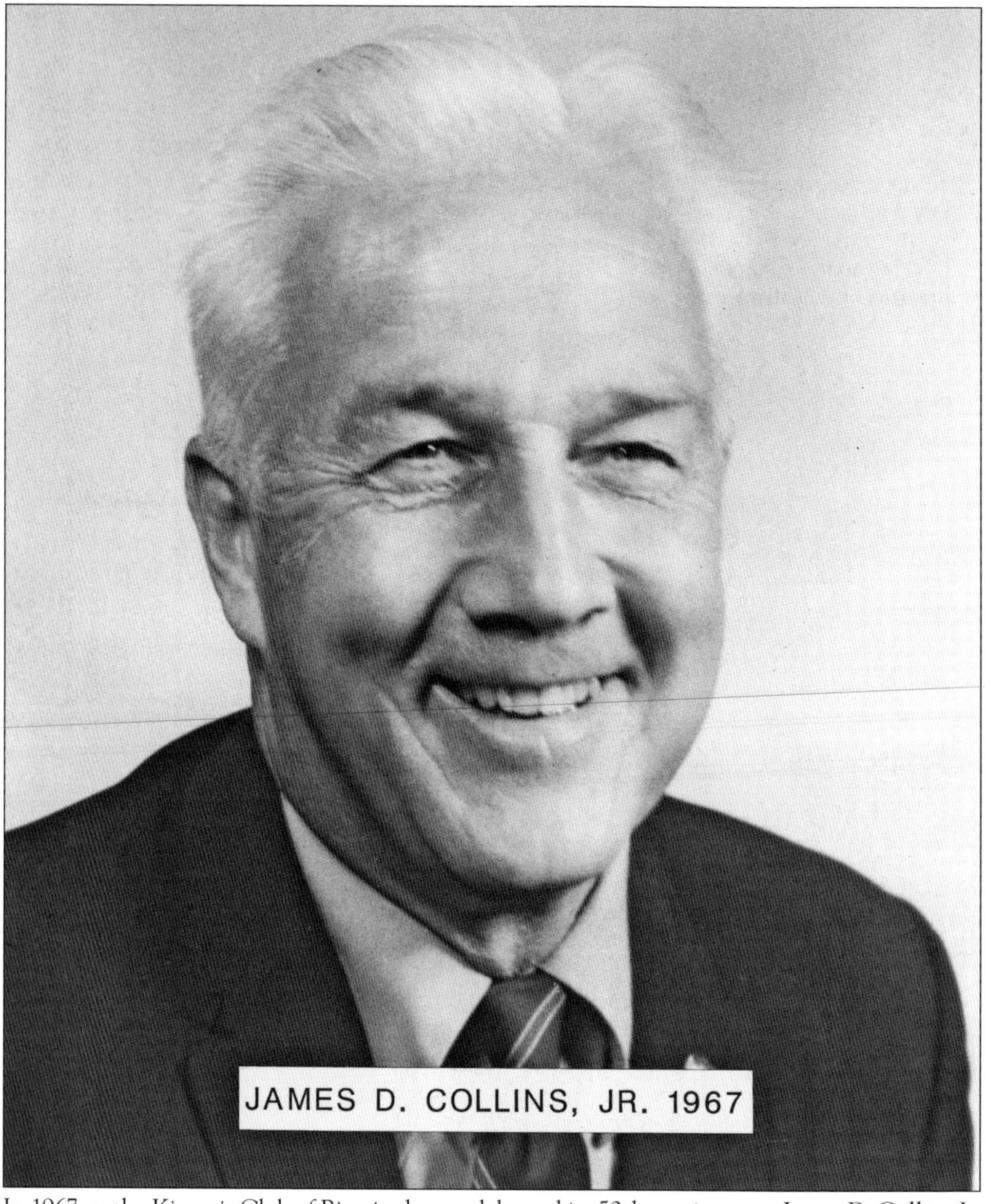

In 1967, as the Kiwanis Club of Birmingham celebrated its 50th anniversary, James D. Collins Jr. became the club's president. A graduate of Georgia Tech with a degree in chemical engineering, Collins came to Birmingham as general sales and marketing manager with the Birmingham Stove and Range Company in 1946, ultimately retiring in 1967. By then, as the club marked five decades of existence, it could count nearly 300 men as its members. Dues were now $55 annually, and the weekly lunches cost $2 a person. Financial records of the era reveal that the club's activities included the Kiwanis Golf Day Luncheon and a Ladies Valentine Luncheon. Those same records testify to charitable activities that included sending students to Washington, DC, on the Jefferson County Citizenship Tour, supporting the YMCA Youth Legislature, funding Junior Achievement and 4-H Awards, funding Christmas parties at the Boys Club, Girls Club, and Crippled Children's Clinic, and sponsoring a bed at the clinic. (KCOB.)

Carl Wittichen Jr. became the club's president in 1968. A native of Birmingham and a graduate of Alabama Polytechnic Institute, he founded the Wittichen Supply Company in 1946. Wittichen's civic and corporate activities included service as the president of the Birmingham Boys Club and as chairman of the board of directors of the Birmingham Realty Company. (KCOB.)

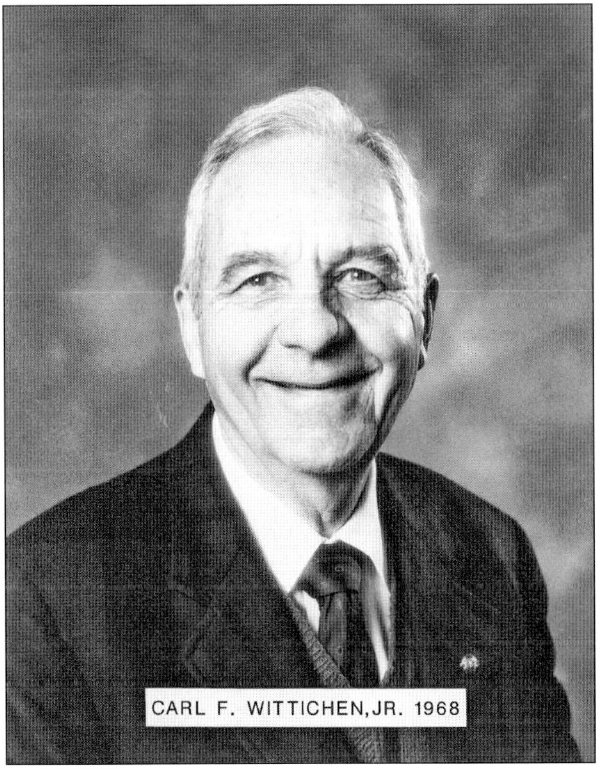

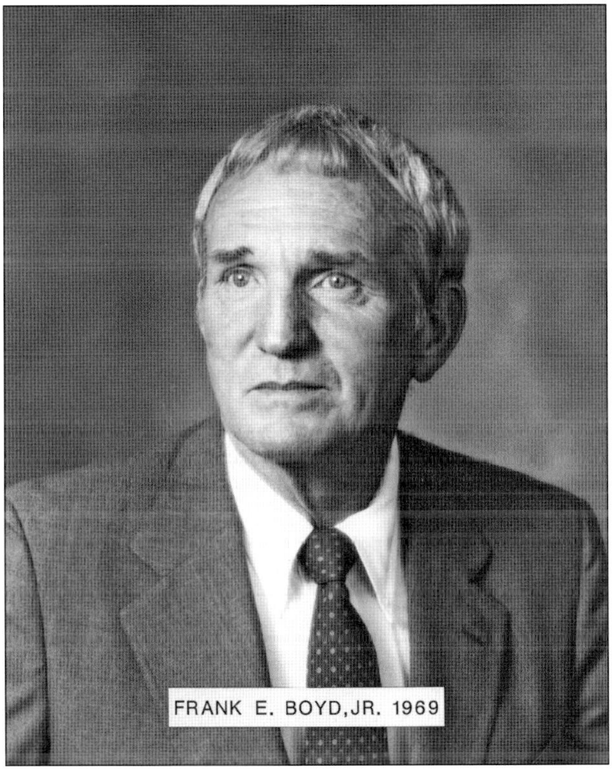

World War II interrupted Frank E. Boyd Jr.'s football career at Auburn; he became a pilot in the Army Air Forces and flew 151 combat missions in Europe. After the war, Boyd completed his education and, after a few years in the oil business in Texas, entered the truck rental business in Birmingham. The president of National Motor Fleets, Boyd became the club's president in 1969. (KCOB.)

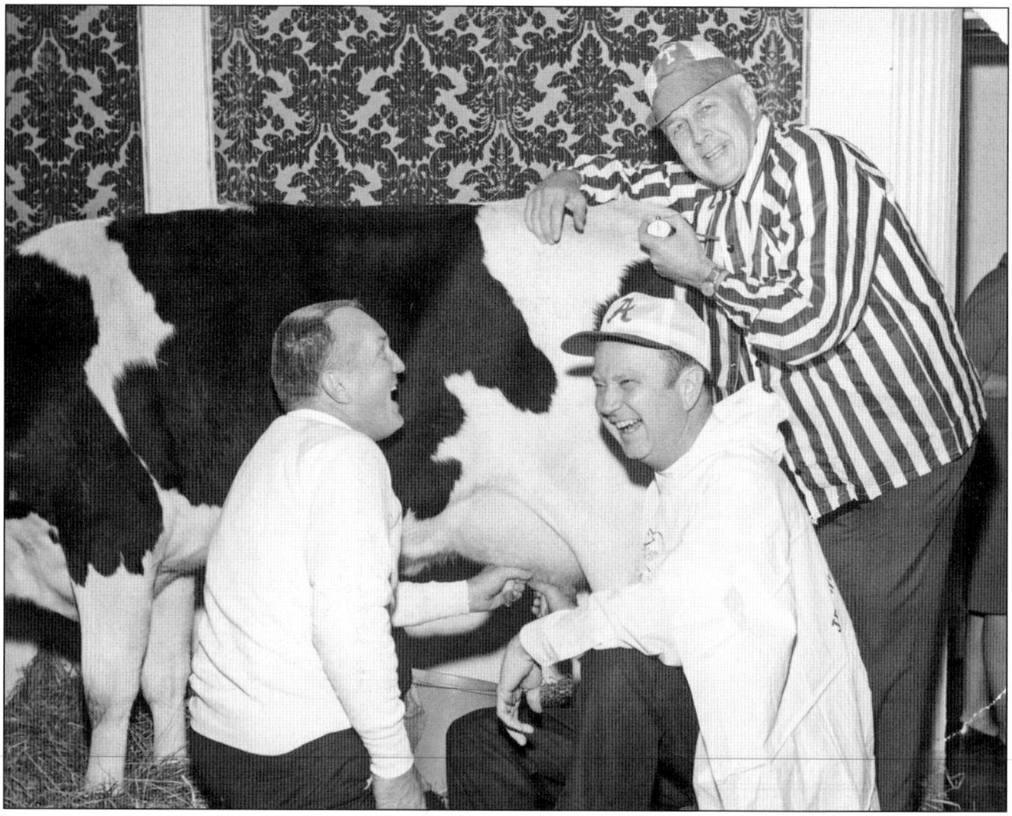

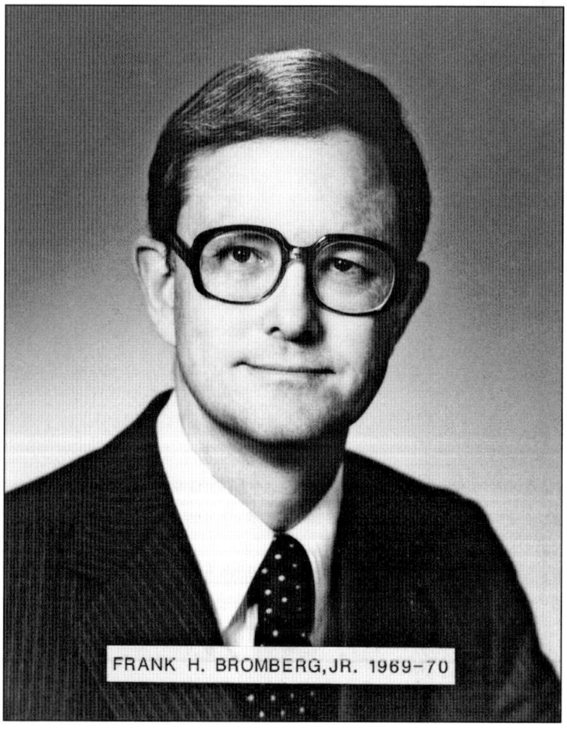

For many years, the Kiwanis Club hosted an annual November luncheon in connection with Farm-City Week. In this 1969 photograph, club members Frank Boyd (left) and Bob McDavid (center) represented the Auburn and Alabama fan bases respectively in a milking contest in the Tutwiler Hotel, while fellow club member Jimmy Collins keeps time. Boyd's team won when the cow kicked over McDavid's milk pail. (IUPUI.)

Frank H. Bromberg Jr. graduated from Ramsay High School. Just like the school's namesake, he was destined to serve as the Kiwanis Club's president. He did so for the 1969–1970 term. Bromberg, a graduate of the University of Alabama and a member of the university's board of trustees, ran his family's business, Bromberg & Company, Inc., as a fifth-generation member of the jewelry store's management. (KCOB.)

From 1970 to 1971, Elmer C. Thuston Jr. was the club's president. A graduate of Birmingham-Southern College and a veteran of World War II, he went to work for the Birmingham Saw Works after the war. It was a company started by his grandfather in 1885, and Thuston ultimately became the company's president. (KCOB.)

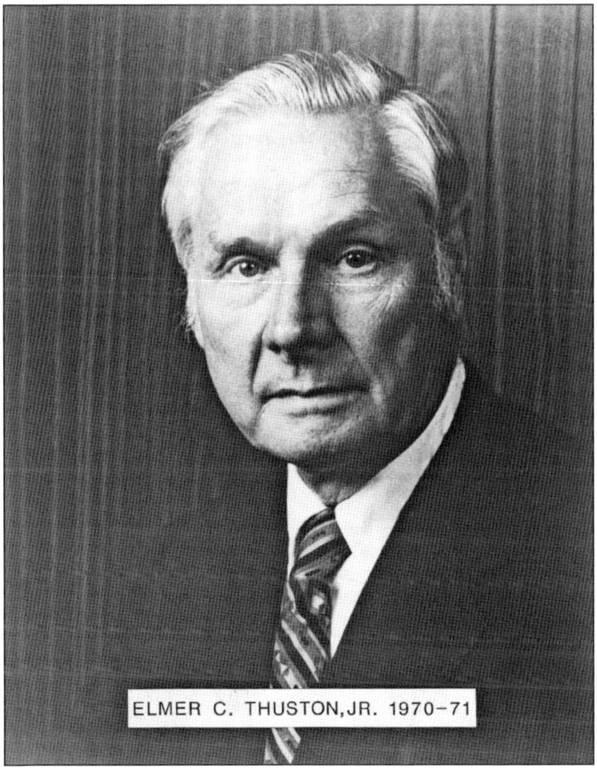

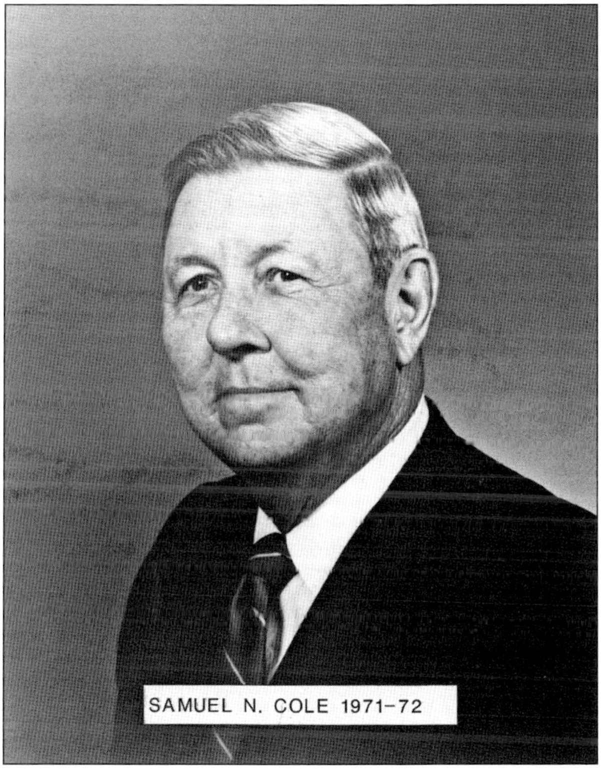

Like previous president Frank Bromberg, Samuel N. Cole was both a graduate of Birmingham's Ramsay High School and a pilot during World War II—in Cole's case, as a B-25 pilot in the Southwest Pacific. For nearly five decades, he was in the trucking business in Birmingham, and he found further success in the field of commercial real estate. He served as the club's president from 1971 to 1972. (KCOB.)

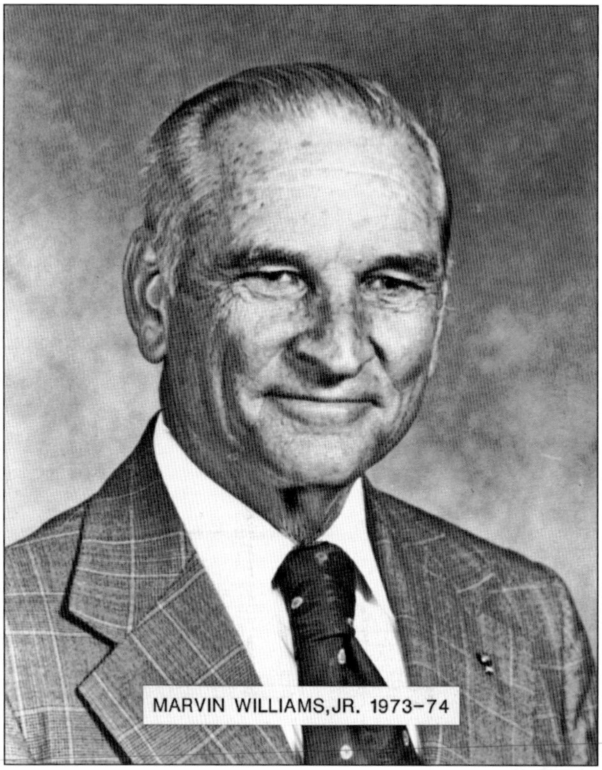

Marvin Williams Jr. served as the club's president during the 1973–1974 term. A graduate of Duke University and Emory School of Law, he saw his legal career briefly stalled by service with the US Navy during World War II. Returning to Birmingham in 1946, he resumed his law practice and ultimately became a senior partner with the firm Davies, Williams, and Wallace. (KCOB.)

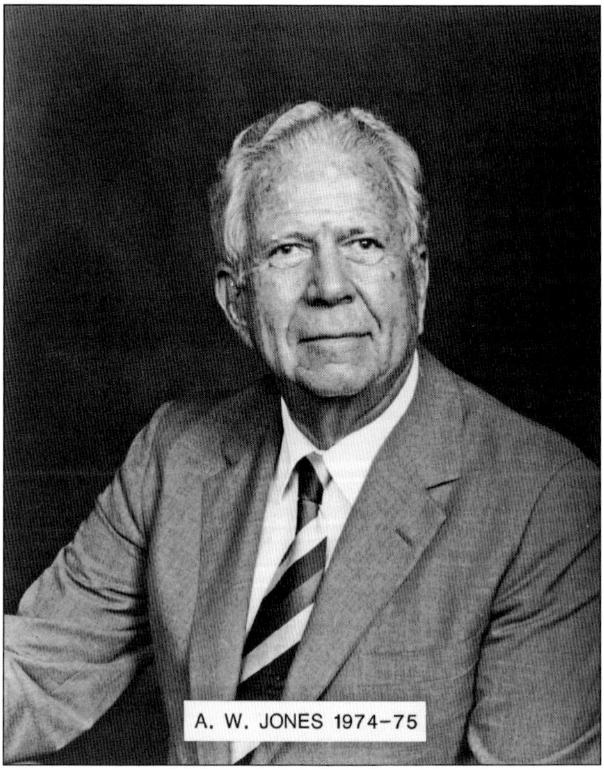

Alexander W. "A.W." Jones earned undergraduate and law degrees from the University of Alabama and went into practice with the firm that would ultimately become Pritchard, McCall & Jones. After taking a significant leadership role in the club's staging of its AFL-NFL exhibition football games, Jones was elected as the club's president for the 1974–1975 term. (KCOB.)

From 1975 to 1976, Peter W. Weston, EdD, served as the club's president. At the time, he was vice president of Samford University. When Weston was designated as a certified financial planner (CFP), he became the first CFP in Alabama to be admitted to the Registry of Financial Planning Professionals. (KCOB.)

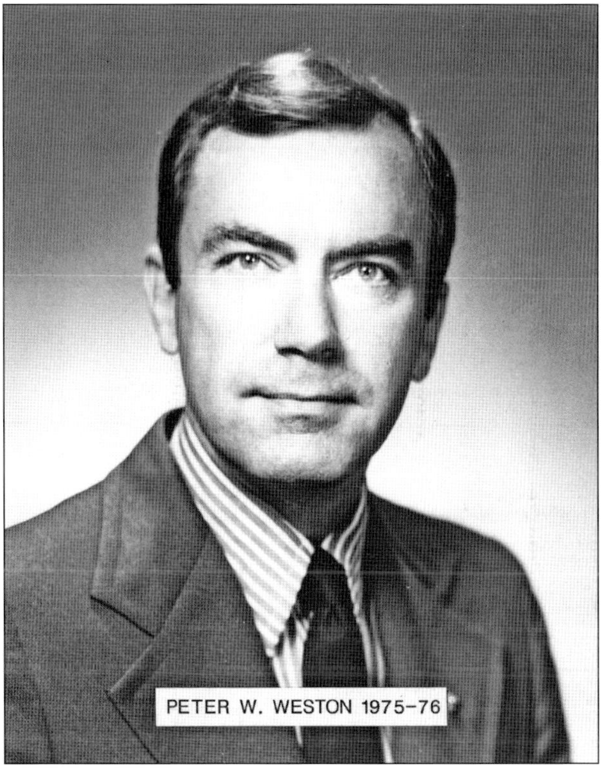

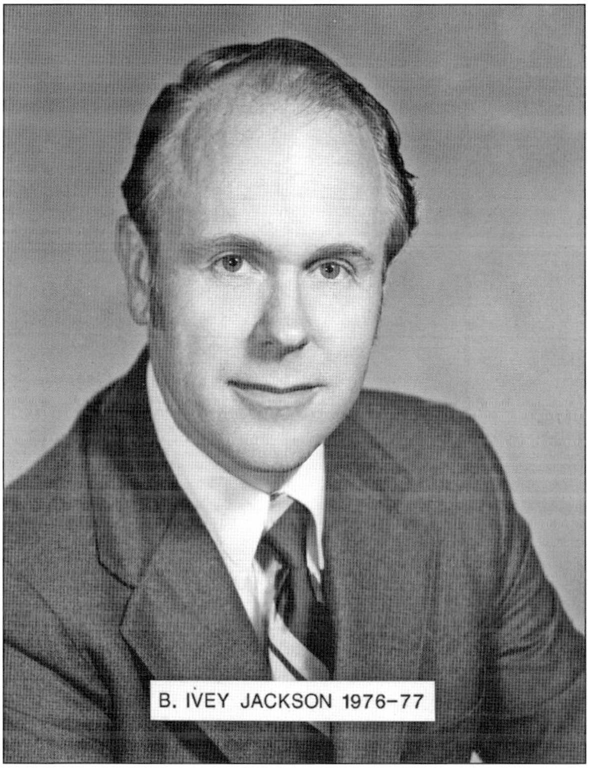

B. Ivey Jackson was elected as the club's president for the 1976–1977 term. A graduate of the University of the South at Sewanee, where he was a star tennis player, Jackson was the chairman of the Jackson Insurance Agency, Inc. A man of many interests and civic endeavors, Jackson is known for his talented photographic work, his array of magic tricks, and his founding of the Greater Birmingham Tennis Association. (KCOB.)

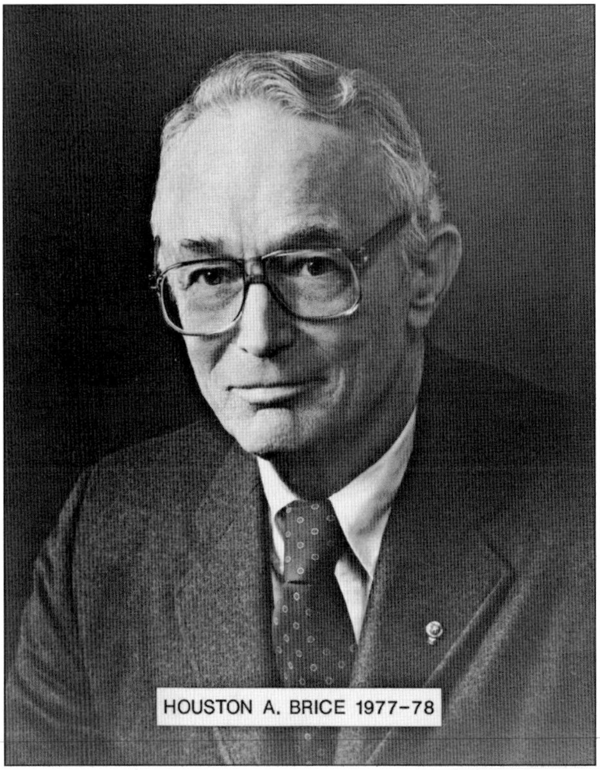

Houston A. Brice Jr. was yet another of the club's Ramsay High School graduates. He attended Birmingham-Southern College but eventually earned degrees from the University of Michigan. A veteran of the US Navy during World War II, Brice went to work for his father's company, Brice Building Company, Inc., and, in 1977, became the company's chairman and chief executive officer. That same year, he also became president of the Kiwanis Club. (KCOB.)

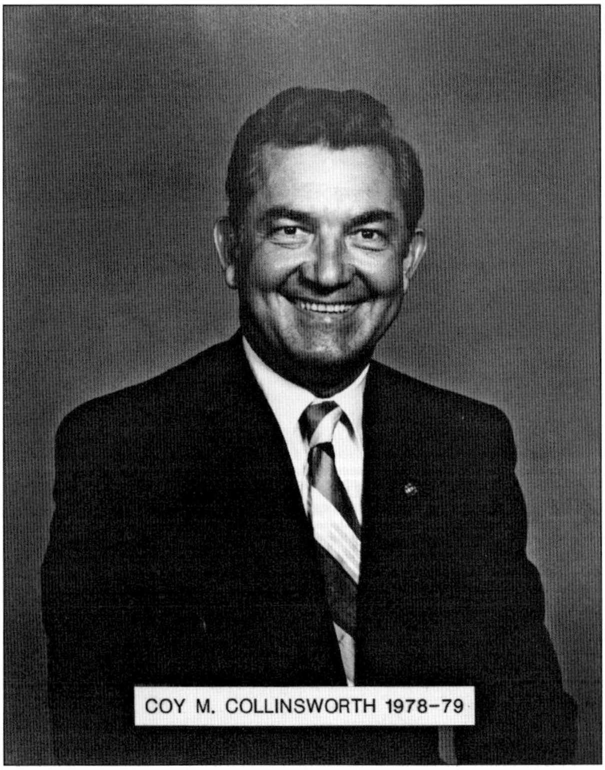

Knoxville, Tennessee, native Coy Collingsworth graduated from the University of Tennessee after earning Golden Gloves boxing honors. He first worked with the Connecticut Mutual Life Insurance Company in Nashville, Tennessee, before moving to Birmingham as the company's general agent for Alabama. His term as club president in 1978–1979 complemented such other civic endeavors as the serving as president of Birmingham's All-American Bowl and on the board of directors of the Salvation Army. (KCOB.)

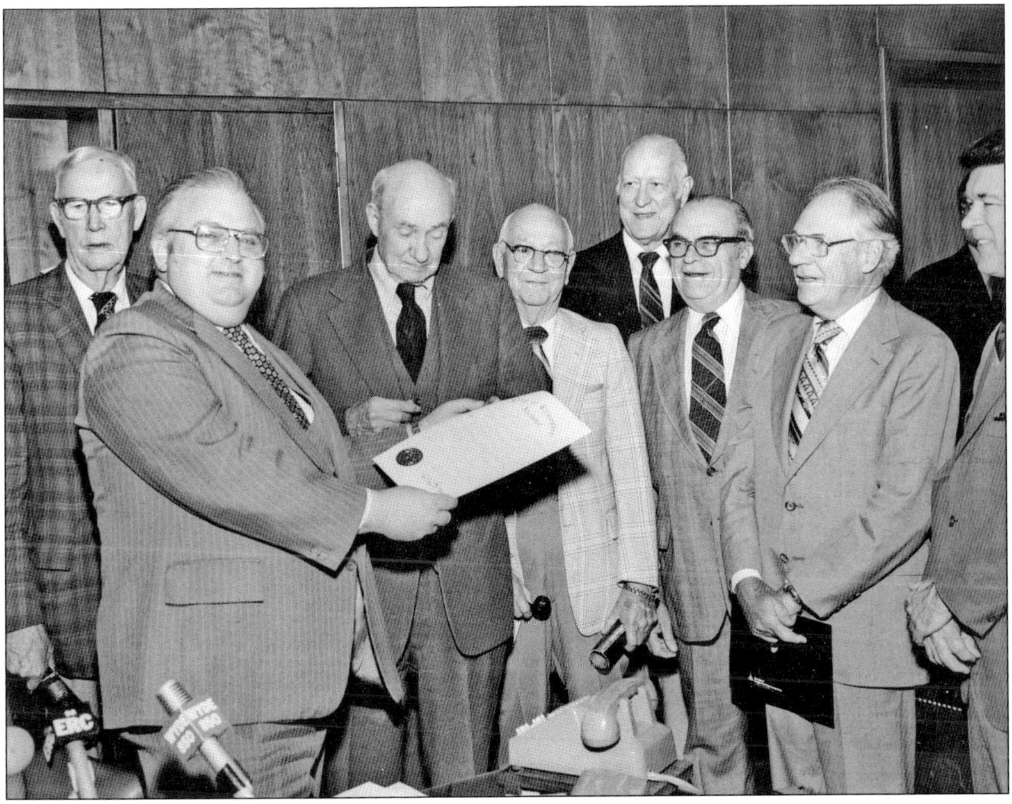

On May 21, 1979, Birmingham mayor David J. Vann (shown with paper in hand) declared the day to be Kiwanis International Independence Day in Birmingham. With his proclamation, Vann harkened back to the days of Kiwanis International's 1919 convention in Birmingham 60 years earlier, when the various individual clubs successfully negotiated their independence and the name "Kiwanis" from organizer Allen Browne. (KCOB.)

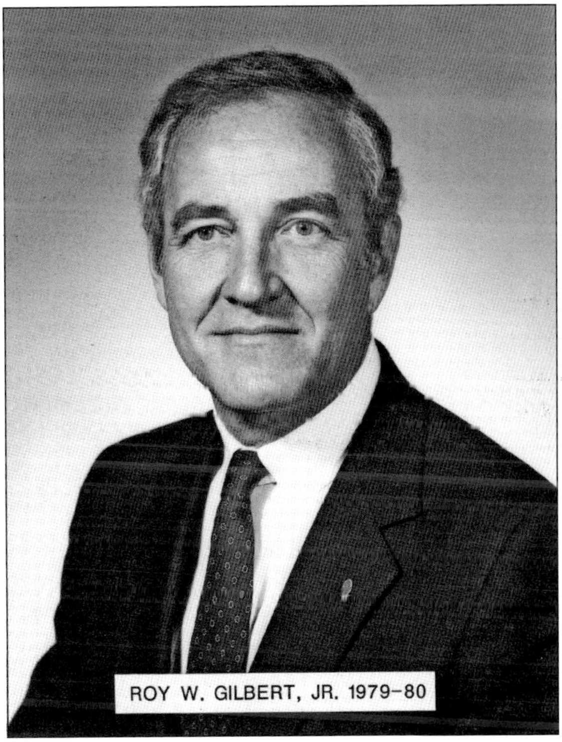

Roy W. Gilbert Jr., a Birmingham native and a Davidson College graduate, earned Samford University's first Distinguished MBA Alumni Award. He was president and chief operating officer and member of the board of directors of SouthTrust Corporation. Gilbert served as the club's president from 1979 to 1980; other notable civic work included service as a trustee of the Southern Research Institute. (KCOB.)

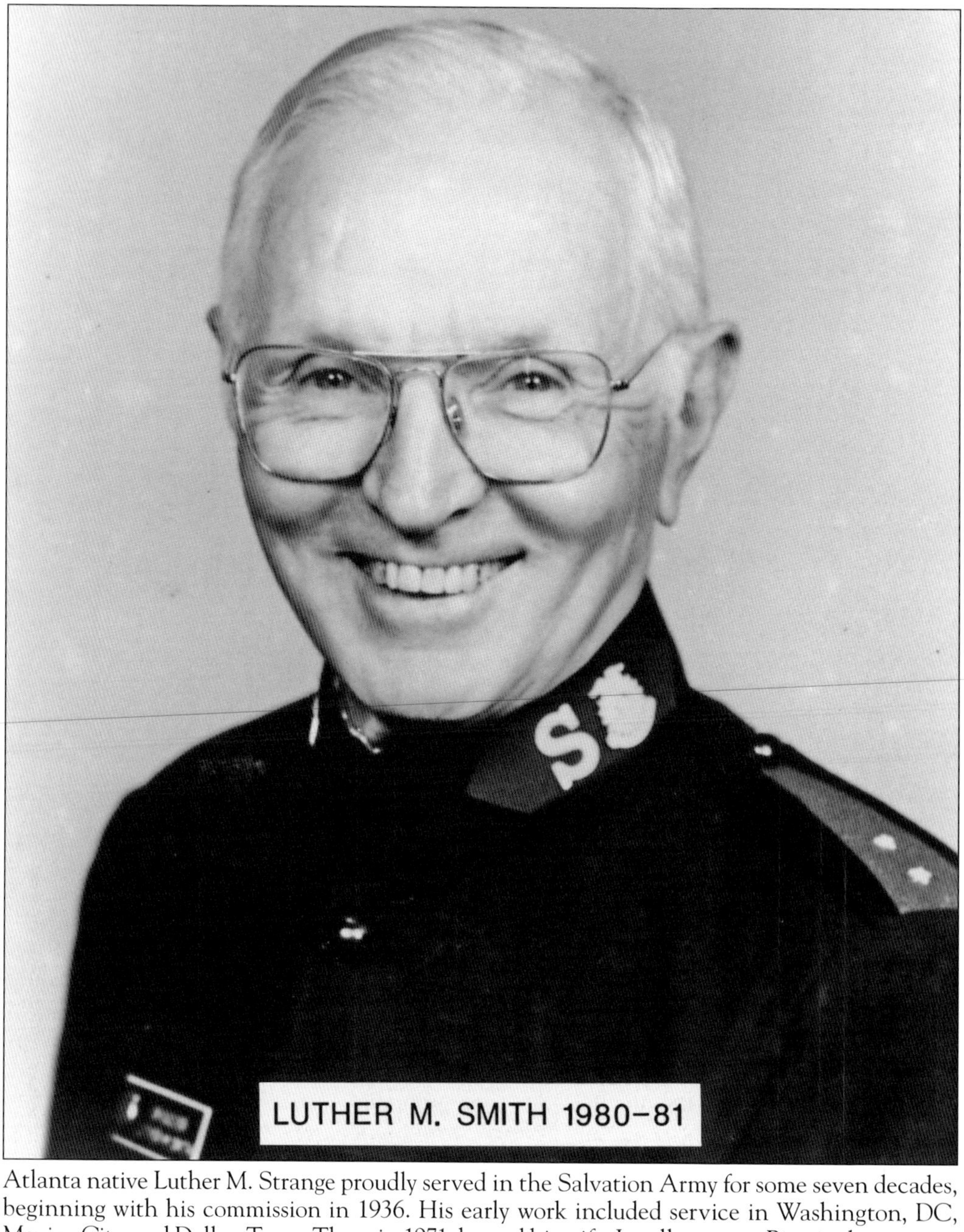

Atlanta native Luther M. Strange proudly served in the Salvation Army for some seven decades, beginning with his commission in 1936. His early work included service in Washington, DC, Mexico City, and Dallas, Texas. Then, in 1971, he and his wife, Jewell, came to Birmingham as city commanders. Even from Birmingham, Strange served extensively in leadership roles in Salvation Army disaster work, especially in Central America (including Honduras and Costa Rica), the Dominican Republic, and Mexico City. In 1980, Strange became president of the Kiwanis Club, and six years later, he was elected Alabama district governor. He also served on the Kiwanis International Committee of Support of Spiritual Aims. A licensed commercial pilot for single-engine airplanes, Strange was also a 35-year veteran of the Civil Air Patrol, ultimately becoming the national chief of Civil Air Patrol chaplains. Understandably, manning the Salvation Army kettle at Christmas on a nearby street corner became a holiday tradition for the club. (KCOB.)

Four

The Kiwanis in Today's Birmingham

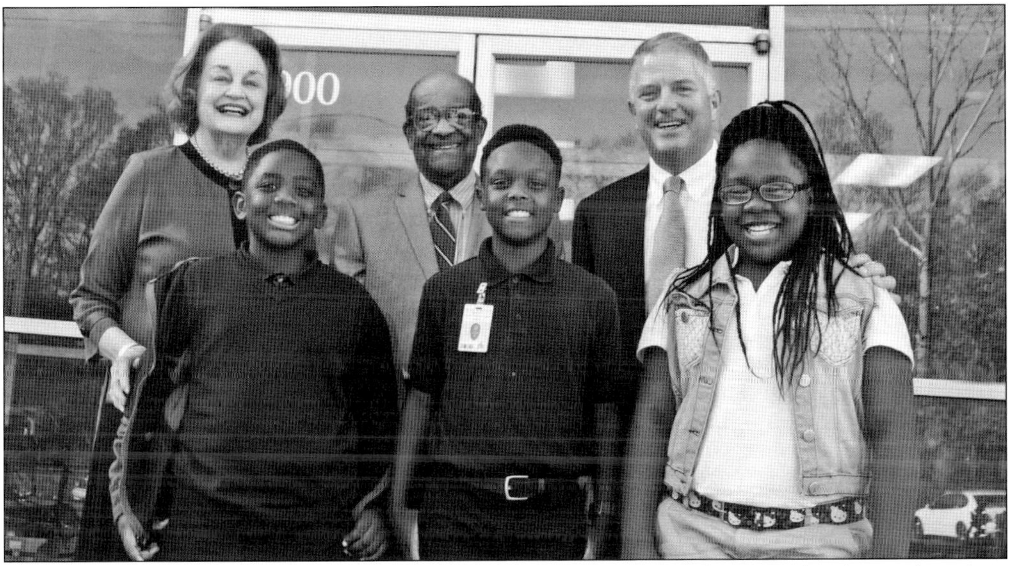

The 1980s marked the beginning of the club's evolution into its modern membership and modern sensibilities. Thanks to the foresight and hard work of earlier members and the continued support of current members, the Kiwanis Foundation would provide thousands of dollars to facilitate the growth and well-being of children such as the ones shown here in front of the A.G. Gaston Boys & Girls Club. (KCOB.)

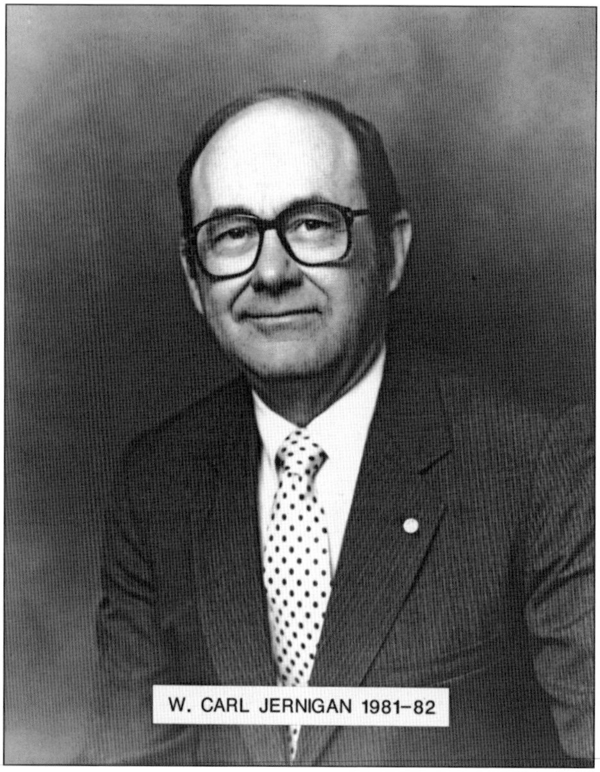

W. Carl Jernigan, whose military service included the Seabees during World War II and on board the USS *Wasp* during the Korean War, led a varied business career ranging from vice president of Plantation Patterns to president of Jernigan Corporation. He was also the president of the Boy Scouts Council of Greater Birmingham and chairman of the board of trustees of the Eye Foundation Hospital. Jernigan became the club's president in 1981. (KCOB.)

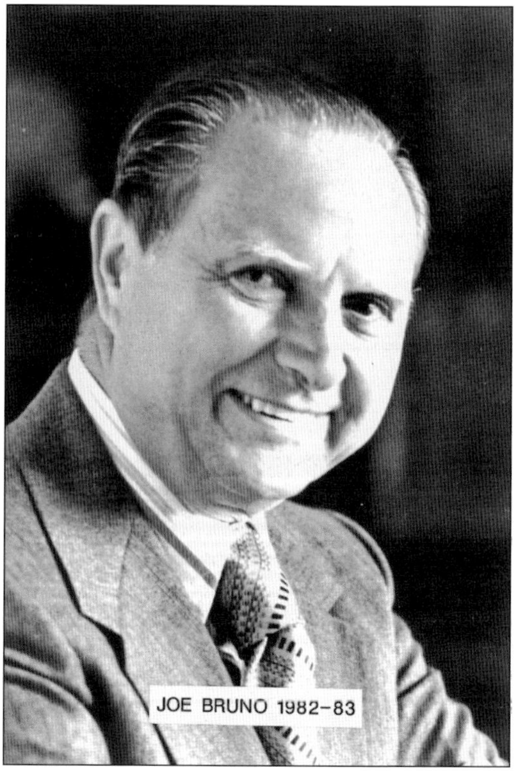

A club history describes Joseph S. Bruno as "a true American success story." He began a grocery store in Birmingham that ultimately expanded into the multistate Bruno's, Inc., and Big B Drug Company. His civic contributions and honors are too many to mention, but his funding of the Bruno Cancer Center at St. Vincent's Hospital was particularly noteworthy. Bruno was the club's president from 1982 to 1983. (KCOB.)

Like his father in 1957, Frederick W. Renneker III served as the club's president. A graduate of Auburn University, Renneker was vice president of the Hilb, Rogal & Hamilton insurance company when he was elected the club's president in 1983; later, he became the company's president. His myriad civic roles ranged from chairing the board of trustees of Children's Hospital of Alabama to the presidency of the Birmingham Jaycees. (KCOB.)

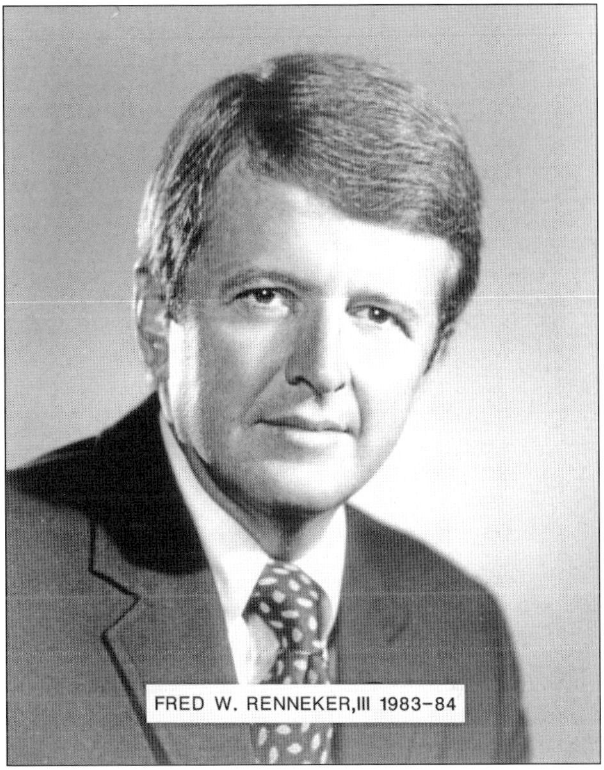

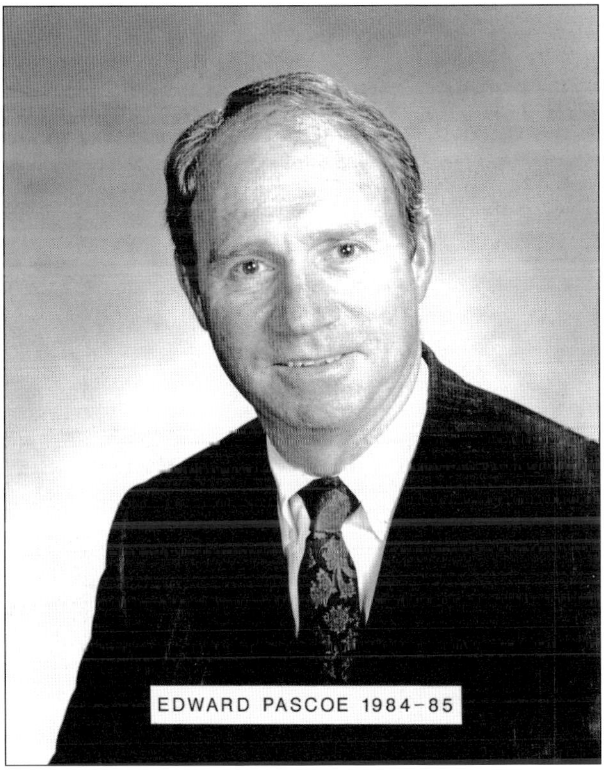

From 1984 to 1985, Edward R. Pascoe served as the club's president. A graduate of Samford University, Pascoe was not only the president of Steel City Bolt & Screw, Inc., but also the senior warden of St. Mary's Episcopal Church and the president of the National Fasteners Distributors Association, among many other civic endeavors. (KCOB.)

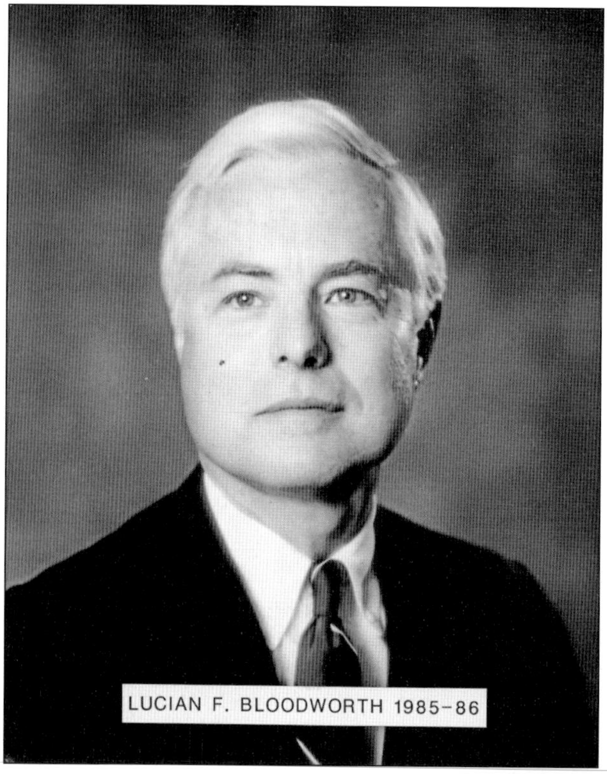

Lucian F. Bloodworth, who attended Auburn University but earned his bachelor's and master of business administration degrees from the University of Michigan, was a former executive with Protective Life and was currently the executive vice president of National Bank of Commerce when he became the club's president for the 1985–1986 term. Bloodworth was also a longtime member of the Mountain Brook Board of Education. (KCOB.)

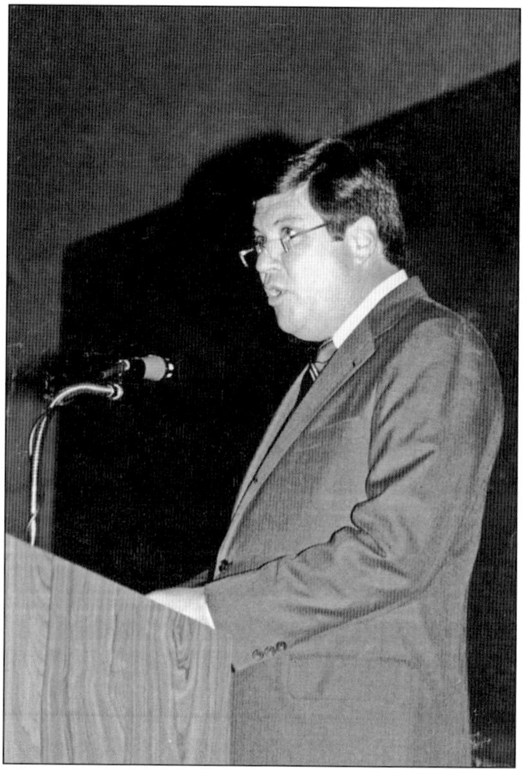

Ehney A. Camp III followed in his father's footsteps and became the club's president in 1986. A graduate of Dartmouth College, Camp also attended the University of Alabama School of Law. After working for Cobbs, Allen & Hall Mortgage Company, Camp was employed by the Rime Companies before founding Camp and Company, a commercial mortgage banking firm. Here, he speaks at the dedication of the Harbert Center. (KCOB.)

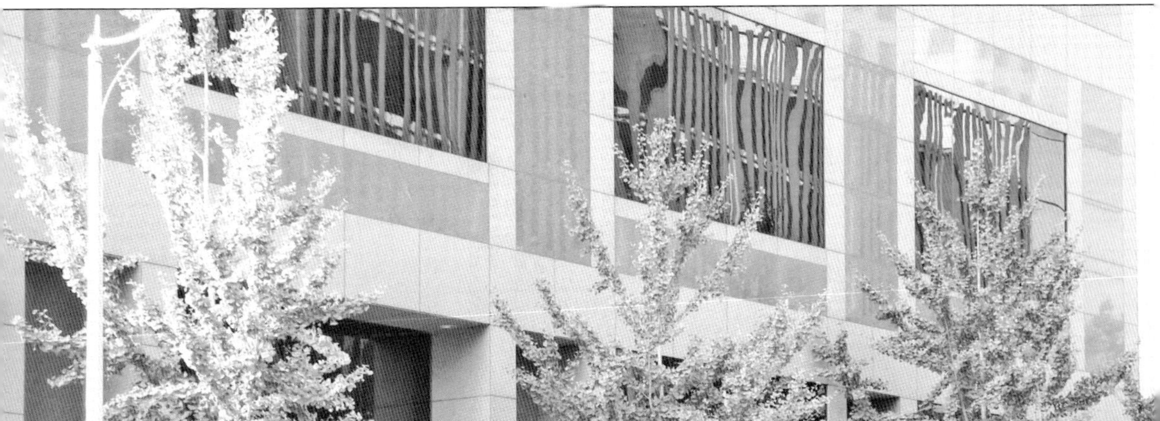

In the wake of the closing and demolition of the old Tutwiler Hotel in 1972, the club struggled for several years to find a suitable home base for its weekly luncheons. For a time, the club operated out of the Daniel Building, the First Alabama Bank Building, and even the Birmingham Jefferson Civic Center. Other civic clubs, notably the Rotary Club and the Monday Morning Quarterback Club, were in a similar predicament. Joining forces in the early 1980s, the organizations worked together to form the Civic Club Foundation and pursue the construction of a facility that could provide a home for all the clubs. Business magnates Hall W. Thompson and John M. Harbert III spearheaded the effort to seek donations and plan construction of the facility. On June 16, 1986, the Harbert Center opened in downtown Birmingham at 2019 Fourth Avenue North. (Harbert Center)

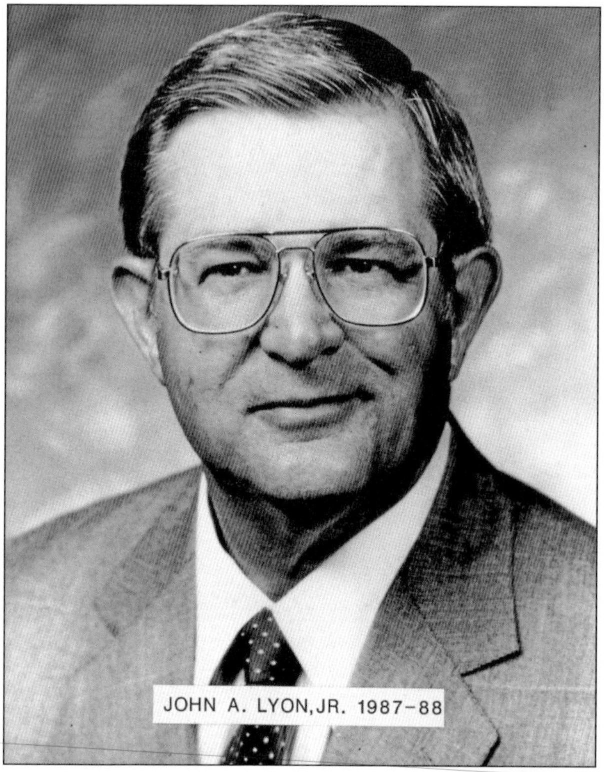

John A. Lyon Jr. served as the club's president for the 1987–1988 term. A University of Alabama accounting graduate, he began his career with the Atlanta office of Arthur Andersen & Company in February 1951 and in September 1960 opened the firm's Birmingham office. He was also elected president of the Alabama Society of CPAs. In addition, he served two years with the US Air Force Office of Special Investigations. (KCOB.)

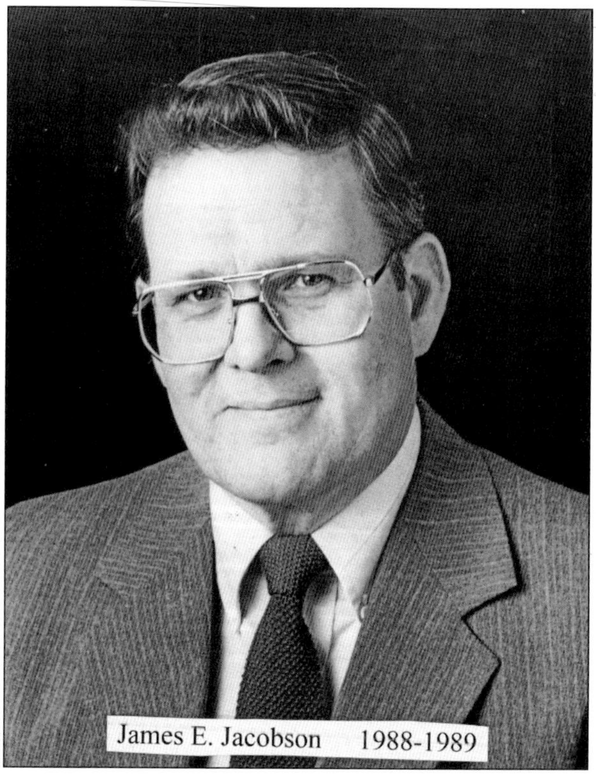

Mobile native James E. Jacobsen earned his bachelor's and master's degrees in journalism at the University of Alabama and, in 1959, joined the staff of the *Birmingham News*. He ultimately became the paper's editor. At the time, it was the state's largest newspaper. Jacobsen served as president of the Alabama Press Club and, in 1988–1989, became the Kiwanis Club's president. (KCOB.)

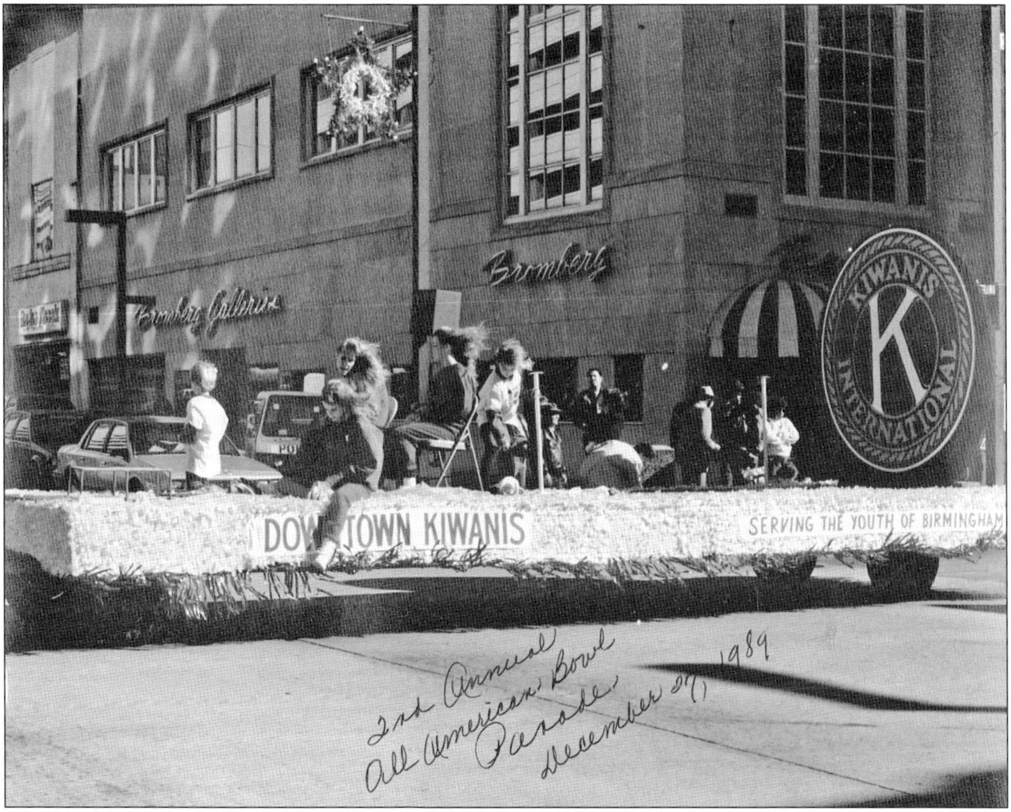

In 1989, Birmingham welcomed Texas Tech University and Duke University for the fourth of five annual All-American Bowls (from 1977 to 1985 called the Hall of Fame Bowl) played at Legion Field. Here, the club's float participates in the city's downtown bowl parade. The following day, Texas Tech beat Duke 49-21, providing an ignominious ending to Steve Spurrier's last game as Duke's head coach. (KCOB.)

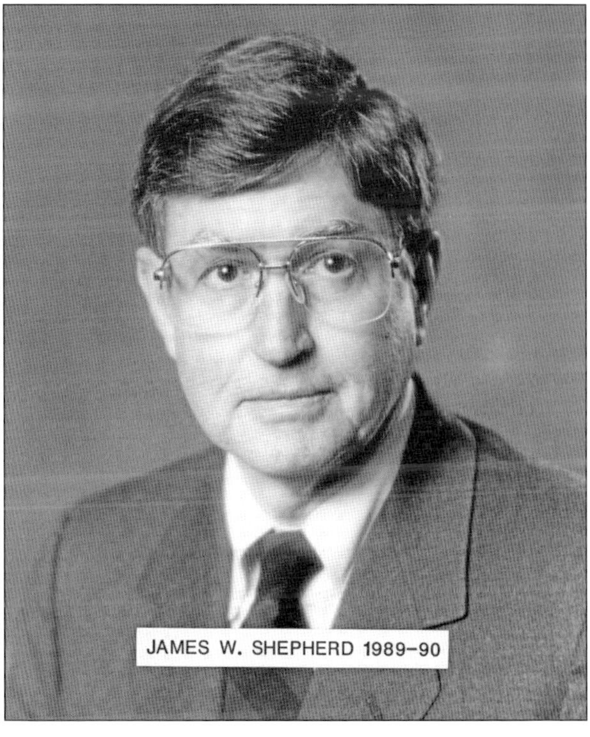

James W. Shepherd, a graduate of the Virginia Military Institute, served as the president of the club from 1989 to 1990. The president of Shepherd Real Estate Company, he also chaired boards of directors for Lakeshore Hospital, the Altamont School, and the Metropolitan YMCA. The James W. Shepherd Observatory at the University of Montevallo is named in his honor. (KCOB.)

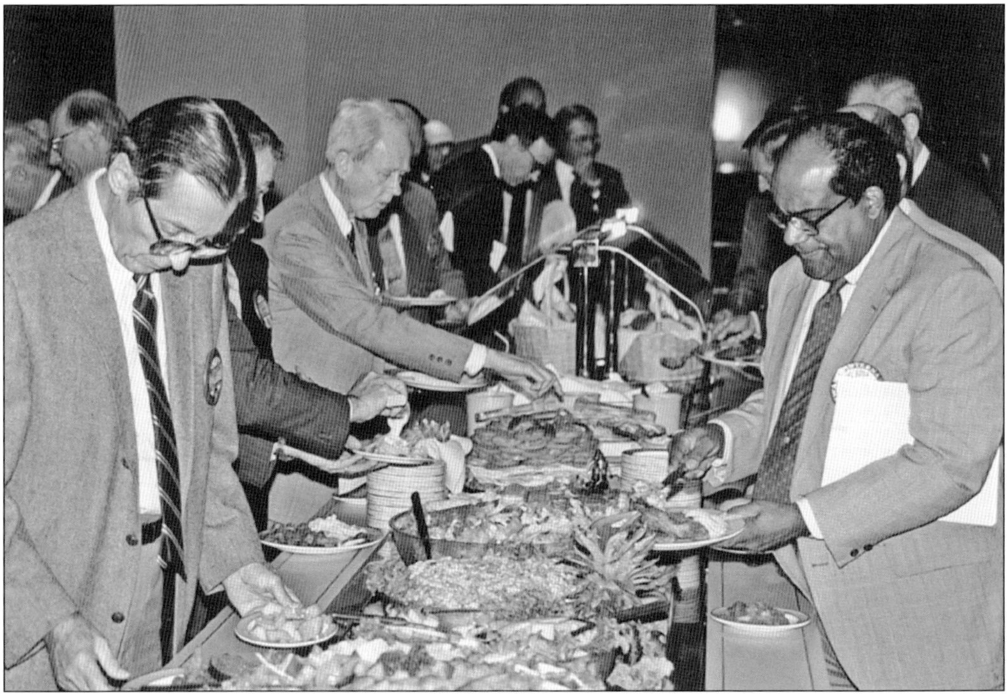

By the 1990s, the club was happily ensconced in its new home in the Harbert Center, where club members would go through a well-stocked buffet line before joining their fellow Kiwanians in the dining room. Although the days of singing before each meal were long gone, the club still began each program with an invocation and the Pledge of Allegiance (and still does). (Both, KCOB.)

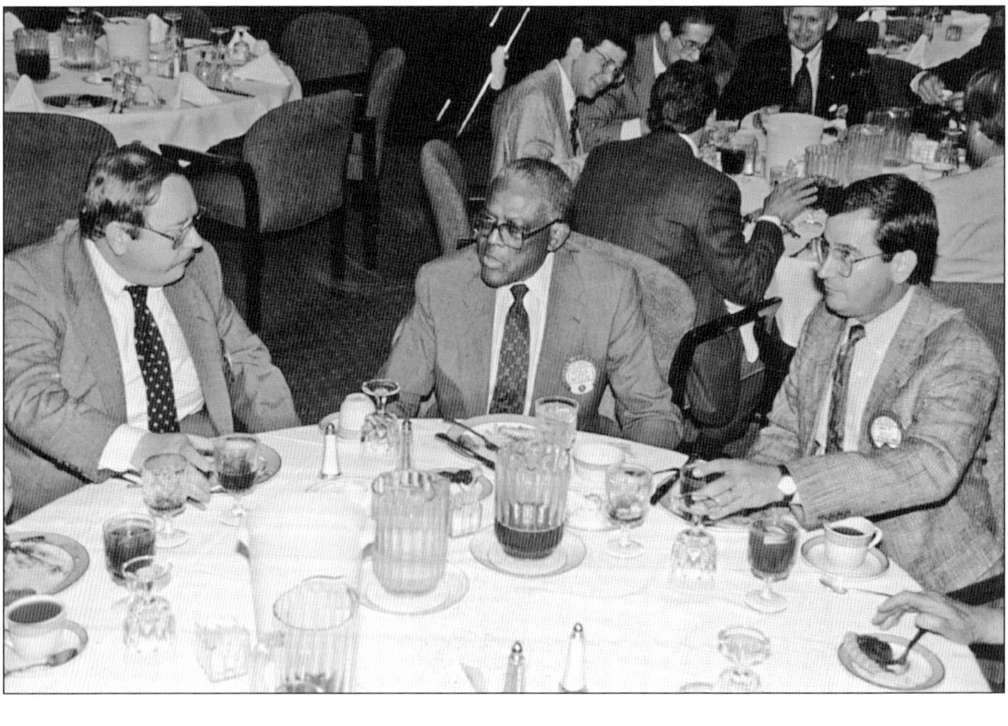

Warren B. Lightfoot earned Phi Beta Kappa honors at the University of Alabama and a bachelor of laws from its School of Law. In 1990, as he became the club's president, he founded the law firm Lightfoot, Franklin & White. His professional and civic honors are manifold; his election as president of the American College of Trial Lawyers and service as the president of the Alabama State Bar were particularly noteworthy. (KCOB.)

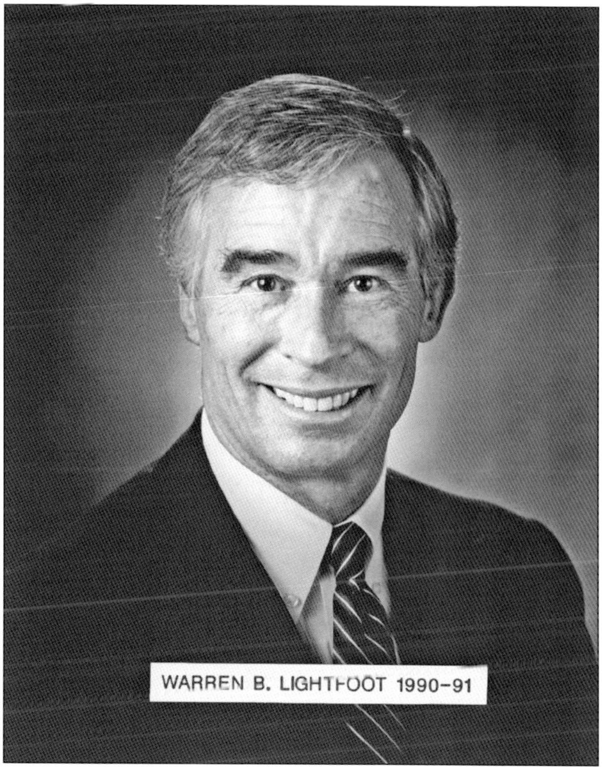

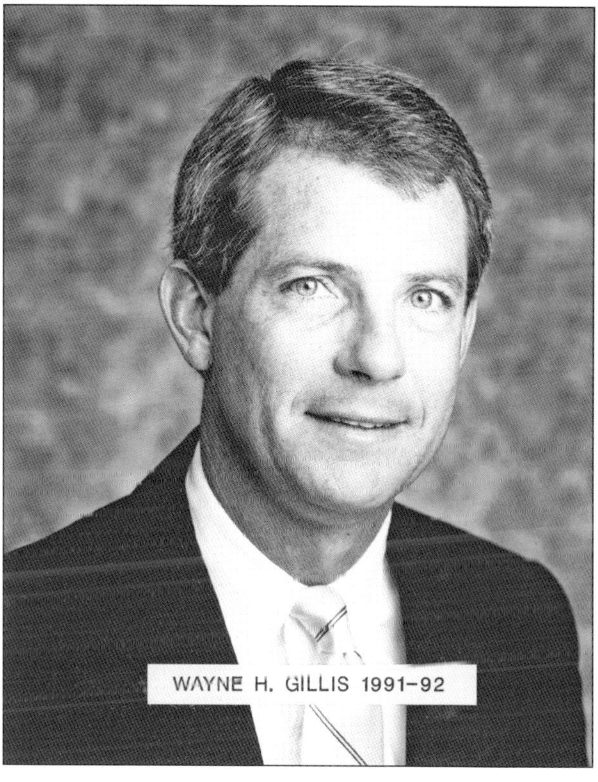

Wayne H. Gillis, of Brewton, Alabama, earned a degree in advertising from the University of Alabama and made advertising his career. In 1973, he founded Gillis Advertising, which eventually grew to become the largest independent advertising agency in Alabama. In 1991, he became the club's president, just one of numerous civic leadership positions that included, among others, service as a director of the Alabama School of Fine Arts and the Birmingham Museum of Art. (KCOB.)

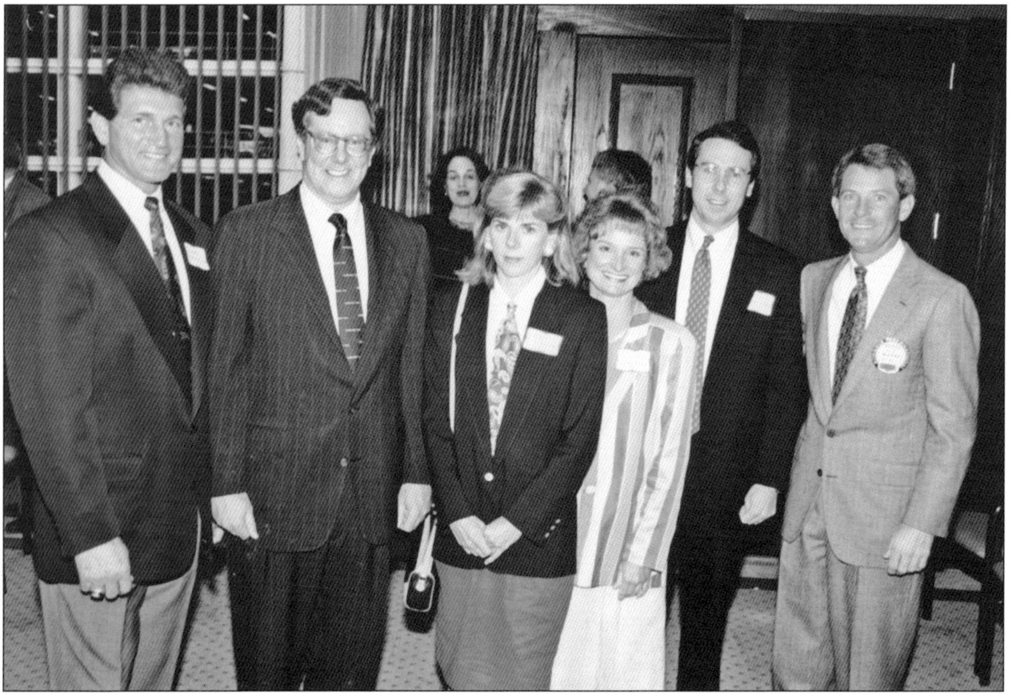

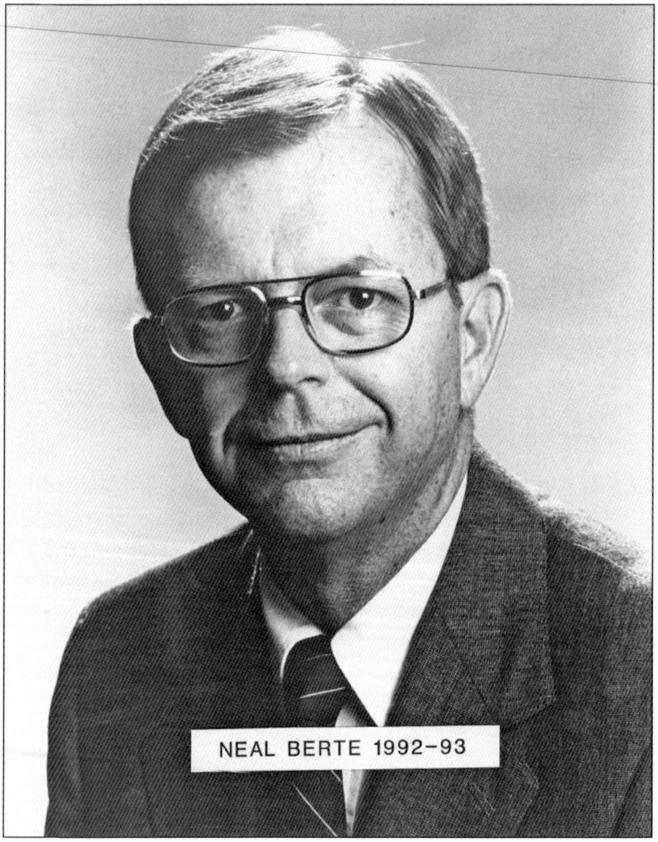

Former Washington Redskins quarterback Joe Theismann (left) and publisher Steve Forbes (second from left) visited the club in 1992. At the time, Theismann was retired from professional football, and Forbes was within a few years of his first presidential race. Club president Wayne Gillis stands on the far right. (KCOB.)

Neale R. Berte, EdD, a native of Cincinnati, Ohio, became the club's president in 1992. At the time, Dr. Berte was the president of Birmingham-Southern College, the alma mater of many former club presidents. Dr. Berte's presence was felt in practically every aspect of Birmingham's civic life, and his honors—including selection to the Alabama Academy of Honor—are too many to list. (KCOB.)

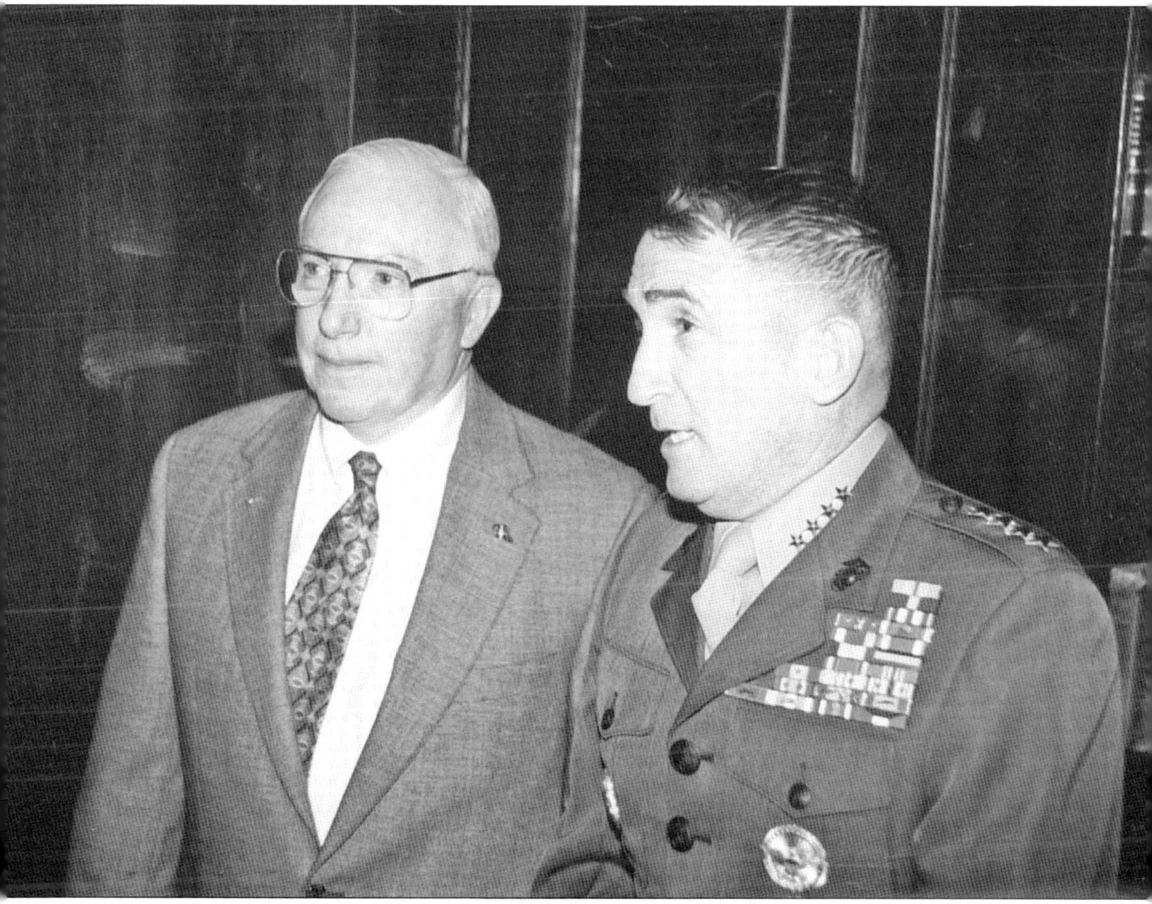

Dave Carder (left) was born in Brooklyn, New York, the son of Baptist missionaries home on furlough from serving in the Canary Islands. He graduated from Wheaton College and earned a master's degree in international affairs from the Fletcher School of Law and Diplomacy at Tufts University, served as an officer in the US Marine Corps, and, when he became the club's president in 1993, was the president of Vulcan Lands, Inc. Over the years, the club, through Carder's assistance, hosted a number of commandants as honored speakers at its luncheons, including Gen. Carl Mundy and, shown here on the right, Gen. Charles Krulak. General Krulak later returned to Birmingham and, for four years, served as the president of Birmingham-Southern College. Today, one of the club's standing committees is its Military Affairs Committee, which has undertaken recent initiatives ranging from providing college scholarships to local JROTC students to making annual donations in the club's name to the Folds of Honor Scholarship program for families of killed, wounded, or disabled service members. (KCOB.)

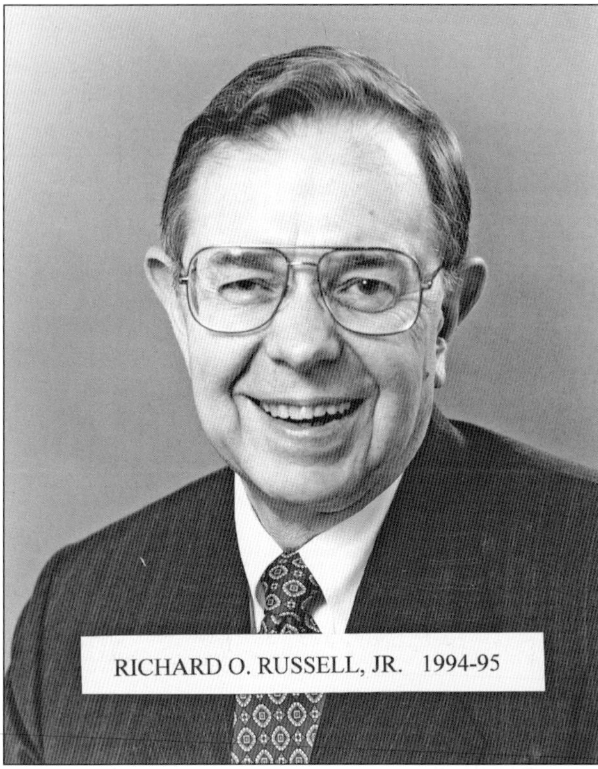

In 1994, Dr. Richard O. Russell Jr. became the club's president. A Birmingham native, Russell graduated Phi Beta Kappa from Vanderbilt University and earned his doctor of medicine from the university's medical school in 1956. A highly respected cardiologist, Russell became a professor of medicine in the University of Alabama's School of Medicine. He also served as chairman of the Jefferson County Board of Health and was chairman of the American Heart Association. (KCOB.)

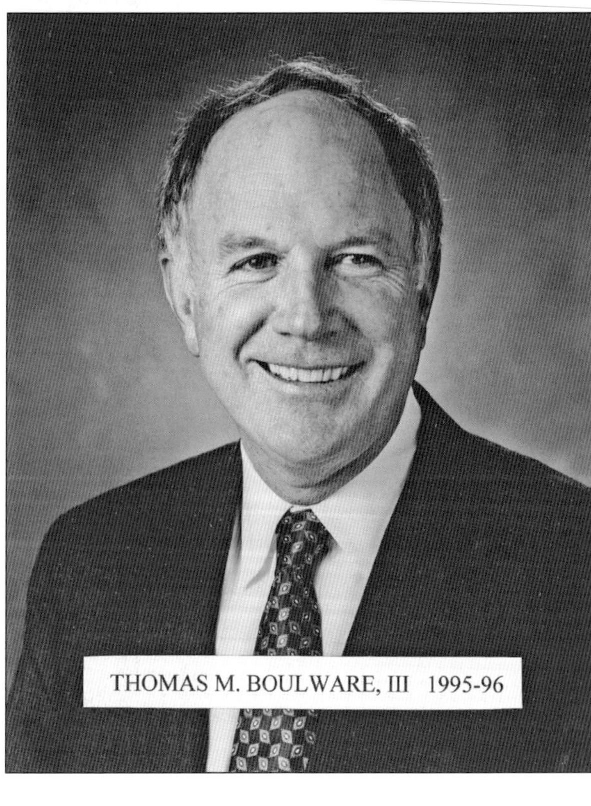

Thomas M. Boulware III was elected as the club's president in 1995. A graduate of the University of Alabama, he was the president of Brown Service Funeral Homes and Brown Service Manufacturing Company. In the broader community, Boulware served as president of Girls, Inc., of Central Alabama, president of the Country Club of Birmingham, and on the boards of the Birmingham Baptist Health Foundation and Vulcan Park Foundation. (KCOB.)

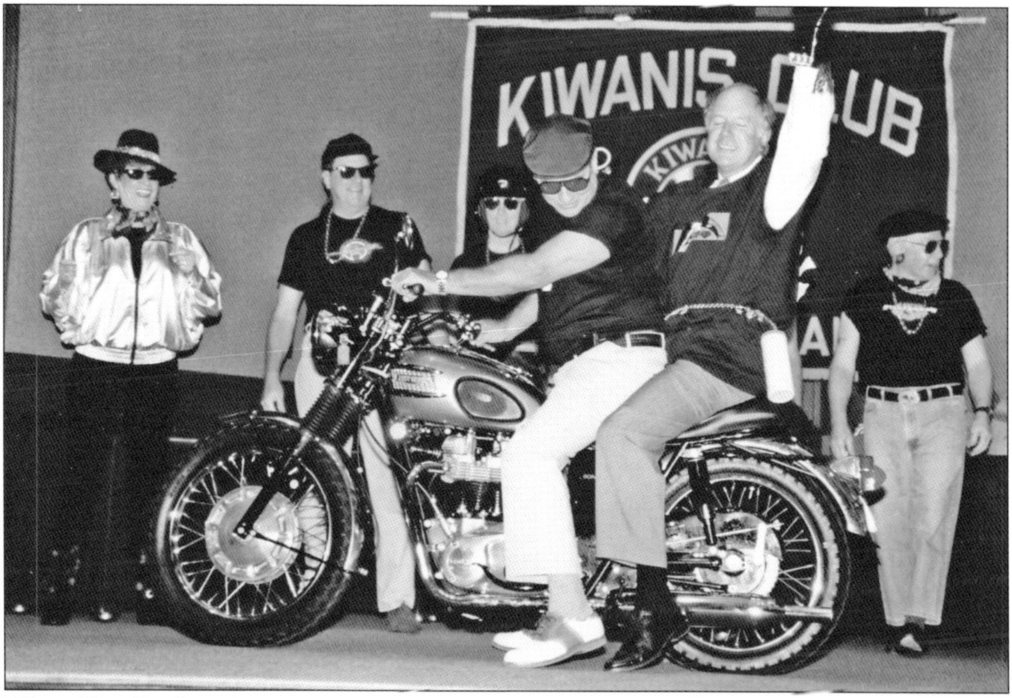

When Tom Boulware's tenure in the club's presidential office drew to a close in 1996, the club pulled out all the stops—literally and figuratively—in sending him off in style. Over the years, the club has seen cows, mules, and horses brought in by mischievous members and speakers, but this was the first time a Harley-Davidson made an appearance. (KCOB.)

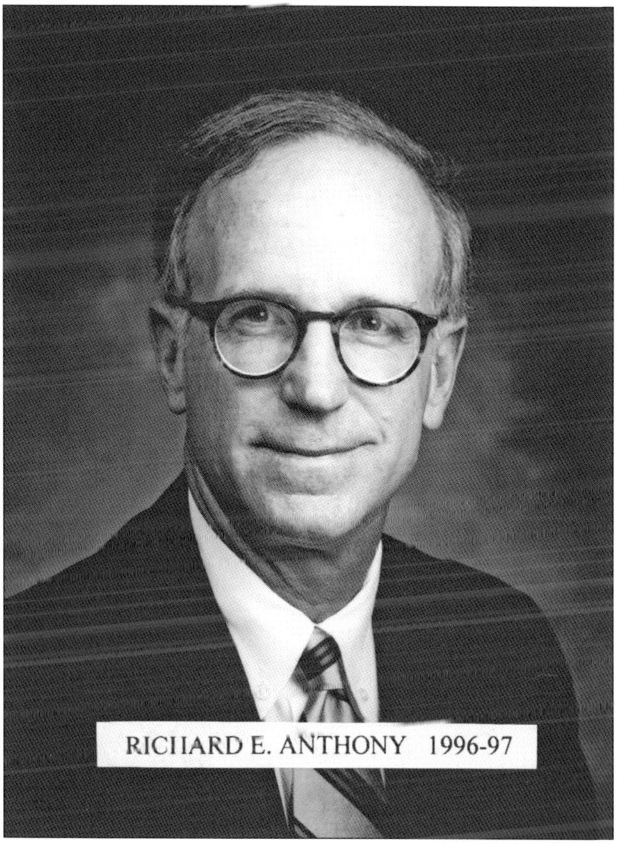

In 1996, Richard E. Anthony became the club's president. After graduating from the University of Alabama and earning his MBA at the University of Virginia, Richard began his career with AmSouth Bank. He later became president of First Commercial Bancshares. First Commercial Bancshares became a member of the Synovus family of companies in 1992 and, in 2005, Anthony became Synovus' president and chief executive officer, adding the title *chairman* in 2006. (KCOB.)

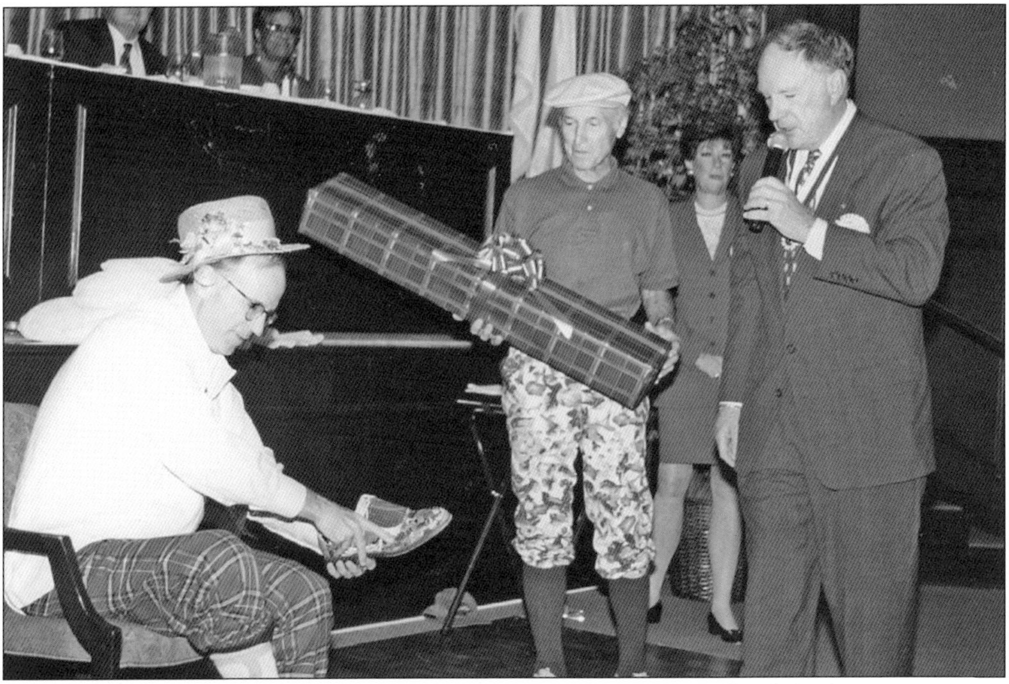

Richard Anthony was one of Birmingham's leading bankers. Nevertheless, his stature in the city's financial community did not protect him from a traditional good-natured roasting at the hands of his fellow Kiwanians when his term in office at the club came to an end in 1997. (KCOB).

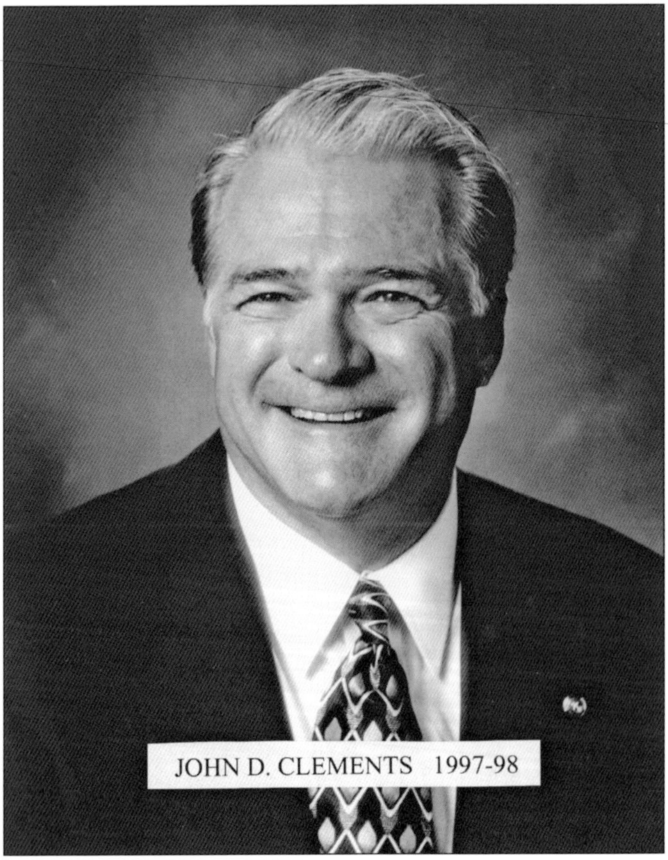

John D. Clements, a partner with the law firm Burr & Forman, became the club's president in 1997. Clements received his undergraduate degree from the University of Alabama in 1963, followed by a law degree in 1966. Recognized as the university's Outstanding Alumnus in 2008, he served his alma mater as president of the National Alumni Association and as the chairman of the Denny Chimes Restoration Fund Campaign. (KCOB.)

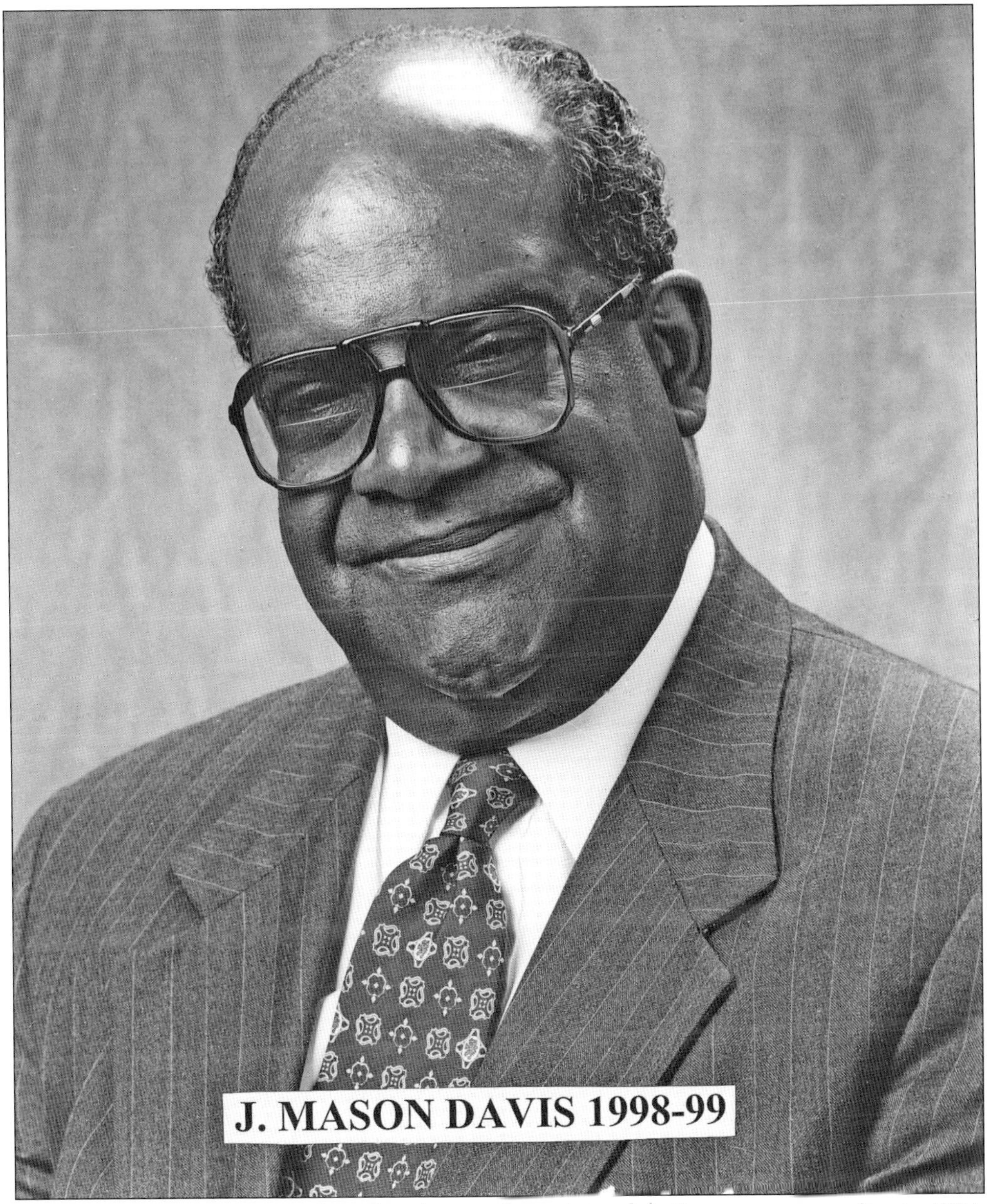

In 1998, J. Mason Davis was elected as the president of the club. Fourteen years earlier, in 1984, he and Louis Willie, chief operations officer of the A.G. Gaston family of companies, had become the club's first African American members. A Birmingham native, Davis graduated from Talladega College and then attended the State University of New York at Buffalo School of Law. Returning to Birmingham, he earned a reputation as an ardent and effective civil rights litigator. In 1984, he was elected president of the Birmingham Bar Association. That same year, he joined the law firm Sirote & Permutt. A distinguished member of Alabama's civic community, Davis served on the board of trustees of Talladega College, chaired the Birmingham Area Chamber of Commerce and the United Way of Central Alabama, was a member of the Alabama Board of Bar Commissioners, and sat on the boards of numerous businesses. In 1999, Davis was inducted into the Alabama Academy of Honor. (KCOB.)

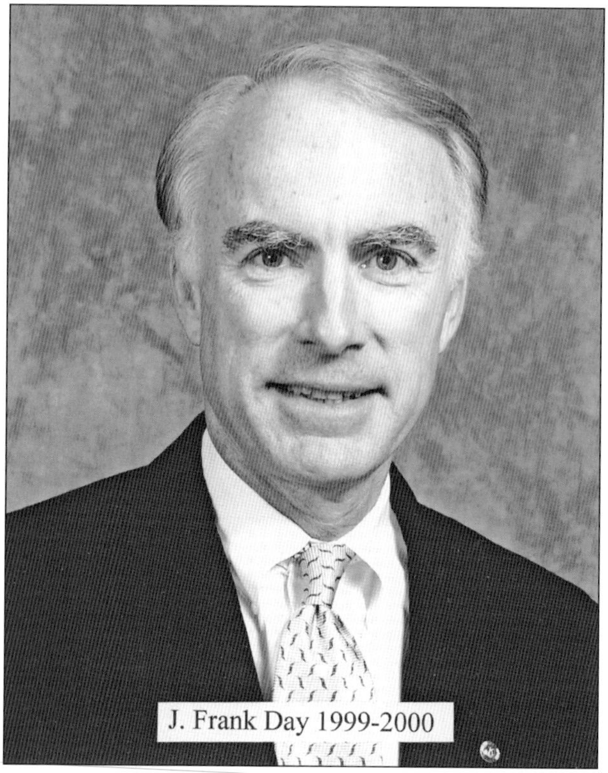

J.F. "Frank" Day III became the club's president in 1999. A graduate of Vanderbilt University with a bachelor of science in political science, Day followed tradition and joined the family business of J.F. Day, the Birmingham-based southeastern dealer of Pella doors, windows, and skylights. Today, Day organizes private chief executive officer advisory boards for Vistage. (KCOB.)

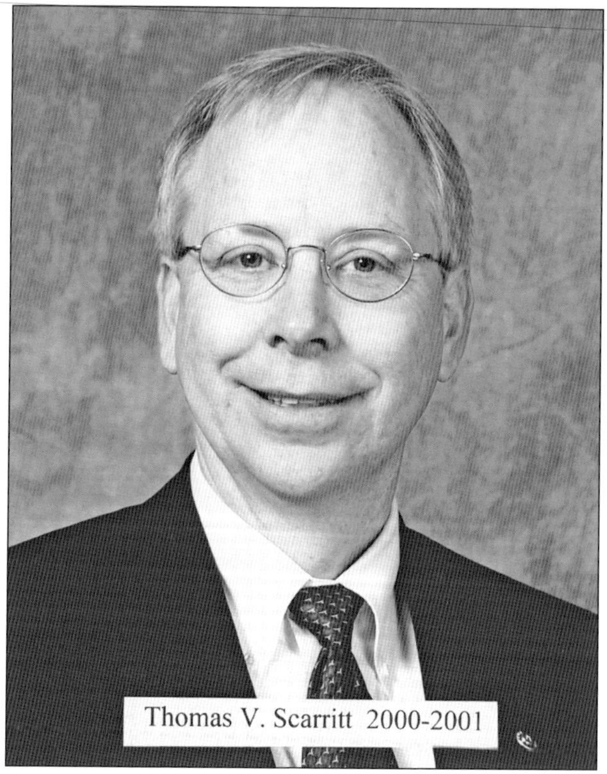

Thomas V. Scarritt went to work for the *Birmingham News* in 1975 after graduating from the University of North Carolina; in 1997, he became the newspaper's editor. He worked at the newspaper for 37 years; under his watch, it earned a Pulitzer Prize for investigative journalism. In 2000, Scarritt became the club's president. (KCOB.)

A graduate of the University of Alabama, Robert E. Luckie III realized his childhood dream of joining his father's advertising firm in 1971. At the firm, he ultimately rose from assistant account executive to the company's president. Further following in the footsteps of his father, who had been the club's president in 1964, Luckie became the club's president in 2001. (KCOB.)

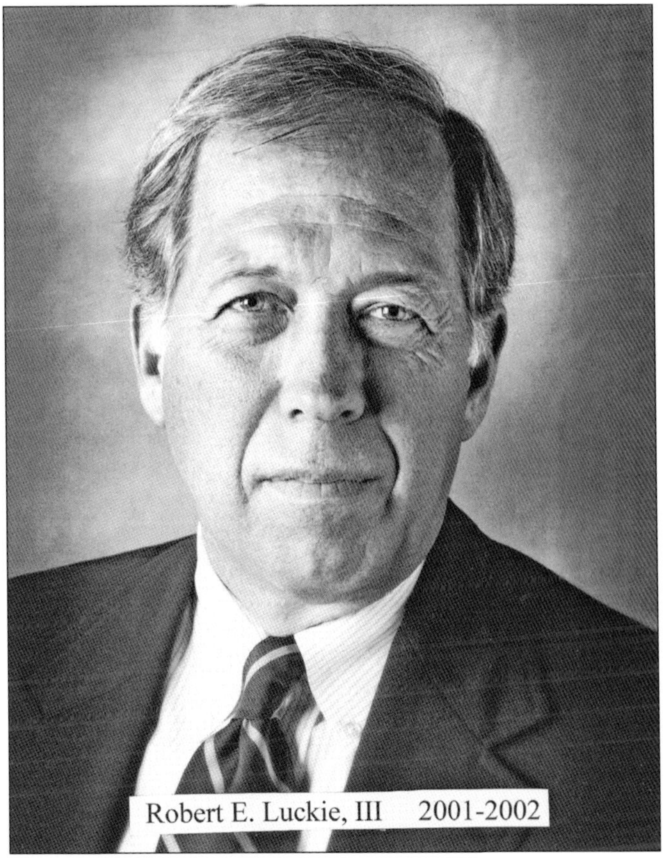

The Kiwanis Club of Birmingham's philanthropic outreach extends well beyond Birmingham. As an active club within the Kiwanis International organization, it has regularly supported such initiatives as Kiwanis International's $80 million toward the global elimination of iodine deficiency disorders and maternal and neonatal tetanus. (Kiwanis International.)

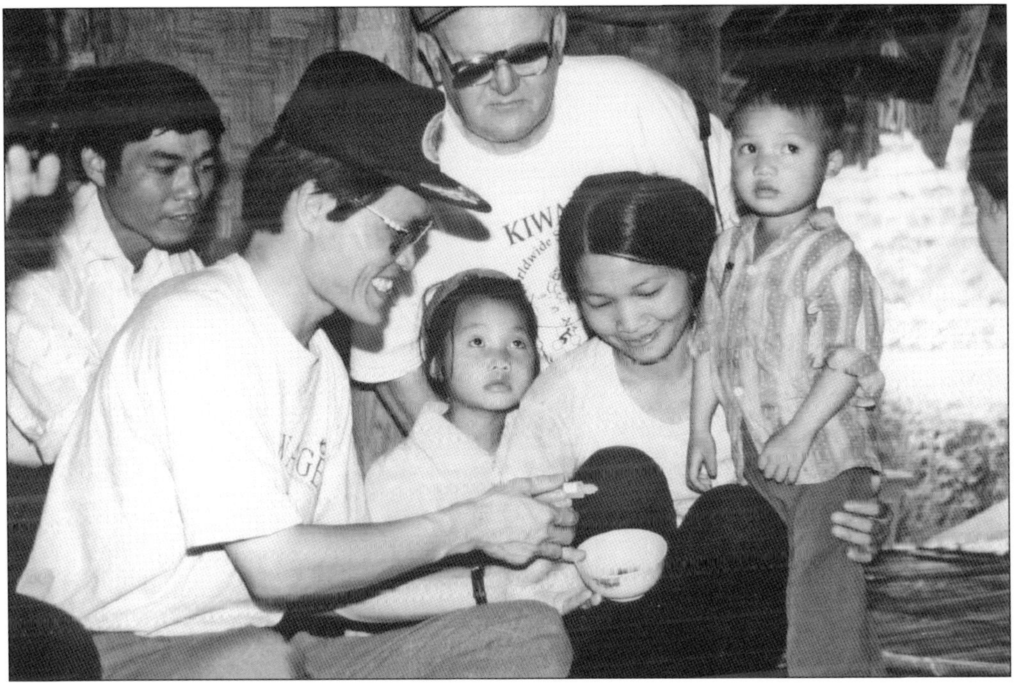

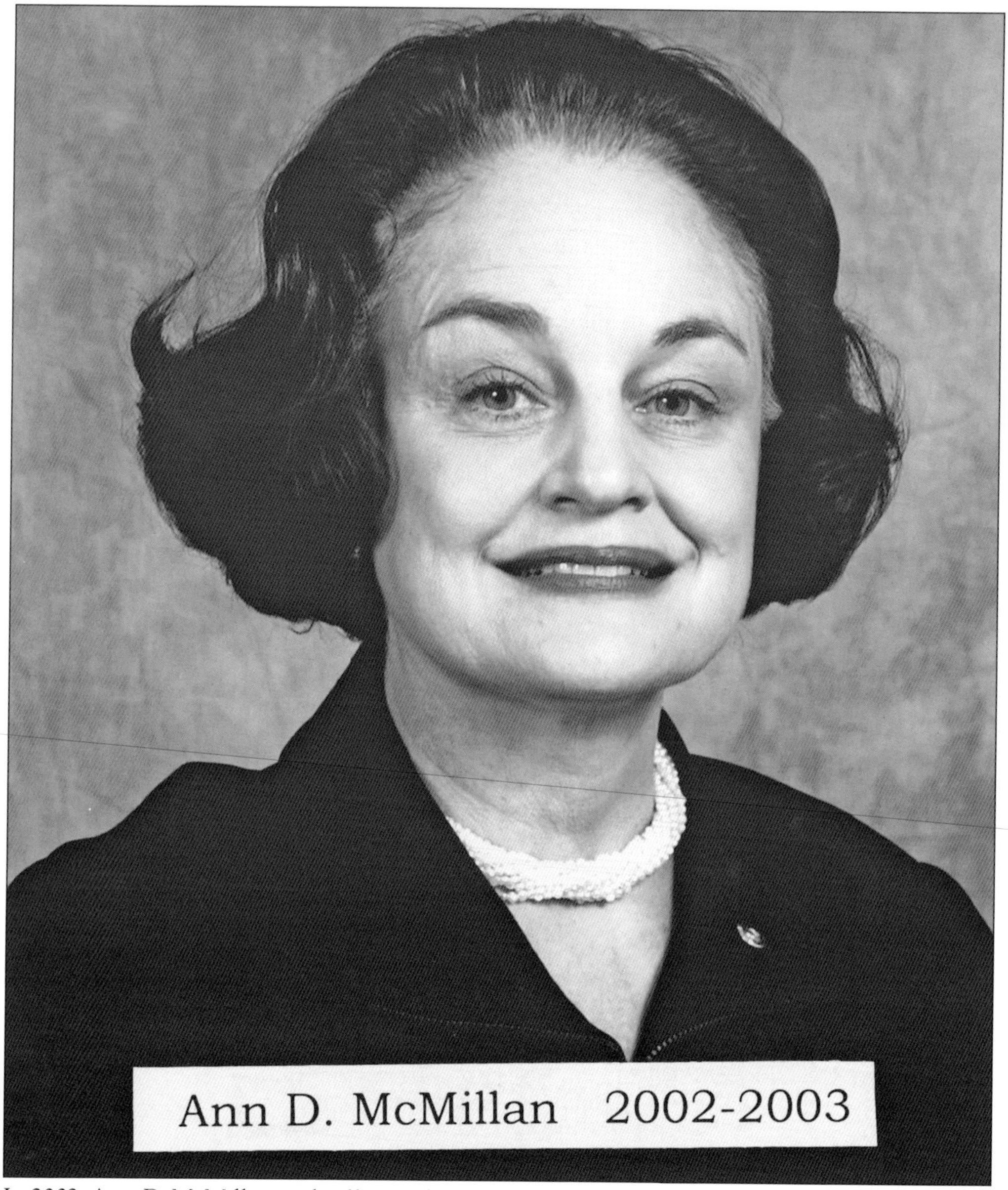

In 2002, Ann D. McMillan took office as the club's first female president. Five years earlier, in 1987, McMillan and Judge Sandra Ross Storm had become the club's first female members after Kiwanis International opened its membership to women. At the time McMillan became president, she was the vice president for community affairs at SouthTrust/Wachovia Bank. In addition to her services to Kiwanis, McMillan was active on numerous community and civic boards, including Children's Health System and the Birmingham Area Chapter of the American Red Cross, both of which as board chair, and the Women's Fund. She also held leadership positions in such community organizations as Leadership Birmingham and Leadership Alabama, as well as the University of Alabama–Birmingham (UAB) Leadership Cabinet and the Dean's Advisory Committee for the UAB School of Public Health. Her husband, attorney George McMillan, is a former Alabama lieutenant governor, and McMillian worked tirelessly in her husband's unsuccessful gubernatorial campaign to unseat George Wallace in 1982. (KCOB.)

In 2003, Matthew H. Lembke became the club's president. He graduated from Rhodes College and the University of Virginia School of Law, clerked on the US Court of Appeals for the Fourth Circuit, and then clerked for US Supreme Court justice Anthony Kennedy. Today, Lembke is a partner with Bradley Arant Boult Cummings. Befitting Kiwanis' historic ties to *Vulcan*, Lembke is a past chairman of the Vulcan Park Foundation. (KCOB.)

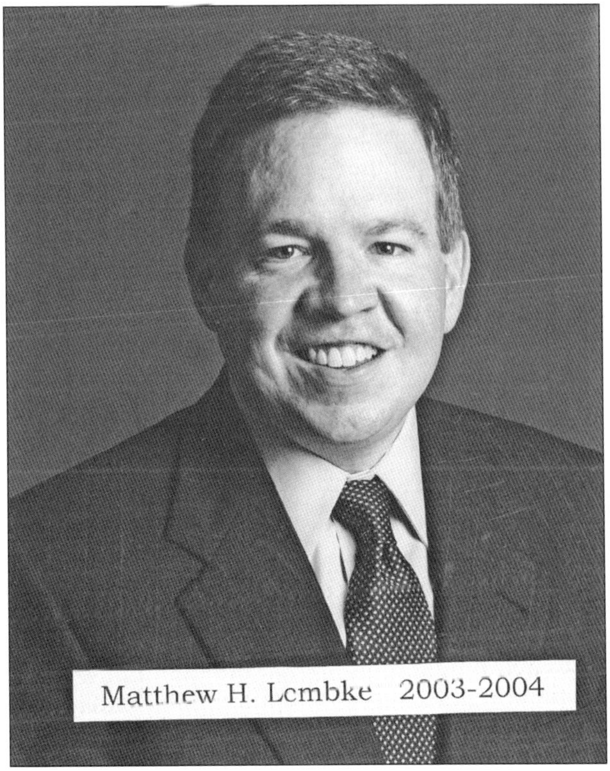

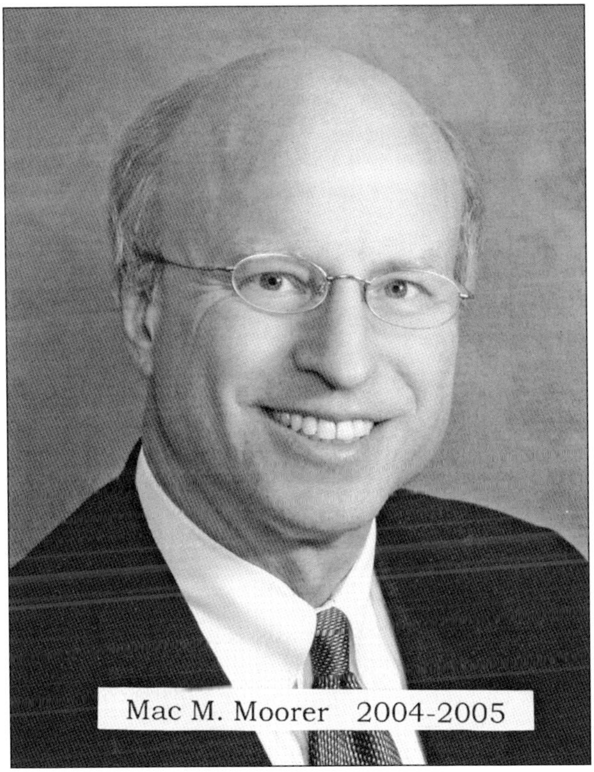

Mac M. Moorer was elected the club's president in 2004. He earned undergraduate and law degrees from the University of Alabama, clerked for US District Court Judge Sam Pointer, and ultimately became the managing partner of the law firm Lightfoot, Franklin & White, from which he retired in 2015. (KCOB.)

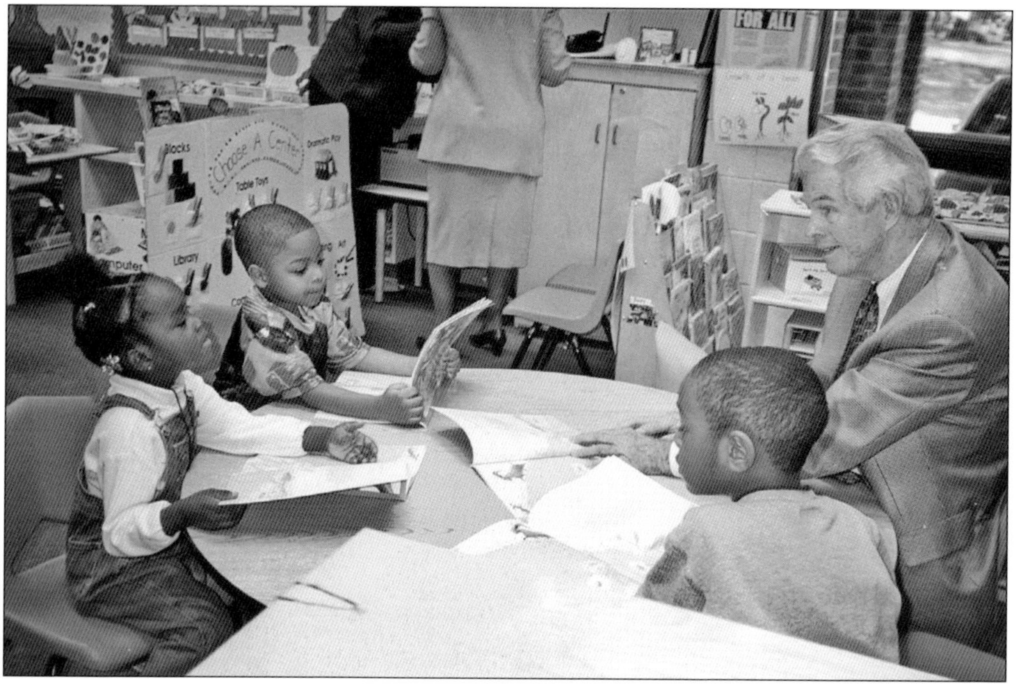

In line with their continued focus on service projects designed to help children, one of the Kiwanians' most popular and enduring community outreach efforts is the Reading Is Fundamental program, which sends club members into local schools to provide reading mentors to elementary school children. (Both, KCOB.)

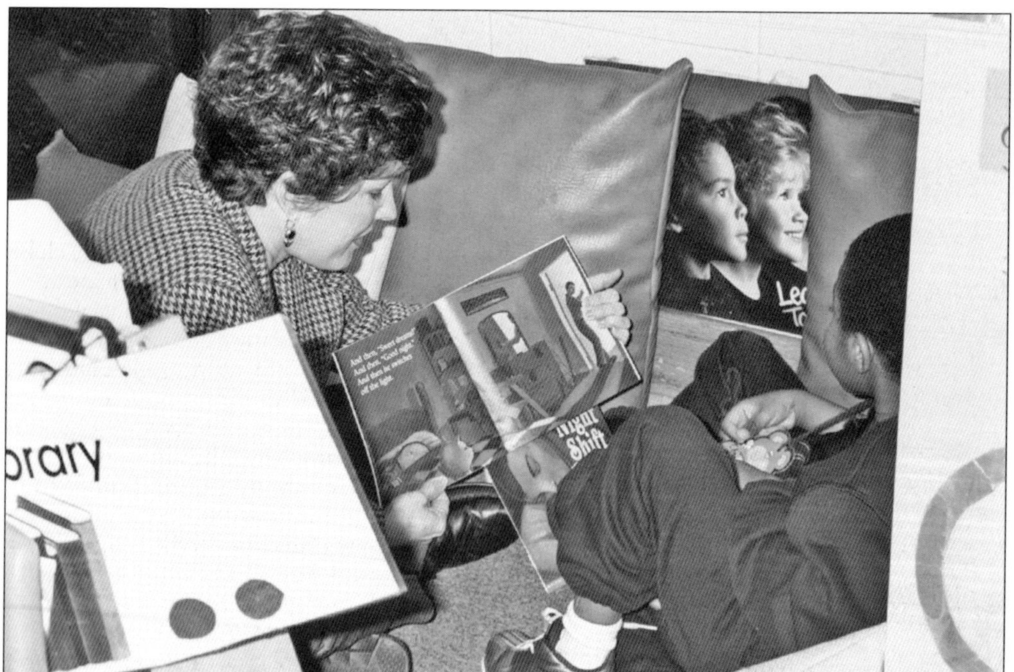

In 2005, William A. "Tony" Davis III became the club's president. A proud native of Talladega, Alabama, Davis has been with the law firm of Starnes Davis Florie since 1976. His service to the greater Birmingham community has included terms as chairman of the University of Alabama President's Cabinet, captain of the Monday Morning Quarterback Club, and president of the Crippled Children's Foundation. (KCOB.)

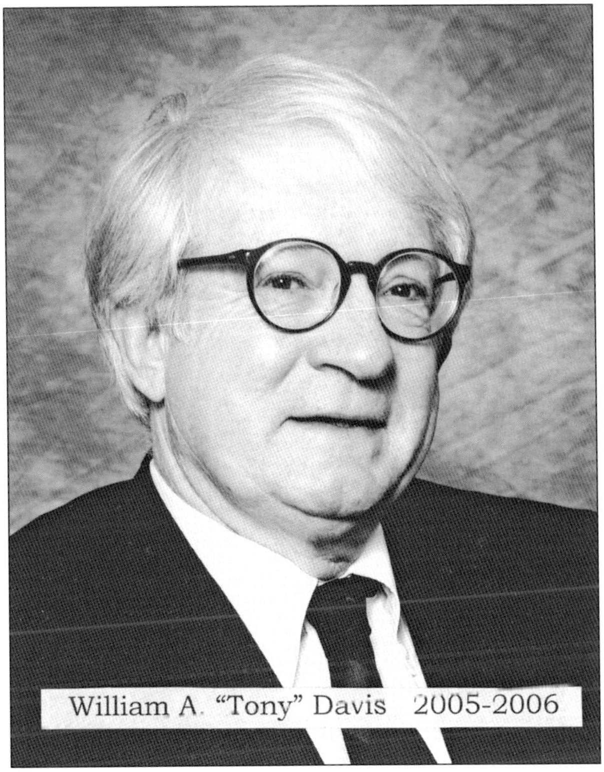

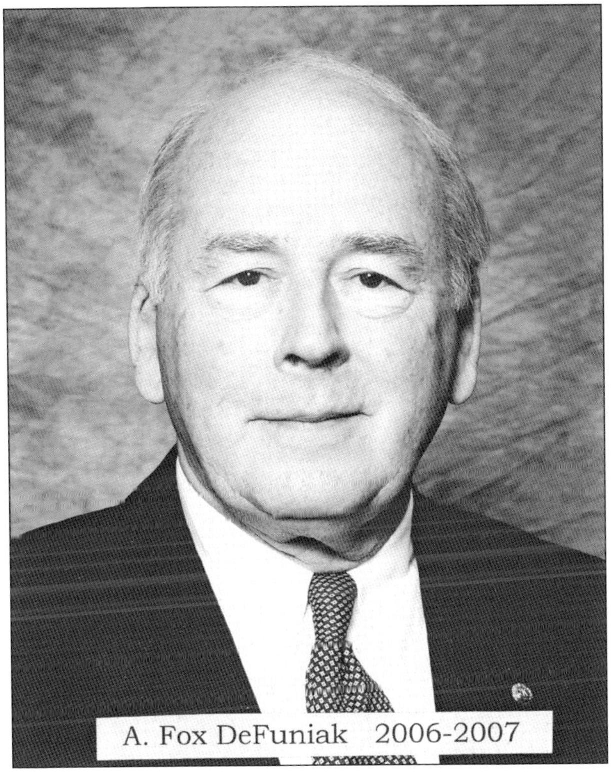

A. Fox DeFuniak became the club's president in 2006. A graduate of the University of Alabama and the Louisiana State University School of Banking, DeFuniak spent 32 years at AmSouth Bank, eventually becoming its Birmingham City president. He joined the investment firm Sterne, Agee & Leach in 1995 and, 10 years later, joined the community bank known as the Bank as the Birmingham market president and a member of its Executive Management Committee. (KCOB.)

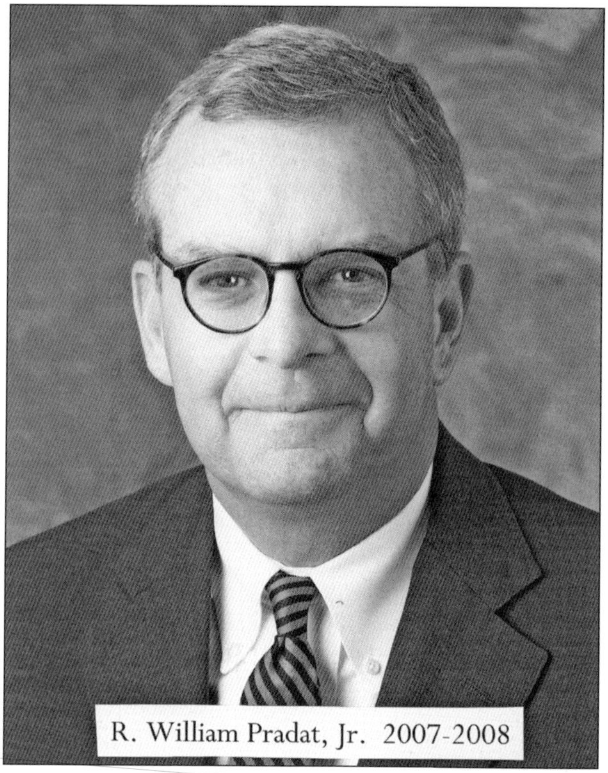

R. William Pradat, Jr. 2007-2008

R. William Pradat Jr. became the club's president in 2007. A native of Birmingham with undergraduate and master's degrees from the University of Alabama and a master of business administration from Samford University, he has been involved in Birmingham's real estate industry since 1984. Today, Pradat is a partner and president of Cushman & Wakefield/EGS Commercial Real Estate. (KCOB.)

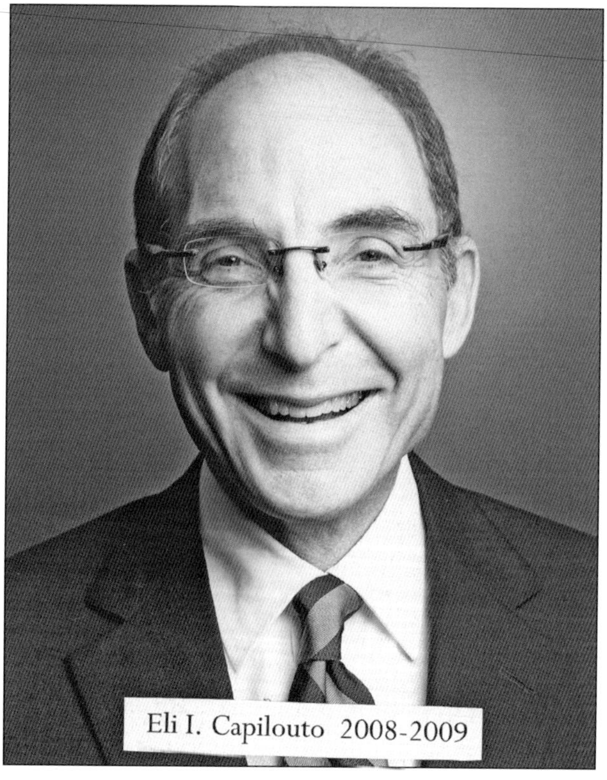

Eli I. Capilouto 2008-2009

From 2008 to 2009, Eli Capilouto, DMD, ScD, served as the club's president. A native of Birmingham educated at the University of Alabama, the University of Alabama at Birmingham, and Harvard University, Dr. Capilouto was the provost at UAB when he was elected president. Today, he is the president of the University of Kentucky. (KCOB.)

In 2009, Joe Dean Jr. became the club's president. A three-year basketball letterman at Mississippi State University, Dean was a head coach at Birmingham-Southern College and at the University of Central Florida before returning to Birmingham-Southern and becoming the school's athletic director. For over 20 years, Dean has also worked as a TV color analyst on SEC basketball games. (KCOB.)

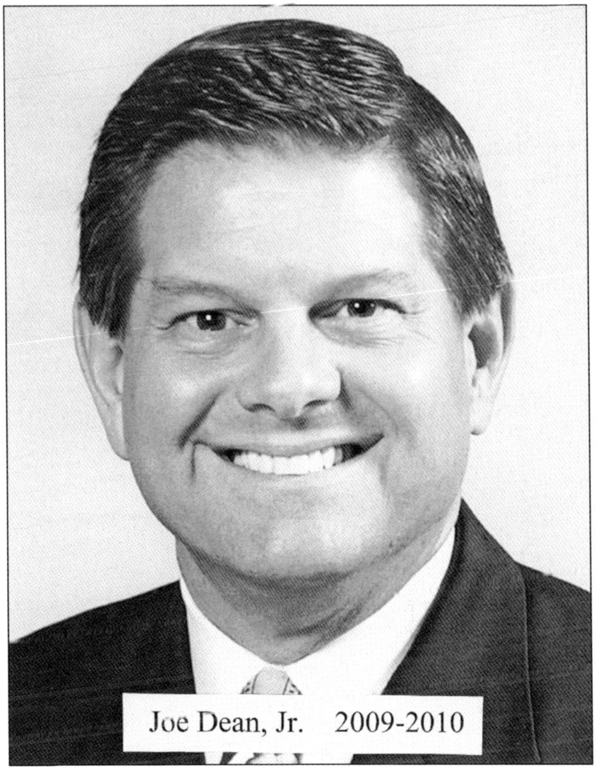

Joe Dean, Jr. 2009-2010

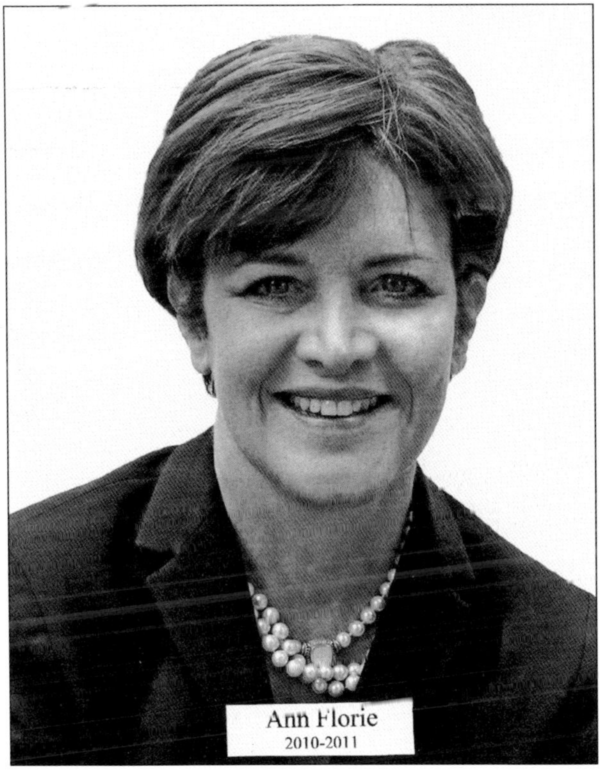

Ann Florie 2010-2011

Ann Florie, a graduate of Tulane University, is currently the executive director of Leadership Birmingham. Previously, she was the founding executive director of Region 2020, Inc., which led efforts to promote regional cooperation and citizen involvement in the areas of affordable housing, education, arts and culture, transportation, and land use in a 12-county area in central Alabama. From 2010 to 2011, she served as the club's president. (KCOB.)

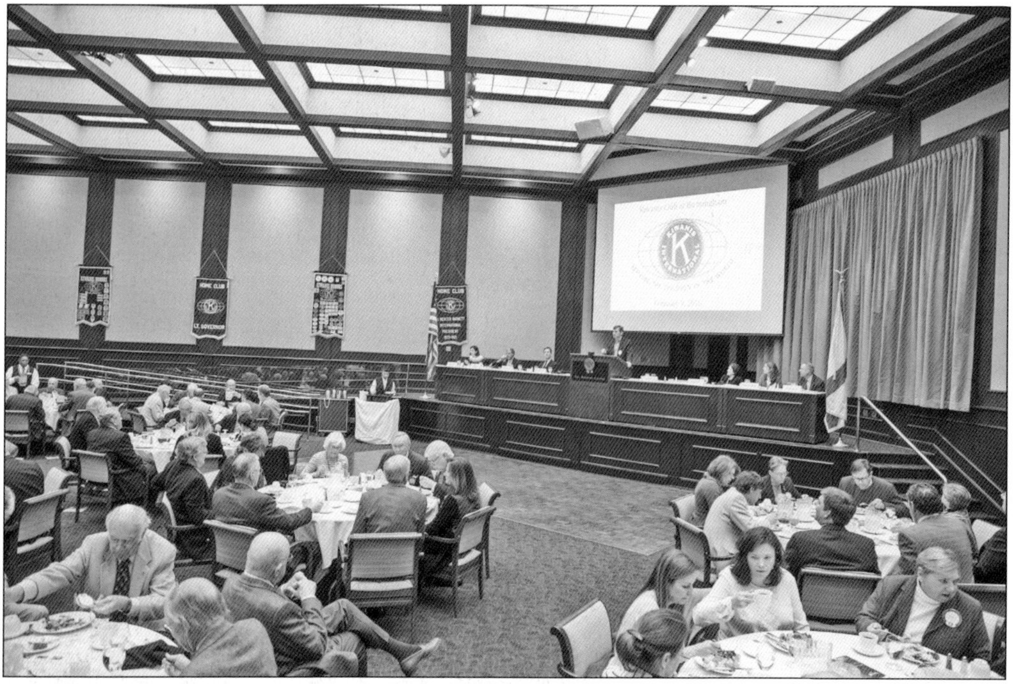

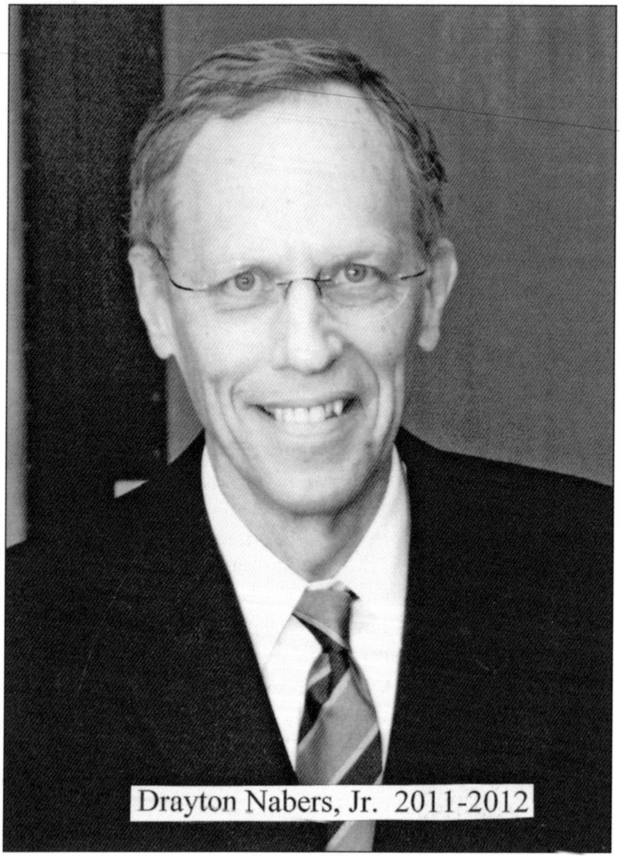

Inside the Harbert Center, in its third-floor main dining room, lunch crowds of 150 or so Kiwanians come together for food, fellowship, and a 30-minute talk from an eclectic assortment of speakers. In recent years, the club's visitors have included governors, US senators, federal judges, presidential candidates, and speakers ranging from the president of the National Rifle Association to the president of the American Civil Liberties Union. (KCOB.)

Justice Drayton Nabers Jr. was the club's president from 2011 to 2012. A graduate of Princeton, he earned his law degree from Yale University and was a law clerk to Justice Hugo Black on the US Supreme Court. After serving as chief executive officer and chairman of Protective Life Corporation, Nabers was Alabama's finance director. In 2004, he was appointed to the Alabama Supreme Court and served as its chief justice. (KCOB.)

In 2012, Harry "Buck" Brock III followed in his father's footsteps as president of the club. A graduate of the University of Alabama, he eventually became president of Central Bank (today's BBVA Compass) in Huntsville and later in Birmingham. He left banking in 1994 to become president of the Express Oil Development Company. Today, Brock is the vice president of business affairs at Samford University. (KCOB.)

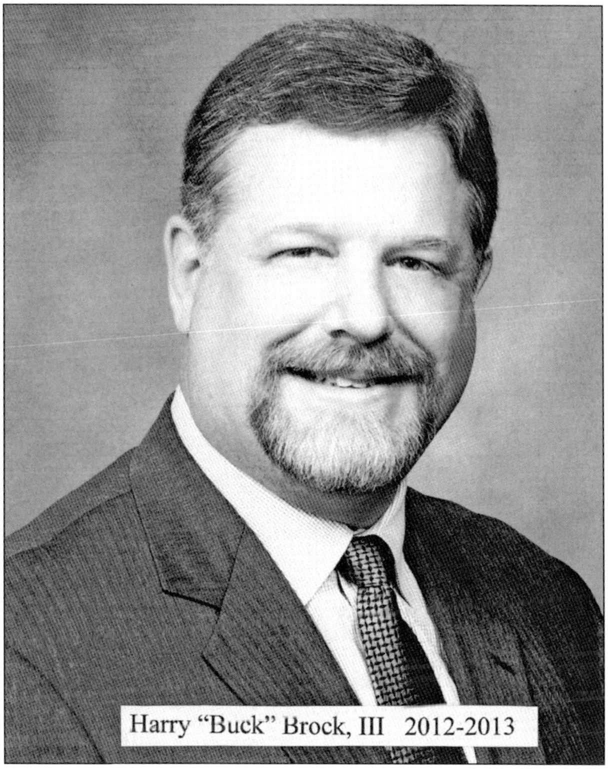

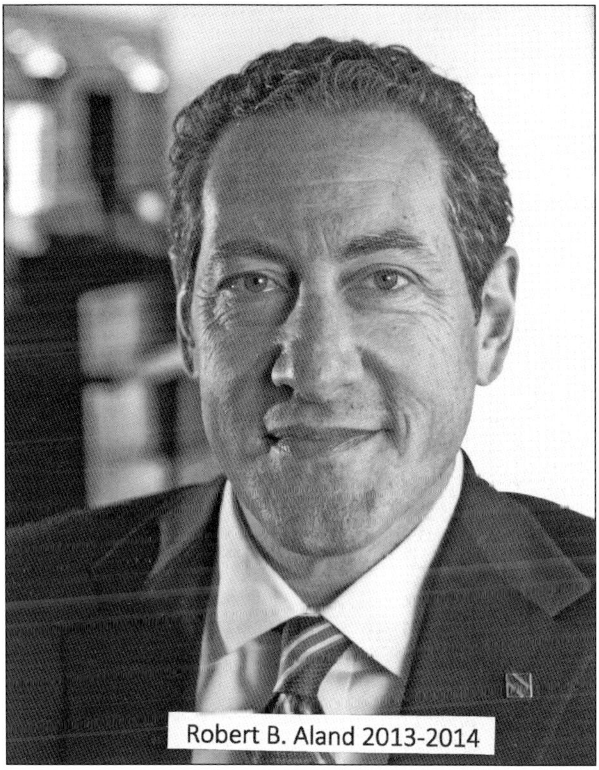

Robert B. Aland became the club's president in 2013. He earned an undergraduate degree and a master of business administration at Vanderbilt University, went to work in his family clothing business, Aland's Department Stores, and then pursued a career in banking. He now is Birmingham market president of National Bank of Commerce. Among his many civic roles, Aland chaired 2011's United Way campaign for central Alabama and currently serves on the board of governors of his alma mater, the Indian Springs School. (KCOB.)

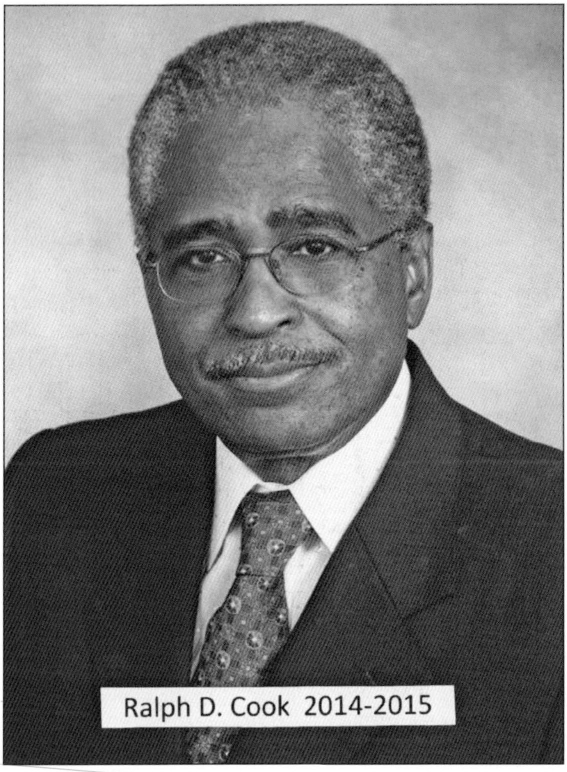

In 2014, Birmingham native Justice Ralph Cook became the club's president. Admitted to the Alabama Bar in 1968, Cook was the longtime dean of the Miles College School of Law. He also served as a Jefferson County Circuit Court judge and, from 1993 to 2000, was a member of the Alabama Supreme Court. A wide range of civic leadership positions have included, among others, chairing the board of directors of the Birmingham Museum of Art. (KCOB.)

This photograph, taken in 2015 during a club visit to Birmingham's Trim Tab Brewery, shows club secretary Carol Hines (left), Trim Tab chief executive officer Harris Stewart (middle), and club president Ralph Cook. It provides a telling snapshot of how far Birmingham and the club had come in the club's 100 years. In 1917, when the club was founded, it only had white male members and Alabama was a dry state. (KCOB.)

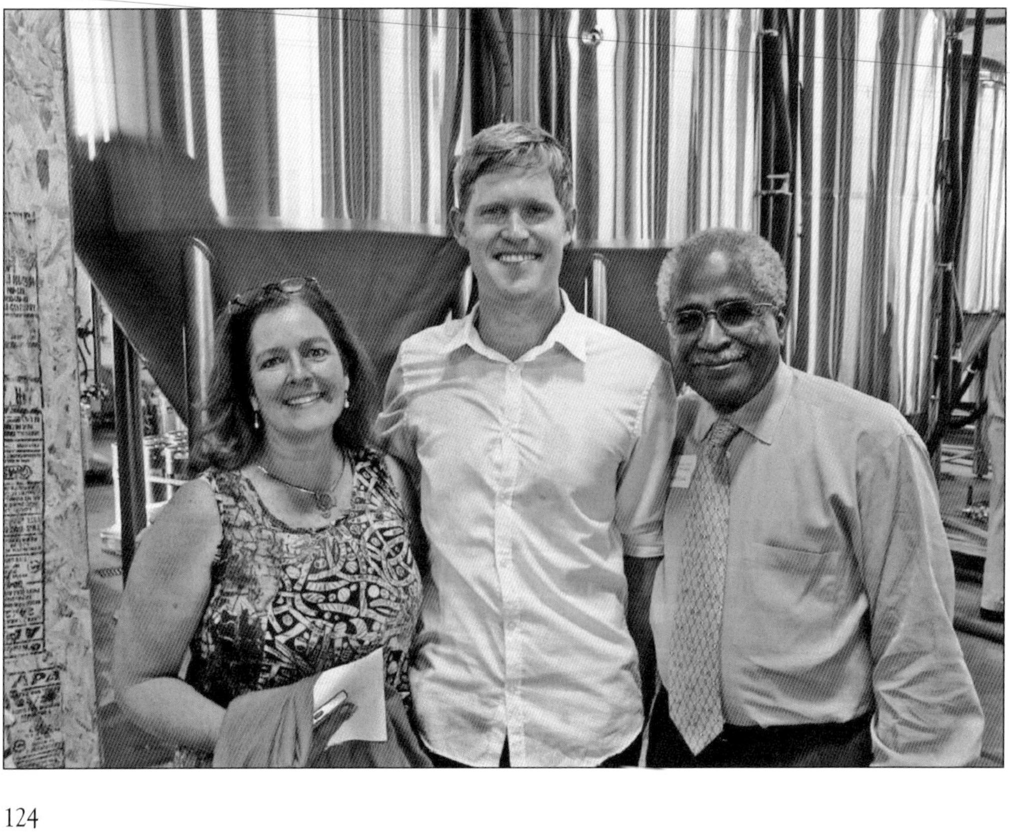

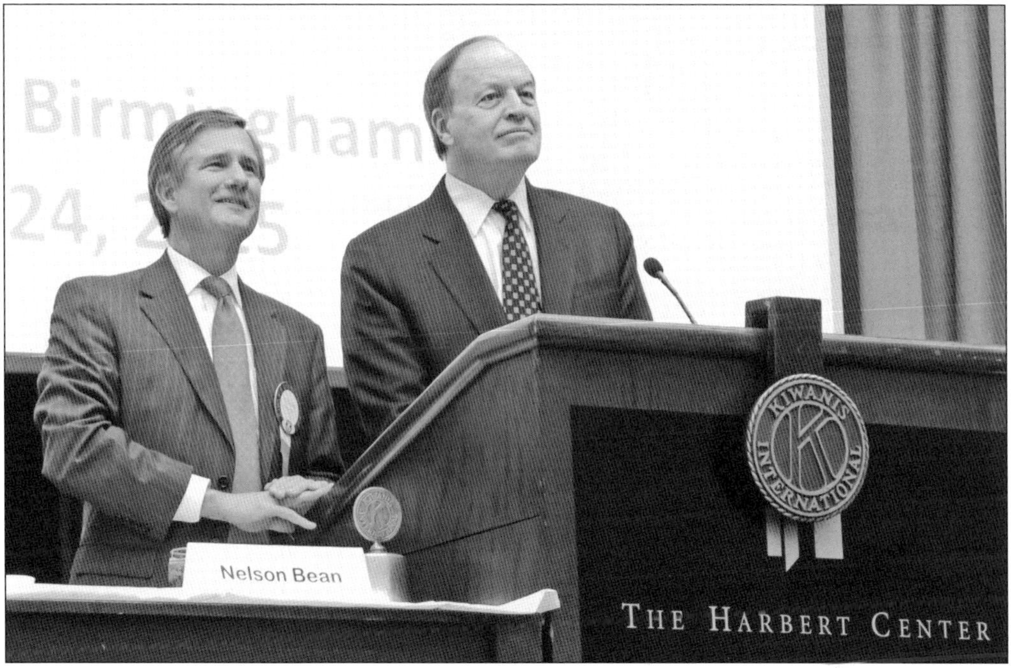

Nelson Bean became the club's president in 2015. A graduate of Vanderbilt University, Bean returned to Birmingham to join First Commercial Bank and became its president in 2004. Bean's civic duties include serving on the board of United Way of Central Alabama and on the executive committee of the Birmingham Business Alliance. Here he stands next to US senator Richard Shelby, one of the club's speakers during Bean's tenure. (KCOB.)

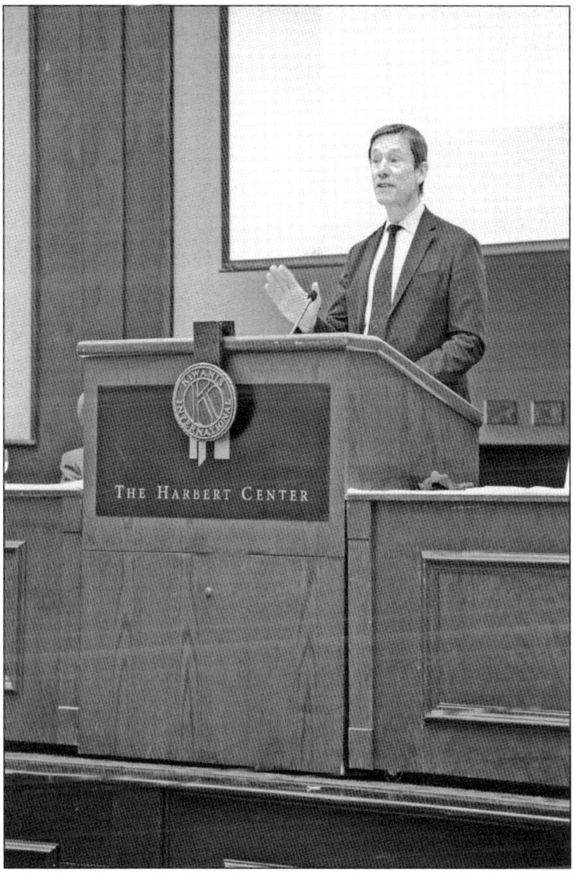

On February 9, 2016, Mark Tercek, president of the Nature Conservancy, made a special trip to Birmingham to speak to the club. In a city founded on coal and iron and known as the "Pittsburgh of the South" at the time the club was founded a century earlier, Tercek argued that the imposition of a carbon tax was necessary to counter the climate change his organization was committed to combat. (Nature Conservancy.)

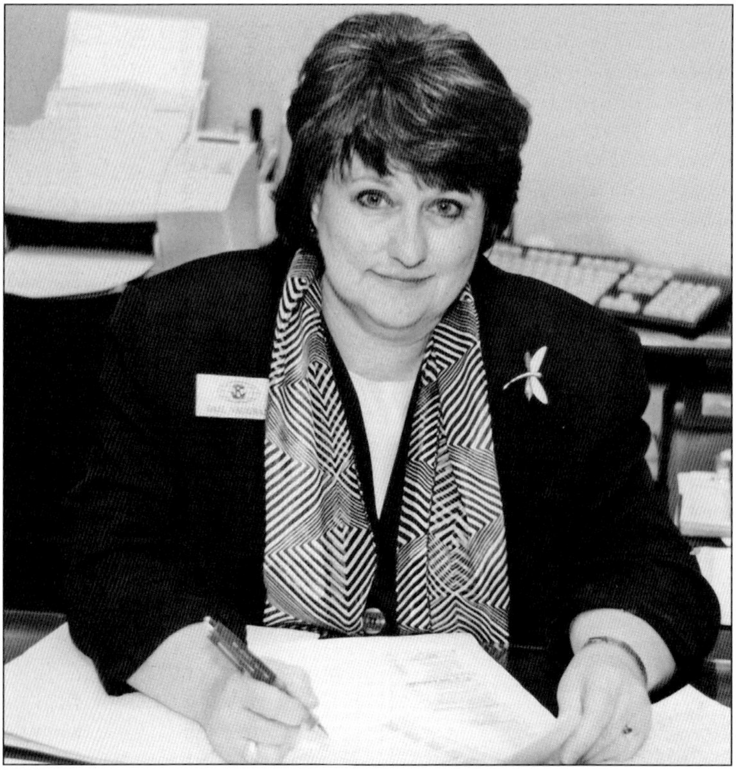

As the club approached its centennial year, it could, with 565 members, proudly claim to be the largest Kiwanis Club in the world. The task of managing the club's day-to-day operations, including its weekly lunches, a steady array of speakers, and daily interaction with the Harbert Center and other tenant clubs, is the responsibility of executive director Gail Vaughan (left) and executive assistant Janet Byrd (below). (Both, KCOB.)

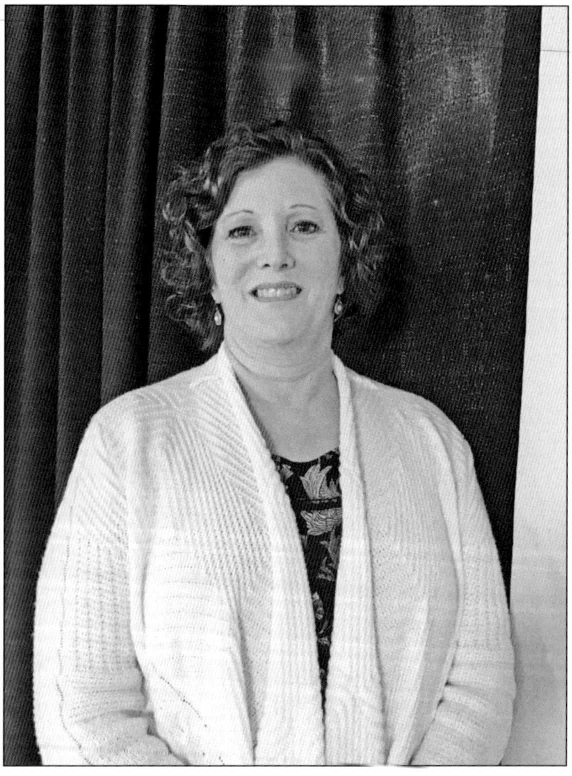

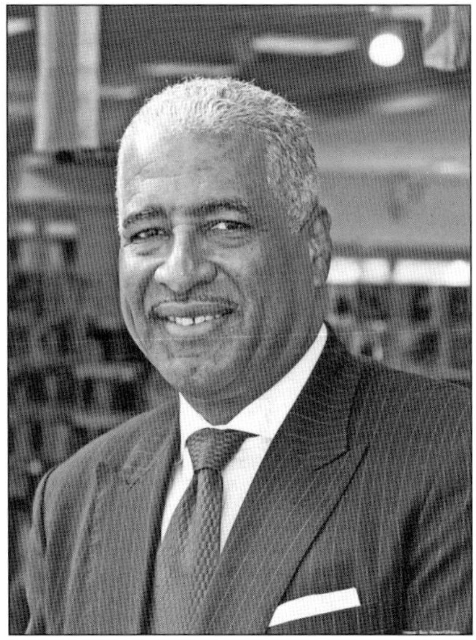

On January 10, 2017, Mayor William Bell continued the long-standing Birmingham tradition of the city's mayor providing his annual State of the City address to the Kiwanis Club. One hundred years earlier, Birmingham was an industrial workshop of a city with a population of 150,000. Today, the population is 212,000, with institutions such as the University of Alabama at Birmingham as its largest employers. (City of Birmingham.)

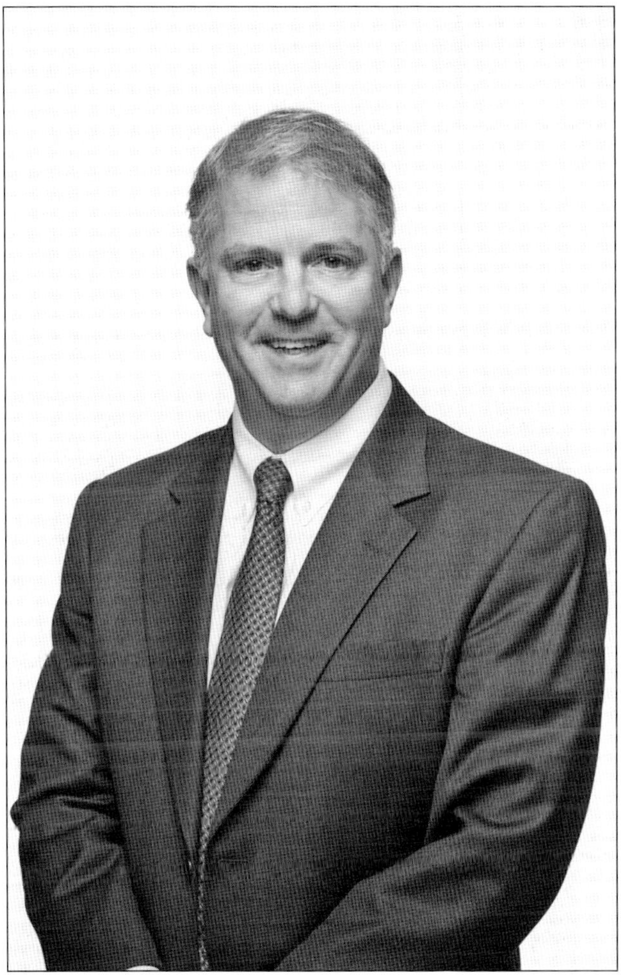

Thomas W. "Tom" Thagard III is a shareholder in the law firm Maynard Cooper & Gale, where he cochairs the firm's litigation practice. He received his juris doctor from the University of Virginia School of Law after first graduating magna cum laude from Washington and Lee University. In 2017, Thagard became the club's president to guide it through its centennial year and, with the support of the club's board of directors and membership, embarked upon the Kiwanis Centennial Park project. Once completed, the $4.5 million project will build a new park on the northern slope of Vulcan Park to link Birmingham's iconic statue with the city's Southside neighborhood, complete a key link in the city's Ridges and Valleys urban trail system, and enhance *Vulcan* with a state-of-the-art, colored LED light display. In many ways, this project will build upon the urban park design work first envisioned by the club in 1923. (Maynard Cooper & Gale.)